KNOW THE TRUTH
AND BE FREE

CENTRUM Publishers

KNOW THE TRUTH AND BE FREE

Wanda Pratnicka

Translation: **Marlena Romanczuk**
Copy-Editing: **Roger Williams**
Cover: **Łukasz Rutkowski**

Printed in Poland on acid-free paper

Library of Congress Cataloging-in-Publication Data is available

CENTRUM Publishers
P.O. Box 257
81-963 Gdynia / Poland
Phone: + 48 58 522 9497
Fax: +48 58 550 6812
E-mail: office@WydawnictwoCentrum.pl
Web: www.WydawnictwoCentrum.pl

ISBN 10: 83-60280-75-4
ISBN 13: 978-83-60280-75-1

CONTENTS

PREFACE

This book is addressed to everyone irrespective of race or religion because one day we will all experience our own or someone else's passing. Do you realize that the fear of death is the primary cause of most, if not all of our internal adversities? The fear of death is like the interior of a simmering volcano. It is that hidden, constant fear that no amount of money or superficial effort can neutralize. This fear is the essence of all things. It is a fear that emanates not only from death itself, but also from a lack of understanding of this very emotional subject. Traditional media is not making it any easier to understand death. Death is either not shown or, for example in movies and video games it is presented in a banal or unrealistic way.

Therefore most people leave things up to chance, not knowing how to control their life on Earth as well as after death. When you familiarize yourself with the information introduced in this book you will no longer waste your life. You will begin to make different, more conscious choices. Who knows, maybe you will become amazingly wise and happy. Once and for all you will get rid of your fears and stop living in constant frustration. You will understand that what you fear the most (most often unconsciously) doesn't even exist, because what you call death is just taking off your body in the same way that you take off and throw away the old clothes that you don't need anymore. Meanwhile you, the essence of you, moves forward. Where? Well, to understand this is extraordinarily important because what you know about death, what you think about it during your life and what you expect from it, will determine what you will experience in the future. Therefore, the knowledge you acquire about death in your lifetime is as important as the air that you breathe because your future depends on it. I hope that you will come to understand that everything that happens to you depends only and solely of you. You must take your life into your own hands because nobody else will help you with it.

Nobody can get by in life without the knowledge provided in this book. It is especially important when you are sick, aged or you have someone in your family who is quickly approaching the transition commonly known as "death". If you have lost someone close to you and you are mourning then this book is appropriate for you. This book will explain every tragedy and it will help you heal any wounds in your heart caused by the loss of someone dear to you.

INTRODUCTION

Dear reader, we are living in times of great change. We should be very happy about this, but many people are constantly worrying about impending doom. It is causing people great, unconscious fear. I took on this task to not only mitigate this fear, but to permanently remove it. It is not possible for us to live with such a burden and function normally. It will negatively affect not only your life, but life in general.

No matter what you are afraid of right now, with this fear there is a fundamental, overarching fear associated with your death and non-existence. You are not even conscious of this fact. This is the reason why many people object to closely looking at this subject. These people are thinking naively deluding themselves into thinking that if they don't touch this subject, death will pass them by. In reality, it is the other way around. Only when you get to know the phenomenon commonly known as "death", when you understand and accept it then you will have a chance that this so-called "death" won't return to haunt you.

Perhaps, like many other people you are afraid to think about death. This is because you know nothing or very little about it. Therefore, you don't understand what happens in the moment of "death" and as a result a great fear paralyses you about this occurrence.

The word "death" should be written in quotes because in reality there is no death. You never die. Only your physical body dies. During so-called "death" you take off your body in the same way you take off old, used, unneeded clothing and you - as the essence of you - still exists, and this is the eternal life. The transformation called death is in reality a movement from one state of consciousness into another one. It is as if you were moving from one classroom to another.

The purpose of this book is to help you get rid of your fear of death and to inspire you. My desire is for you to move through life filled with peace and trust, and not to flit by death secretly and in constant fear of your own life and the lives of others.

Dear reader, I realize that this is an abhorrent subject and that you might approach it with antipathy. But you have to understand that sooner or later you will have to face this problem. This way it will not surprise you or suddenly hit you like a lightning bolt later on in life. Now you have enough time to calmly prepare yourself and your friends and family (only if they are willing) to make a conscious and safe transition to the other side.

You cannot assume that the people close to you will be open to the knowledge introduced in this book. You can't do anything about that. You can't forcefully make them aware of it. Obviously, it would be better if your friends and family also had this knowledge and live in peace. Then they would be growing and thinking just like you. However, you can't force them into anything. You can just wait and hope their beliefs will change. But keep in mind that they might never get there. Therefore start the change with you and quietly hope that they will follow in your footsteps. Otherwise you will end up wasting your chance in the same way as they wasted theirs by not taking any action. So, don't rush them or pressure them to grow and follow your lead because none of you will gain anything from it.

I am addressing this book to everyone, not only to sick, elderly or dying persons. By making yourself familiar with the information presented here you will stop fearing death and you will prepare for it as one might prepare for a trip, in the way you find most convenient. You will get used to death and as a result your fear will disappear. Consequently, you will stop being afraid in general and you will learn to become fearless in this world as well as in the next one.

If you have somebody in your family that is very sick or if you are mourning someone, this book will help you to get through tough times like these now and in the future.

The knowledge introduced here is also useful for people who take care of sick people professionally. Thanks to this knowledge the quality of live will improve for both the people who we call alive and those who we refer to as dead.

If you are young and healthy then this will still be very appropriate reading material. It's about time you became familiar with this topic. Don't leave it for later because you are not living in a world where death only comes to the elderly who have lived a rewarding life. It is the opposite – death seems to lurk around each corner. Isn't this why you should want to know more about death now?

In bookstores there are thousands of books on different subjects. There are books that tell you how young women should give birth, how to raise kids, how to pick schools for them, how to decorate an apartment, what to eat to live up to a certain number of years and even what to wear. We also have many books on salvation of the soul. But there are only a limited number of books that touch on a topic that involves all of us without any exceptions, namely the topic of "death". What is it and what happens to us after it. I am writing "death" in quotation marks because we use this terminology to refer to a deceased when his/her body is not showing any signs of life. Obviously, this is an illusion because in reality after so called "death" this person is even more active than ever before. Something like "death" doesn't exist because you, the essence of you lives eternally.

In this book, I will summarize the concept of "death" in a very simplified way. I will narrow it down to a physical body which we discard in the moment of "death" like used clothing that is no longer needed. And, I will mention only a little about the essence of the person who after leaving the physical body still exists and functions as during physical life. This is all too broad a knowledge to fit into one book.

If you read books covering a similar subject matter before and think that you know everything about it, remember that this area of knowledge is similar to a poem. By reading it once and twice you will not remember much about it. However, by reading it repetitiously it will sink deep into your memory such that you will never be able to forget it. This is the point – to permanently retain this material in your consciousness. Then you will not only have this knowledge in an intellectual way, but you will also be adept in this area on a deep, personal level. At that time you will have something like a map or compass with which you can peacefully move around in this world and in the next world.

What you are going to read here is for each one of us the most important things in the world. From this basic knowledge or from lack of it, *Who You Are in Essence,* will be determined the quality of your everyday life here on Earth as well as after your departure.

Perhaps you are thinking that you had no influence over the fact that you appeared here and over what you will do after the death of your physical body. In that case you will constantly feel enslaved and everything that you do will be loaded with antipathy or feel like a great burden. However, if you can have influence over those things, I think that you would like to know what kind of influence you have in that regard. It will give you a feeling of freedom, lightness and it might bring about great inner changes. It is very important that you come around to understanding the following: this knowledge has an assertive influence not only on your evanescent life, but on all events that will come after the death of your physical body.

I hope that by reading this book you will look at your life from a different perspective and free yourself from the pretense or illusion which up until now you considered life. Everything that I am writing here you already know somewhere on the deeper level of your being and my role is only to remind you about what is already inside of you.

This book as well as my previous books, took up such a task. My intention was fulfilled because they brought up to the consciousness of readers matters that were up to that point untapped, which in turn changed the lives of many families. Does it mean that I discovered something new? Of course not, because this knowledge was known for the longest time, long before Jesus came to Earth, though many events during the development of the church, especially during the times of the Inquisition. This knowledge was erased from our collective consciousness therefore also from our memory. In my first book – *Possessed by Ghosts* – I pointed out innumerable examples of what has led to this lack of a very basic knowledge.

Obviously, almost each person knows that the ghosts of dead people exist, but I wanted to show how tragic are the effects of the connection between the astral and physical world, especially when we approach life frivolously.

Most people don't assimilate these laws; as a result they die in unconsciousness and then are afraid to cross to the other side of death's curtain. Many persons are deluded into thinking that after the death of their physical bodies they are living the same life as they had been to that point and that nothing has changed for them. However, after their death, the lives of those who remain in the physical life may change greatly, just because the deceased remain next to us. Most people don't realize that and therefore the results of such things turn out to be in most cases lamentable.

I am not talking about the extreme cases which I described in the book *Possessed By Ghosts*, but about people who didn't completely break down yet, but their lives are as hard, and uncompromising, whether we are talking about a single person, entire family or entire social groups.

Through this book, my desire is to ensure that you will come to understand on your deeper level of consciousness that what we call "death" is nothing else but abandoning the physical body like used clothing. My wish is also to present here what will happen to you after this happens. Based on my forty years of experience and knowledge and the analysis of tens of thousands of cases of people that asked me for help, I certainly know that there is far too little of this basic knowledge. This is why I am addressing this book to everyone, not only to the readers who are now dealing with their own loved ones death or those who are in mourning. I obviously don't wish to impose on anyone the principles presented here because everyone has a right to the way they choose to live their lives and behave. I am only trying to point out the road that is suitable and simple, tried by many people and found to be very satisfying. Dear reader, what you are going to do with this knowledge and whether you will learn something from it is your decision. Let your heart suggest to you. You can also do nothing and dwell in ignorance, because you have done this for a very long time already. What you will decide and do, won't make a greater difference for God or universe. However change resulting from adopting the principles described here, could turn out to be very helpful and felt by you and your surroundings.

A Few Words about Myself

I had always been sensitive to people's hardships and I often had asked myself whether people's suffering is inevitable, is a result of bad fate or whether perhaps something could be done about it. Often I would dig deep into the cause of a person's misery and investigate until I found the reason for his misfortune and what's more important, its solution.

In that way I recognized that the cause for some problems were often ghosts although even the youngest kids knew about this. What is more important, I was able to recognize any dependencies between the cause and effect, not only in this world, but also in the other world. Most of all I would discover then that a person is never born nor dies. What we commonly call "death" is nothing else, but putting away a physical body, in the same way we throw away old, used, unneeded clothing (I repeat this sentence every so often, because I want for it to sink deeply into your memory). I noticed that many souls (ghosts) who didn't have a physical body for a long time weren't aware of their death and in the so-called "netherworld", functioned in the same way as during their physical lifetime.

I also understood why ghosts remain among the living and what the cause for their influence on our life is. In my research I went even further and discovered unremitting, even for a second, continuity of life in this and in the other world. These are not my guesses or fantasies. These facts are supported by my research and gathered knowledge based on analyzing thousands of similar cases of people who reached out to me for help.

I am an exorcist, psychologist and parapsychologist, but most of all a researcher and scientist although for the area that I address here, there are no schools of higher education. For people that only use their senses and don't have developed extra-sensory perception I may seem to be someone not worthy of trust, maybe even dangerous. For I look into the areas that are completely inaccessible to many, areas that they have no idea even exists. How could we live without this knowledge since it is for a human as important as the air that we breathe? I am not talking here about a simple person who in reference to any knowledge seems to be ignorant. I am talking about people who consider themselves educated, intelligent, even religious or spiritual.

These persons' sense of logic is deceiving them, not allowing them to understand something which (only at that moment) is beyond their ability to perceive and subsequently also understand. We can't see without the right tools, telescope or microscope something very far away or miniscule. Similarly many of us are not able to notice something that is directly accessible to us, but indistinguishable for our physical senses. That "right tool" didn't develop in us yet. As a result it becomes impossible to perceive the reality in a way that really is.

Most people are only able to appreciate the materialistic – what could be touched, seen, smelled, measured and weighted. They are not able to believe in other things they can't see them for themselves, for example, ghosts, subtle bodies so-called auras (although there are special cameras created that could photograph such phenomena). They are saying that such things are nonsense. However, what for some people is impossible, for others is a completely natural thing.

Many people have a gift of multisensory perception, but only a few have any knowledge on this subject. They can see and everything is alright until they share their insights with others. Then the problem starts, because the latter's sense, not that it doesn't want to, but it can't accept the perspective of such a perception. Simply it is not adjusted to it. The atomic structure of the brain cells does not allow for this comprehension. Only when most people accept a certain phenomenon, then the logic minds of others make it their own reality.

It happened often in the past that something was discovered that people couldn't understand because their senses couldn't grasp it. At first, in their own defense they resisted the discovery and oppressed the discoverer fearing that it will disrupt their world, position and wealth. The list of such people is long and could easily fill a few volumes.

I was also publicly condemned and called a deceptive person in front of an audience of millions. Such was the magnitude of the viewership (it was record breaking) of the television show on which they were trying to condemn me. Who was behind this attempt? An editor who at all costs was looking for a sensation and a psychiatrist who no matter what was presented didn't want to accept the knowledge I was offering. If he would and most importantly, if he could embrace this knowledge, his clinics would be empty and he wouldn't make a fortune prescribing psychotropic medication in his private practice. These people thought they would harm me in this way… On the flip side though, of the four million people who directly watched the show and the hundreds of thousands of people, if not millions of people, who later found out about it, not even a small percentage of them came forward to say that they had been deceived as a result of my help as an exorcist.

I don't hold a grudge against anyone because I know that the creators of the show were guided by their logical mind which we know contains only a small part of the entire human mind. And if the rest of the mind is closed then such persons would be unable to learn anything new. A closed mind rejects everything different which contradicts its beliefs although it could be (and usually is) mistaken. One force that closes people's mind is fear. Only open minds can look beyond logic and accept and process new knowledge.

Dear reader this explains why many people don't want to know about matters which impact their fate and upon which their existence depends; in this and the other world. Don't you think they behave like an ostrich hiding its head in the sand? Or like a hiker who chose to take a walk through a dangerous, unknown area without a compass or map (currently substituted by a GPS). Nevertheless, many people who travel through foreign places don't want to learn anything about it because they are afraid of that knowledge and what they would possibly see.

This is precisely how most people around us behave, including some priests who we are accustomed to calling our shepherds. Considering what happens to them after the death of their physical body, they are in no better situation than most people. Some people ignorance this because they lack basic information, while others do this out of fear, and yet others who are conceited claim to be great and already have this "knowledge". The last group is in the worst position. They think they know enough, but in reality they are blind and deaf to everything that could be helpful to their soul's development. However they would first have to admit this to themselves and accept the fact that in reality they know nothing. This is well illustrated by the saying: "A wise man learns constantly, a stupid man already knows everything".

You can't see, touch or fix a soul with your physical senses. This is why many materialistic people think souls don't exist and is part of an old belief system. They then however let go of the steering wheel and drift on the waters of life from situation to situation. It is possible for someone in their physical state to lead a decent life and hide behind the academic titles. After death though, they become frightened because they don't know what to do with themselves next.

Society seems to be rapidly progressing. In many areas we see progress, but this is only materialistic progress. In matters regarding our inner selves nothing or very little has changed. In private live, at own homes, in relationships, at work most people desire steadiness above all else. They would eagerly stop everything around them so that nothing changes. However, the world and life is continuously moving forward. There is constant change that forces us to constantly develop. Spiritual growth requires constantly working on yourself and this means there is a need of constant change and this change provokes new changes and thus the process goes on and on. This is what it means to go with the spirit of the age, in agreement with the necessary life changes and the need to move forward.

Nonetheless, many people are very afraid of changes and retreat from life and in a short period die thinking that "THERE" they will finally achieve happiness, peace and solace. In other words, everything that they were lacking here on Earth. Unfortunately, that "THERE" is not in reality any new, amazing place with amazing life that is freeing us from being responsible for ourselves. Rather, it is an extension of our existing life "HERE". Therefore, if our life was happy here on Earth, then it is also going to be the same "THERE", on the other side of the curtain. Conversely, an unhappy life here as a consequence will lead to a continuation of the present adversity faced in life. Readers of my previous books *Possessed by Ghosts* and *In the Wheel of Life* already know about this. We don't have any other choice but to try to achieve happiness now, when we still have our physical body. Otherwise we will be unpleasantly surprised.

It is incredibly important, dear reader as you go on the journey of reading this book that you maintain a logical and rational mindset. But at the same time, I want you to look beyond it. It is as foolish to accept everything without consideration, contemplation and afterthought, as it is to immediately deny that which is new. The former and latter functions do not operate on the same principle. Know that solely thinking logically is keeping you on the leash and not letting to perceive your own life from a broader perspective.

I hope that your experiences from reading this book will help you, to transform you, into a loving being that feels safe, avoids violence and is fearless. It's true that we hear voices coming from everywhere about impending doom and evidences of global warming are shown to us which foretell huge changes. Humankind expropriated and manhandled for too long the good energy which is God, so we shouldn't be surprised that we witness so many cataclysms (which are always the reflection of what is happening in people's souls). If we don't change, there will be more catastrophes. I am not writing this to make you scared, but to encourage you to change your way of thinking. We can't pretend any longer to be cat's whiskers and live with the delusion that from us, from each of you dear reader, nothing is required. What is happening around us depends more and more on you than it seems to you, meaning each one of us separately creates the reality that we live in. Therefore, we must act in harmony, let go of hatred, anger, fear and pride. We must have the courage to act in the right way. We must love and respect ourselves and others, recognize and appreciate the beauty and dignity of all people including ourselves and those close to us, because we are all souls made from the same matter. Only through cooperation, becoming one huge family, can we avoid the storm. If we can't achieve this collaboratively then each one of us individually, one after another has to find the way Home.

In order to have a full appreciation of things we must start with the most basic principles to gain a better understanding not just superficially or even rationally, but on all levels of our being. We must recall *Who We Are in Essence*.

WHO ARE YOU

If I were to ask you, who you are, probably you would immediately tell me your first and last name or you would point with your hand at your body. Right?

If you haven't had deep thoughts about yourself, you haven't asked yourself these type of questions before then most likely you will just identify yourself with your physical body. That is because your body seems to be the very exterior of you, is the most visible and the most tangible. If you are religious then your answer could be slightly different, deeper. Religions generally say that inside you there is "something", which is called a "soul" or spirit. It's that hypothetical "something", that most people find difficult to quickly define.

Certainly you are that "something" that desires, envies, acts, misses, is happy, pleased, calm or opposite, helpless or furious. During your lifetime you constantly repeat: "I am this", "I am that", "I have this", "I have or I don't have that". During any given day you play many roles. At your own home you must be a father/mother to your kids, or a son/daughter to your parents. At the same time you are, for example, a wife, housewife and in the evening a lover. At work you are a boss or employee and at the same time a friend. We can go on and on counting the roles. And if a person is more active, then he/she has even more roles. In addition there are all the roles that we play to ourselves: I am resourceful, poor, loser, I love and I am loved, I am happy or not happy. Your personality puts on a mask, in fact many masks to as it plays all these roles.

Therefore, your "I" creates a specific "you" which causes your consciousness to also say "I", "I", "I" – Although more often than not you repeat the "I" which you identify with your body. However you have to deny this rationalization because you certainly are not only your body with all its functions. There is also in your body something more and that something, dear reader, you also call it "I". What is that "I"? You say: "I have a hand", "I have a head", "This is mine", therefore this belongs to you, to your "I". However if your "I" has that then that cannot be you. Therefore your "I" is not your hand, not your leg, not your head, because your "I" has them, your "I" owns them. Your hand and your head only belong to you, but they are not you.

Since you are not your body, then what are you? What is that "I" that owns your body? If you are not what you are on the outside since you are not your own body, then does this mean that you are "something" what exists inside. So, some interior being moves your body, thinks for you, feels, and acts according to your will. A body which up until now you considered as yourself, in reality, is like clothing for your inner being. In the material world you wouldn't be able to do anything without this clothing; you wouldn't be able to perform the simplest material-istic, physical actions.

You are wedded to this illusion because you perceive yourself in the form of a personality, and your body as your property. However you are not the personality that you consider yourself to be, but a soul, the Divine Spark of God. Living in the illusion you don't bear in mind that your "own" body doesn't belong to you at all, but it's the home of God. You are looking for Him intensely in the outside world meanwhile He is inside you, as well as inside every other person. Divinity exists in the innermost depths of your being. At this point we arrive at a par-adox. Although the world in itself reflects completeness and ex-cellence, in reality you don't have access to it. You don't know that you can only have access to that truth through the truth of your own interior, through discovery of your inner being, your true "Self".

However to get to that inner being you have to declutter your interior through constant cleansing and healing of a huge space of your subconscious inside which mills around the entire accumulation of pent up emotions, ousted desires, unconscious conflicts and frustrated needs. They cause blockades inside of you. In order for the energy to flow effortlessly, all of that has to be cleansed and healed. It is only possible to achieve contact with your own inner being, with your own self, in other words, with what is the best, purest and most excellent in you when nothing blocks the free flow of energy in your body as well as in your mind.

YOUR BIRTH

When you think about your birth you might form an impression that you are here on Earth for the first time and appearing in the body of a small child was the beginning of your being. However, a baby's body was not the beginning of your life. Perhaps, dear reader, you don't agree with me on this matter, because you don't feel the continuity of your life. You may think that if you lived before then you should remember at least a little bit about what was happening with you before you were born. You don't have that memory because if you did it would completely overwhelm you and you would be unable to function and experience *Who You Are in Essence*. Nevertheless, that memory has your Self, your inner being. You also lose the memory of your previous incarnations in order to significantly improve your fate or your destiny in the current stage of your growth. If you had, dear reader, the memory of your previous incarnations

you would also have the knowledge of how to avoid much needed growth experiences and how balance out certain causes. And,
if you immediately balance out those causes you would be leading a boring, unsatisfied, stereotypical life. Therefore you would
not be interested in life at all. Life would stop being a mystery to
you and it would become only an existence resembling a boring
game that you had already played many times before. You
would exactly know how to go through "life's pitfalls" and perfectly know the end result of the game.

The entire process of life is just based on constantly
searching for the truth, constantly reminding yourself *Who You
Are In Essence*, and I would like to help you find this truth, dear
reader. You will only understand how important it is to awaken
that memory in you when you realize what we call "death" really is. Understanding death allows us to fully understand life, this
in turn allows us to understand ourselves. Only then you begin
to remember *Who You Are in Essence* and what all of this is really about.

I would like you, dear reader, to look at your life from a
broader perspective, be present here and now in your physical
body, but at the same time know and always remember *Who You
really Are*. I understand that it is hard for you to realize, *Who
You Are*, when you look at some tiny being that was just born to
this Earth and you see his fragility and helplessness. That perspective so strongly acts on your senses that it gives you the impression that you are just a small child just starting out in life. In
a way, it is so, because your old, experienced soul receives a
new chance to experience new desires.

This is why a soul is born in new circumstances, a new
environment, and amongst new people. When you realize this, a
new, broader perspective of *Who You really Are*, will unfold in

front of you, a perspective not resembling the picture of who you think you are. Then you will also stop feeling fear and instead a zeal for life will awaken in you. This is exactly why you came to this Earth, to always have zeal, vigor and constantly derive pleasure from your creative life without even the smallest deviation from this. Every second of your life you are creating something, if you want to or not, whether you are aware of it, or whether you are doing it unwittingly. Creativity starts with your thoughts, but are you aware of all your thoughts? This is why consciousness is needed. By living a continually growing, creative life you will achieve well-being in every category of your life. Well-being means a good state in all, facets of life without exception, including health, finances, relationships, etc. Life is offering you thousands of opportunities to achieve this, but you must decide whether you are open to them or not and which of these opportunities, if any you will choose.

You didn't come to this world just to be here. You were brought here by a desire. You planned your life in a specific manner when you were still in the non-physical world, in the non-physical nonmaterial space, before you adopted your physical body. You planned to face new challenges linked with own desires, but most of all to derive from your own life everything that was in the best interest of your own development.

WHAT IS SOUL?

All religions agreeably speak of a soul. Since I was young I heard that every person had a soul which leaves the body after death and goes to heaven, hell or purgatory. If a soul leaves the body then to me that meant it was still alive. No matter where it goes it is still going to "exist" somewhere. Oh God! I was almost jumping with happiness. If my soul still exists after death, doesn't it mean that I will never die, that I will still be alive? At that moment I stopped being afraid of death and concerned for my well-being, but continually other questions were popping up in my head.

I was asking: "Is my soul me – little Wanda?" "Probably yes" – immediately I was answering myself – "but is my soul my body? No, it can't be my body, my hand or leg, because my next door neighbor doesn't have legs and still lives." Suddenly, I thought that my soul, my "I", is my brain: "Yes. It is my brain.

Because when I say: I Wanda, I feel that in my head. Yes, it's the head that is guiding my life, certainly my soul is in my head. However if a soul leaves a body then it cannot be a body, it cannot be in my head" – I was intensely contemplating all of this. Adults continually repeated to me that it's in my body. Where? Is it in the heart or in some other place?

If my soul is so important to me and since it determines where I will go after death, why do I know so little about it? I don't even know if I treat my soul good or bad. Can I feel, see, touch, or even fix it if it is malfunctioning, cheer it up if it is suffering, or comfort it if it feels lost? If yes, then who can do this or is this doable at all? Who is guiding it? I – little Wanda – or perhaps that great, dangerous God who exists somewhere far away in Heaven like they taught us in religious class.

When we are young we develop a fear of a dangerous and spiteful God. We wonder how we could love Him and if it even makes sense to ask Him anything since He has treated us so cruelly just for eating an apple. So what is awaiting us when committing even greater mistakes?

From that moment on, even as a young child, I was no longer indifferent to what was going to happen after I rid of my physical body or what I do, think and feel. I knew that these things would determine where my soul ended up and what would happen to me. Such contemplating led me to the research and work which I currently do.

Dear reader, tell me what you think about where your soul is? Is it in the head, because you use it to think and make decisions? It is not there? Perhaps is it in your heart? In the end, it is your heart that is the engine for your body and when it stops beating you stop living. Not there either? Perhaps it is in your stomach because there you feel your emotions. Not there?

Where then? Even if you looked through the tiniest parts of your body you would not find it there. Therefore, dear reader, do you have a soul or not?

Of course, you have one! You have a soul since you are aware that you exist, this consciousness, which is your real, true "I".

We are looking for a soul in our body because throughout the ages we have heard that our body has a soul which leaves after death and wanders... It may seem that way, but the truth is absolutely different.

When we are here, on Earth, and we look at ourselves from the perspective of only one life, it seems to us that we are a body that has a soul. When I did further research, I reached a conclusion (like many greater people before me) that humans not only have a soul, we are a soul that has a body. Much later I also discovered that each one of us has many bodies which in different spheres (on different planes) are vessels and tools of our soul. If you are more interested in this subject I recommend my book *In the Wheel of Life.* The task of that modest, "little book" is to outline that subject to you.

Therefore, what we call "death" is merely a parting of the soul from the form that exists in the lowest sphere, or energy plane, in other words from the physical body. Meanwhile, the soul or the essence of our being which resides on a higher plane doesn't change, just as a physical person/body doesn't change when we take off our clothes.

TABOO SUBJECT

Dear reader, you need to know that in our modern world religion and science, in a way have conspired to make immortality and life after death taboo subjects. Obviously, this didn't happen on its own. Once the leaders of the Church noticed that more and more followers were turning away from the Church they came up with the idea to join forces with the world of science. Since then they started directing followers' attention to science as the provider of solutions to all humanity's agonizing problems.

As a result of that people for hundreds of years mistakenly believed that if science could only reach a certain point in development, it would solve all the humanity's problems. Science was supposed to become a path to freedom from illnesses, poverty and suffering. Currently, we know that science and technology can't solve such problems on its own. They could be used for good as well as bad purposes. Actually, technology can only help us when we use it consciously, wisely and above all in moderation. Humanity itself must find inner harmony and balance. It cannot be given as a gift for anyone from the outside (even by using the most amazing technology). Not all people realize that the basis for balance and harmony is love, and love we can only find inside of us.

Putting the power in the hands of science caused the teaching system to be distorted and it contributed even more to our mental confusion. Such flawed teaching meant that only materialistic ways of explaining the world were considered. As a result this seems exceedingly attractive to people and they don't consider other options. Obviously, mere science and scientists should not be blamed. It is us (each person individually) that allowed these false perceptions to control our thinking and gain more and more followers. They don't present anything other than what can be seen, tasted, touched, heard, smelled, measured, weighted, bought or sold. This is humanity's legacy of which we are so proud. We don't realize that this is leading us to a dead end, which we realize only after the death of our physical body when it's too late to do anything about it. There is a saying "A Pole is wise after the event". It should be changed to "A human is wise after the event" because obviously this phenomenon can be applied globally.

More and more people are trying to get out of the darkness into which humanity has descended over centuries. The limitations of the material world still bother most people, especially educated persons because they rely how things appear based on their five senses. This applies to individuals as well as entire institutions. At first glance it seems that there are people who are impervious to reason. How should we refer to people who never controvert their convictions and belief system? New explanations can't be accepted and consequently new knowledge either. It is not even allowed for by others as our minds are blinded by outdated convictions and ideas. This is why people pay so little attention to their roots which can be traced to long before the moment of their physical birth or their future which, dear reader, goes far beyond the death of the physical body. Although we have many scholars, in matters regarding life itself we only touch the surface of the phenomenon. Most often we rely only on what we already know and that doesn't allow us to realize the nature of things that exist beyond the perception of our five senses. Scientists look for, for example: life on distant planets where it absolutely exists, but they can't perceive it. Hence, they remain unaware of the amazing spaces that stretch out to the furthest horizons. How many letters I receive regarding such subjects. Individual persons see the non-material world or notice some anomaly, but are afraid to openly talk about it. They write: "Mrs. Pratnicka, you are so brave. I agree with you, but I am too weak to change anything in the way which people think. Readers of my books make up a relatively small group of people. They deeply believe in life after death and accept their immortality.

Meanwhile, sceptics continue to contemptuously burst out laughing at the very thought of life after death and with arrogance they reject the world that are unable to see. They shrug their shoulders and prefer not to care for, what according to them is a distant and uncertain echo from a different world. In any case sooner or later their doubts will also be removed. At the latest, it will occur after the death of their physical body when they will find out how things really are. Older persons say: "How can we know what you write is true? Nobody certainly came back from there yet..." However, many people came back from "there", for instance people who experienced clinical death or long, deep anesthesia. In any case, you cannot prove to some-body something they don't want to believe (and it shouldn't be tried).

Others not noticing those spaces unconsciously deprive themselves of their cosmic identity and consequently deny their spiritual being. By rejecting this legacy they are at the same time denying the essence of their existence. I know this from my dai-ly work experience because I often deal with cases such as the one I describe below.

Once I met a scientist who was a physics professor. Let's call him Karl. He was a hardened materialist who completely didn't believe in life after death or in reincarnation. He spent many hours on debating these topics with me or with bigger groups, with his scientist friends and priests who he liked to bring to our meetings. Karl was a traveler. He was continuously traveling around the world visiting a variety schools. All of that was happening during communism when the topic about live af-ter death was completely unknown. After a few years of such meetings our paths day by day split up in a weird way. He stopped visiting me for no apparent reason. Eventually I found out that at the age of almost forty he fell down the stairs of his department and died before the ambulance came. He didn't visit me after his death either. In a meantime many people from his work environment and his family (who I didn't know before) started to reach out to me as an exorcist for help and continuous-ly described anew the same phenomenon. It turned out that the professor was a tireless and frequent visitor of many debates, and although he was already dead a long time, he was still at-tending them. He died suddenly and didn't understand that his physical body no longer existed. As a result he was behaving in the same way as he did before his death. By actively attending the above mentioned debates he often created terror and confusion in his own home, school and different clubs.

Even when he became aware about the transformation called "death", he still didn't want to leave. Now his goal was to make everyone that had discussions with him aware that he was wrong and he was the apparent proof. Most of them didn't hear him because of fear or lack of faith in life after death. Unwittingly I was forced to mediate in many of his talks until he would get things done, meaning make his friends, colleagues, family and neighbors aware. In most cases I was giving messages from him to his numerous family (also with professional degrees), later they by themselves mediated in the conversations. Those more stubborn I had to "take care of" by myself. Anew groups of people started visiting me to understand what he tried to communicate. Karl was determined and only left when his family and friends understood that life after death exists.

However, such conscious souls like Karl's soul are few. Those more conscious ones leave and those unconscious ones stay and this is why so little knowledge gets across our consciousness.

FEAR OF DEATH

In life we are afraid of many things: pain, old age, poverty, loneliness, the unknown, catastrophes, women fear childbirth, students fear exams, but for most people the most dreadful is perhaps dying.

Death seems to be the most terrifying, but as well as the most unavoidable thing in the world. Why are we afraid of it so much? Why is it for us such a painful event? It is because we don't want to leave this world. We hang on to our loved ones: husbands, wives, parents, kids, friends, lovers and etc. The same way behave people who remain alive. They are afraid to be left alone and don't want to let the dying, departing soul leave. Both of them are doing it in the name of love, but this has nothing to do with love. This way of thinking is not caused by love, but by the paralyzing fear of what will happen to us and how we will manage. Others could be due to attachment to material things, careers or power. Yet others addictions-alcohol, drugs, food, sex, gambling.

We are also afraid of death because we don't know what will happen to us, where we will go after leaving this world. We are not ready for death. From early on we were taught a variety of things, even how women should give birth, but nobody taught us how to die, what death is and what happens to us after death. If we would know that in our lifetime, we would acknowledge that dying is a very happy and joyful moment which should not be feared, but it should be awaited with joy. Death and birth are the same thing. In order to be born on Earth, there, on the other side we have too a way die. Conversely, to be born there, we have to die here, but this is nothing else but a transition from one form of existence to another. Coming to Earth we have to put on an adequate body for our tasks, and when we are leaving Earth we have to release ourselves from that body.

We all belong to God and we came to Earth not for punishment, as some people and religions claim, but to learn in the Earth School. When we come to the world full of trust, our lives are proceeding in harmony and love. When we come with feelings of sorrow, fear, distrust then whatever we do, everything is filled with these feelings. We hold grudges against God that he abandoned and left us alone, but this is not true at all. Our mistaken thinking means we live in sorrow, frustration, fear and dissatisfaction. This happens until the moment we realize what this mistaken thinking is all about. This could last one or few lives.

When we come to understand that in fact God never abandoned us, our lives start to change diametrically. We don't have to hold on to what is known and continuously fight, because we know there is an abundance of everything and that

God is abundant in all existence. After such a satisfied life filled with happiness we will be returning into our Father's arms and death is nothing else but a return Home. There is a good anecdote on this topic.

A person goes to heaven and with God looks at his past life like a 3D movie. After a projection he says to God: "Father, when I was doing well on Earth I saw two pairs of footprints on the path of my life. Yours and mine". On the other hand, when I was not doing well I saw only one pair of footprints. Why did you then abandon me, Father? "Beloved son" – says God – "Those were the moments when I was carrying you".

FAULTY BELIEF

There is no faultier way of thinking than the conviction that death is a process that we don't have to know anything about and during which everything will happen by itself. Agreed, the physical body will be put a in a coffin, buried in the ground or burned in a crematorium, but what will happen to the real human? He will still live on and basically be doing much better than in the physical life. He won't be limited anymore by thick matter. He will feel as if he took off a heavy, uncomfortable suit. Is it wise for a person in this situation to lie down as is done with a physical body and wait for the mercy of fate as referred to by different religions in the Last Judgment? He will resemble a cork that is drifting on the water for many, many years or possibly even thousands of years. Is it worth it to leave things up to fate and swim somehow, somewhere, where most likely we won't like it at all? Well, fate mostly supports people that take control and work on it.

Therefore, I think that it is okay to talk about death. Most of us just need to get used to this idea. Once and for all we need to realize that what we are afraid of the most doesn't exist at all in reality. Death doesn't exist. In reality humans live eternally. This is why you had courage to come to Earth. God promised you an eternal life and he always keeps His word. The death of our physical body seems to be the end but it is really the taking off of an old, used, no longer needed body in order for the real human in his faithful form to continue his journey. This form is a precise reflection of a physical body, but for most physical eyes it is invisible. Where are we going? This depends upon us one hundred percent. However, to be able to make a decision about this we at least need to know the laws that apply in that reality. Jesus from Nazareth constantly reminded people: "Know the truth and it will free you" Free us from what? It will free us from the limitations that we put on ourselves when we think according to what our five senses tell us. How do I know this? From the experiences of tens of thousands of people that reached out to me in the last few years, and this should be multiplied by the amount of ghosts that have possessed individual persons. This adds up to a large number of r beings in total.

This is what a person wrote to me after he has read my book *Possessed by Ghosts* and stopped being afraid of death: "Mrs. Pratnicka! At first I didn't realize that I have completely changed, and then when I did, I didn't know why it happened. Indeed, I realized that somehow I am calmer and more patient towards my wife and kids. Next, acquaintances were asking me why I looked so rested and happy, as though I had won the lottery. When I started to think more deeply about it, I came to the conclusion that it was because I no longer feared death which up until then I was very frightened of. I also stopped being afraid of my non-existence and all of that thanks to your book. I am less fearful of losing my loved ones (up until then this was my greatest concern). I realized that I would certainly feel deep sadness, but I wouldn't be in great despair as I was before. This is because I know that death doesn't end my life and I am aware that they won't die at all, but only move to another state of existence. Why would I despair in this situation knowing that they are right next to me? Mrs. Pratnicka, you have no idea, how much this knowledge has changed my life. Only now can I create, be happy and live. Once again thank you, greetings and I wish you the best of luck. Jack Leffers".

How nerve-wrecking and common is the fear of death. Due to this fear there are many strange things that happen with people. Mostly, they want to hold on to their lives as long as they can. When they realize that time is slipping through their fingers they experience a very deep inner crisis which they are not able to handle. This is why people continuously get into new relationships, are obsessed about their looks and the looks of others s, physical function, gathering material things and striving for many completely needless things. All of that makes them forget the true goal of their lives.

Dear reader, what do you think about the moment of your life, commonly called "death"? Do you sometimes wonder what would it be like when it happens to you? Probably you sometimes think about what would happen when a loved one (father, mother, spouse) passes away, if you were suddenly left alone. I doubt though that you wondered about you own departure from the world of physical matter. Don't you think it is about time you changed that? Death constantly occurs to people and it doesn't have to do with old age at all. Do you think that it will avoid you?

THINKING ABOUT DEATH

Dear reader, have you ever thought about death and what will happen when you leave your physical body? What is going to happen with you? What will you do? Where will you go? Are you afraid to think about this? Perhaps, you think that you are young and healthy enough that it is Unnecessary to have precautionary concerns. Do you think that considerations about death should be reserved for old, sick people and until you reach that stage you still have many years to live? Do you believe that only the old and sick die? "Oh yes" – you say – "Indeed, young people also die, but in unexpected accidents and I am always lucky and very careful so nothing like that will happen to me". Maybe you think: "Why care about such an unpleasant topic, what is meant to happen, will happen. In the meantime, I will care for more pleasant things…" You are wrong. If you get used to death now then it won't seem to you so frightening or cruel. Only then will you begin to actually live. Surely you will be offended now and say: "But I live alright now and also fairly well". Indeed, but this life is full of anxiety. Perhaps, you didn't notice it because you pushed it deep into your subconscious. However, that fear is letting you know about its existence every day, every hour and in every second.

I am not asking these questions to scare you in any case. I just wanted to remind you that what you call "death" exists and takes away old, young, small kids, the sick as well as healthy and strong people. Avoiding thinking and talking about death is like running away from something that is chasing you and when you have no more strength to run you fall from exhaustion, suddenly realizing that what you have been running away from is your own shadow. This is not a metaphor, because death is accompanying life like a shadow from the moment of our birth. Accepting death and completely getting rid of the fear of death will not shorten, but will indeed prolong your life.

As you probably know, when you are afraid of something you attract it to yourself even more. You are afraid of an accident and after some time it happens to you; you are afraid of robbery, theft and after some time you experience them. When you are paranoid about death, when you are paranoid to the point of pretending it doesn't concern you, you are attracting it to yourself like a huge magnet.

Now stop and think, meditate. What does death mean to you? Is it the end or the beginning? When you get rid of the fear of death you will become fearless. In fact, there is nothing more frightening than that fear. Besides death what else could you be afraid of?

I would like to tell you that there is nothing to fear, because you never die. No, you didn't misunderstand. You will never die. What you are calling "death" is just abandoning your physical body; it is no different from taking off your clothes. Just like we throw away used clothes similarly we abandon our used bodies. This doesn't mean that we stop existing. "Nonsense" – you think – "everything what is born, must die. This is how it is and nothing can be done about it". I want to comfort you. Nothing that is born dies, it only changes from one form to another. From heavy, thick (this is our physical body) to very light after death as this is what our non-material body is built from. As during life we have a body, mind (which we shouldn't mistake for a brain) and soul, so to after death we have a body, mind and soul.

Your body, mind and soul live eternally. How do you feel about this news? Are you glad? Are you relieved? Are you puzzled? Maybe you shouted that I am writing nonsense? Maybe you are mad at yourself that you unnecessarily feared all your life? Or maybe it would be a shame for you to give up this fear since you like to worry so much? Maybe you simply believe in death and nothing will convince you otherwise? Most likely, you won't recognize this knowledge right away because you believed in death many, many years and for many incarnations. You are not alone in thinking this way. Many people think this way. Our parents, grandparents, great grandparents were thinking this way therefore you too are possibly thinking this way according to tradition.

I am writing this, dear reader, to make you realize that based on what you know about death, what you think about it during your life and what you expect from it, will be determined what will happen to you after death and your further fate. In the following chapters I will provide the examples that will confirm what I write here. If you want more examples I recommend my books *Possessed by Ghosts* and *In the Wheel of Life.*

Now I will describe death, a sudden death. A person is

riding in some sort of transportation and suddenly gets into an accident. At first this person is frightened and shocked. He thinks: "God, I am dying". A moment later he observes that he is not, he was wrong. "Ah what a relief" – for a moment he thought that he had died, but he didn't, he is still alive. Rejoicing! Only how did he survive this accident? It was a hopeless situation, but he made it. Suddenly, he notices that some people are running around, screaming, and administrating first aid. They are screaming that he died?! "Are they crazy, but I am alive. I can hear, see, feel, and move better than before. No, this is insane. Either I have gone mad or they have gone mad". He is trying to tell them that they are mistaking – "I am alive, I didn't die" – but they don't want to listen to him. Suddenly he notices that he is in a way slightly above them, lightly in the air. What about down there? "No, this butchered body in the huge puddle of blood is me? How is this possible? Certainly, I have my body, nothing is hurting me, and I am feeling light, free and strangely happy". The body is being taken to an ambulance; "Wait a moment, what about me?" He is going with them to the hospital. His family was notified. Everybody is in despair. Hearts are aching at the sight of mourning. "I have to quickly tell them so they don't worry. There is no death, I am still alive". What is that, they can't hear me? My wife seems to be looking through me. Even her? We understood each other so well up until now, even without words.

Most ghosts report death more or less in the same way. These people, rather souls experience authentic shock, they are alone, nobody sees or hears them, and they are ignored. It is the same way people who survived clinical death and who were saved describe death. You could say that the shock comes from the fact the person was not expecting the accident and more so

death. Even when death is preceded by a long illness and awaited with anticipation it is described in the same or a similar way.

Those who didn't have knowledge that after death there
is still life are usually greatly surprised by that fact. Their first
reaction is a desire to tell this to their loved ones, for them to
know so some day they won't be surprised themselves. They are
trying in every way to get someone to notice, most often with no
results. Some decide to come back even for a moment to a body
in order to be able to tell them. In the next part of this book I
will describe the instances that I witnessed myself.

LIFE ON EARTH

Our life on Earth can be compared to a great school (I will write more about that in a moment). When we come into this world we are like children who leave their parent's home to go to school, and our death is nothing more than returning Home from earthly school. When a child leaves home to go to school with happiness expecting that he will learn something new, meet his friends with whom he will experience adventure, his life lessons proceed harmoniously. He knows and trusts that all is going to be well no matter what path he chooses because consequently it will lead him to his goal. He trusts that he has enough time to achieve his goals. He also trusts that school is safe and nothing bad can happen to him there. He doesn't have to be afraid, rush or take life too seriously because in fact everything is a learning process. He knows that after classes his beloved parents are waiting home for him.

When a child leaves home for school anxious or distrustful, he is not able to learn much because he doesn't do much besides waiting to return home. He holds a grudge against his parents for sending him to school. He is full of rebellion and hostility. In everything he does he feels the victim of a horrible fate that he was maneuvered into and had no influence over. He has no desire either for learning or living. Most of us have such an approach to life. We are angry at God that He sent us here. Learning we treat us punishment, and not a chance for growth. By continually resisting we are not able to learn much and therefore we go through the same lessons many times like a student who repeats the same grade over and over.

The longer we go to school the more we get used to it and then it develops in us a desire to remain there permanently. We forget that we came to Earth to learn and our life belongs entirely to God. This doesn't happen with all people, but with great number of them. Those people, who forgot this, return to God full of pity that everything they had on Earth they had to leave behind. It's like a student who would like to take home what he plays with at school not considering that at home he has everything he needs, and even more and better things. The death of our physical body is our return Home and for that reason it should be full of happiness, trust, and love because we are going back to our true parents.

UNDERSTANDING LIFE

When we look at life from only one, physical point of view we are unable to understand it and it seems to us that everything is devoid of any meaning. Moreover, we are deluded into thinking that God is unjust.

We wonder why some people are healthy, beautiful, wealthy, have everything that they dream of, live like they are in paradise while others seem to lack everything. They have nothing to put in a cooking pan and sometimes they don't even have a cooking pan or kitchenette. Every day they are struggling with new difficulties, illnesses, adversities and accidents. Or conversely– we can ask why beautiful, smart, wealthy people are sometimes so extremely unhappy while others deprived of all of that are cheerful, full of love and fulfilled. Shouldn't we consider that maybe this is a based on how they behaved at some point in the past?

From the perspective of the life which we are now experiencing we are unable to understand God, ourselves or even the meaning of life in general. However when we look at life from the broader perspective (such as what we deal with daily) suddenly everything becomes clear and understandable, gaining an entirely different meaning. We find in it a deep sense of justice. We don't hold grudges against God because we begin to understand that the conditions in which each person currently lives is the result of their soul's desires. It is the next lesson assigned to them to learn or the result of their former choices. If, for example you are destroying your environment now then some day when you are born again you will end up living in it. This is exactly what justice is. Many people don't get it that their grandchildren and great grandchildren will have to live in such horrible conditions (maybe they don't have them or care very little about them). However, when they come to understand the truth that they themselves will live such a reality they suddenly change their idle way of thinking.

SCHOOL CALLED LIFE

Dear reader, I would now like to show you life as a whole. Looking from the frog's perspective you see little, however looking at the same phenomena from a bird's eye view you are able to see physical life from a completely different point of view. Looking from the spiritual perspective you discover with astonishment that you are not only a physical body, but also a being that lives eternally, the same as the eternal God which created you. Currently you don't feel Him because you are identifying with your physical body and personality instead of your soul. Therefore, you don't understand your own life or life in general. This is why I suggest finding the courage and looking at matters from a broader perspective.

Well from God, The Source of Everything that Exists once erupted energy compounds. This led to matter interacting at various experience levels. The human soul, including your own, set off to new spaces. It decided to gain new experiences through continuous learning and expression. However, each journey, even the longest one someday eventually comes to an end. It is the same with the journey of your soul. The soul then comes back to God, to Father-Mother, to Source, to Light. These are the various names for that same reality.

From the physical point of view everything in the universe works based on waves. As a result of the existence of the progressing wave of the universe, your soul's life, meaning the essence of you, is based on descending into thicker matter (which consists of your physical body and also the physical Earth) and ascending back into higher spiritual worlds. Each time that your soul goes back Home it takes with it an abundant harvest that consists of achievements and accomplishments based on its experiences. To understand each other well, I want to emphasize that your soul doesn't die and isn't constantly re-born, but rather it leads a continuously eternal live.

One such life experience you recognize as the next day in the earthly school. It begins with your physical birth and it ends with your physical death. However, after death you don't start a new life, but continue the current one. Please recognize that you had already experienced and will continue to experience many such days in the future. From this perspective you see that each person has an endlessly long life.

Each person, without exception, has experienced a long history of such incarnations. The average person has many ahead of them because they still have a lot to learn.

During each incarnation the soul puts on new physical body (and subtle bodies) and goes to school, to the physical world to learn its own lessons. What kind of lessons? Everything depends from the real human what he wants to learn. Obviously, this choice is made by self-conscious souls that are willing to learn. Other souls are, in a way forced into learning. However, God doesn't force this upon them; it is due to their unfulfilled desires.

A human's ultimate goal is the attainment of freedom through love, kindness and self-respect. When we take a closer look at these qualities, we ascertain that all of them are the same. When we achieve love, respect, knowledge, kindness and understanding with regards to ourselves, we begin to learn these qualities with regards to humanity as a whole. How long will our lessons last? Try to answer this question for yourself, dear reader. When you take a look around you, you will easily recognize how many of us do in fact have a sense of personal dignity and how many of us have learnt to appreciate ourselves for being unique, excellent souls or individuals. Perhaps you might discover to your own surprise that almost nobody has such an approach and that most of us mistake dignity and love for ourselves (meaning to our true inner "I") with egotism.

Turning Knowledge into Wisdom

Dear reader, your soul needs to get to know the truth from each side to fully understand life. This includes everyone. This is why every few incarnations we change our religion, race and nationality. We experience our incarnations not only in extraordinary wealth, but also in extreme poverty, illness and health, fame and disgrace. During incarnations we also change sex. In one incarnation we have many kids and in another incarnation we have don't have any even though sometimes we want them very much. In one instance we are an oppressor and in another we are a victim, or we might be a criminal and another time almost a saint. We are experiencing this to gain a multi-faceted knowledge (similar to what occurs in every other school). Therefore, is it worth it to judge others if we ourselves were once at some point in the same situation or perhaps we will be?

Sometimes after experiencing their physical life some souls don't learn anything. Many souls learn a planned program only half-way or using the language of earth school, give something a lick and a promise. However despite the amount of experiences, a soul ultimately takes off its bodily clothing and goes back Home to rest and gain strength. "In the morning" of each new life, meaning after our physical birth, a soul undertakes learning in exactly the same place where it left off from the day before. Returning to Earth after, all souls have a feeling that they are dealing with something completely new and unknown.

The movie "Groundhog Day" from 1993 shows this dependence very well. It is worth watching it to understand how through repetition a person learns the same lessons. For example how not to "step into the same puddle you stepped into yesterday and in previous earthly days. A person is learning until he remembers his learning, processes it and goes through life with a "dry foot". Hence, some lessons souls learn within one day, and others after many, many days until they completely internalize enough to pass the exam to a higher level.

What souls have to learn most of all? That a person dying physically doesn't take with them "things", but only their deeds. Those are the fruits that come from the wisdom of their heart.

However, people entering life on earth often forget about this and stand on the doorstep of further existence (after their physical death) empty handed. There, in his true Home, he promises himself that when he goes to school "tomorrow" he will definitely behave differently. After many attempts he is able to remember the lesson which becomes his new habit and because of that the cords of his life changes. This is shown with precision in the movie "Groundhog Day".

Most people don't remember their experiences the first time. Therefore, they have to go through death and birth multiple times (with all the trials and challenges of that process) until the memory solidifies and they become what they learn. The main lesson is to understand that the fundamental nature of the human family is spirituality and not materialism. When this lesson is tackled, death stops to exist for the human race. This subject I described extensively in the book *In the Wheel of Life*, vol III.

How do we remember our experiences? Most of all we have to realize that we are a soul that puts on a physical body just like we put on clothing. A descendent soul on Earth can be compared to a discoverer entering an unknown land. It reminds a diver that he has to put on a heavy suit to face the conditions at the bottom of the ocean. The mission with which a soul comes to Earth is always the same – gathering experiences and broadening knowledge which in time becomes wisdom. And when this is achieved, the soul has the task of helping others achieve this level that it has already achieved. When the journey undertaken in the incarnations comes to an end, the soul lays down the physical body and continues learning but on a higher plane. That in essence is the part of you that lives eternally. A person who fully accepts this stops identifying so strongly with his body. He knows that he is a soul that has a physical body. He will remind himself (and will permanently remember) that being "everything", he is inseparably connected in unity with God, with his Source. He will also understand that with the help of the illusive impression of separateness everything (not only him) is continuously learning and getting to better know itself and through that eternity develops.

SELF-CONSCIOUSNESS

The person who grasps this knows and don't ever forget that whenever he leaves home, on the other side he comes to Earth only to experience and draw from this experience. This is needed for him as he constantly strives for spiritual perfection, for excellence. He also knows that before he comes to Earth, nobody imposes anything upon him. He decides who and what he will be, and even creates his own model or plan guiding him through the experiences of the short journey beyond Home, meaning lessons which he wants to internalize during his journey. He is aware that there are many paths to achieve his goals. He can play many roles to achieve the longed for, final goal of his existence on Earth – obtaining freedom from the desires and needs that are currently on Earth and as Jesus said: "live on this world, but not to be from this world". He repeats his lessons until he achieves complete freedom.

Quite a few readers would ask why we actually have to return to Earth to learn anything. Why can't we stay there and learn in a spiritual state? Obviously, we can and we do it because varied levels of learning exist. However, we don't want to stay there as a matter of course, because our unfulfilled desires from previous incarnations are attracting us to a physical reality. Moreover, we are aware that interactions between people in a spiritual state are based on something other than between people functioning in a physical state. Some things we can only learn as bodily beings. Only then we can create interpersonal interactions in which we feel pain and can cause hurt ourselves. In a spiritual state this is completely impossible, because pain doesn't exist. Perhaps you realize that most people can learn only through suffering, otherwise they are not able to understand anything. This is obviously very exhausting and we can't live like this for long. Then Soul returns Home, rests and reenergizes. This is the time of rejuvenation and mobilization. On the other side it's easy to gain energy and motivation to act. At Source there exists only happiness and satisfaction. After the phase of resting we come back to learning again.

However, not all people that you meet in your earthly journey go through the same system. There are many people here that are only here to teach and help others when they forget, *Who They Are in Essence*. Such person could be even an old lady begging who has a task to teach love and sympathy. Many come to Earth only to live in the impurity of the physical world and not get dirty from it. Some pass and others don't. Then they have to take on the lesson anew. You should know that from the top (from the highest level of consciousness) it is quicker to fall down and sometimes to hit the bottom. The more developed a soul, the more pain it feels which it sometimes can't stand. That pain can blind the soul so much that it loses orientation and sidesteps from the previously picked course. Sometimes the body cannot take the pain any longer, and throws the soul out of the body. Then the physical person dies. Either way, the sequence of earthly lessons is not imposed on us, we choose them ourselves. If you don't like what you previously picked then forgive yourself and change your desires to new ones and then your life will change.

EXPERIENCES

It is most difficult for a person to understand that the current experiences in earthly school are his lessons. And because he is just learning something it is normal for him to make various mistakes. His actions could sometimes be termed stupid, bad or even worthy of condemnation, according to human standards. The soul can develop and undergo transformation even during the most shabby and shameful incarnation. It can draw lessons from it and in the next life use skills and knowledge obtained to help other souls. In one life it can oppress and in the next one help. The feeling of guilt from a shameful incarnation is not necessary. It is important to draw knowledge from the past and not ponder on it and have feelings of guilt. Learning is important, not judgment. That is why we have to learn to reject any biases and hatred. Those people who for some reason won't do that (because don't understand or can't forgive) simply interchange sides, coming back in new incarnations in the bodies of their mutual enemies. This is supposed to help them to understand the lesson. Each action is only a way to express oneself. Actions do not represent us in any way therefore we shouldn't identify with them.

A person shouldn't demand too much of himself, judge or condemn himself for not being able to do something well enough or for acting badly. He also shouldn't judge others because they are in exactly the same situation he once was or will be. When a person as a soul understands this, he will no longer be frustrated which in turn will hasten his learning. He won't judge himself or others anymore. When a person finally understands that something is bad then he simply stops to express that and his perspective and thinking immediately changes. His actions follow accordingly.

It is hard to continuously remember we are a soul and not a body, even when we are aware that we are here in earthly school. If we could remember, even from time to time it would largely shatter our illusions and delusions. Living would be a lot easier for everyone (for us and for others). Moreover we would realize that however individual each person's path, each one of us is heading in the same direction, to Home, the Source, God.

LEARNING TIME

The soul's progress as a student going through earthly school is not always linear. The soul can achieve great successes in one category, for example: it can be caring, thoughtful, sympathizing, but failing in another category, for example: it can be angry, jealous or lack patience.

If a soul in earthly school is an eager student then it learns very quickly. Not only what it planned to internalize but it can also look for an additional program. It tries to understand its rights as a student and at the same time get to know the school's rules which consist of the laws of the universe. When it grasps them, it knows how in the best and most effective way to adapt to these rules. The soul then begins to swim on the waves of life and it is not like it is resisting, or in other words swimming against the current. It also understands that those laws pertain to our entire life, at all levels, and not only to our physical existence.

The educational life of such a student will be relatively short on the physical plane. After it ends he moves on with all his resources of knowledge and wisdom to life in the higher worlds. As I mentioned before, there learning continues, as life in the lower worlds is only a preparation for the essence of living. It resembles graduating from elementary school to middle school, and later to high school and then on to higher and higher educational institutions.

Unfortunately, for some souls physical life does not work out. They try as best as they can, but nothing good comes of it. For some learning is tough, because their lessons are still too demanding. Perhaps they are learning these lessons for the first time. The problems of the latter group are karmic burdens. They are currently overwhelmed by what they previously planted. Yet other souls undertake some tasks as a result of their own decisions. This group includes overambitious souls, who most of all come to help others, but overestimate their own strength. The weight of undertaken tasks transcends the strength of their human, in other words physical possibilities. Behind death's curtain everything you dream of could be easily achieved. Hence, for some souls it seems that they can handle everything on Earth even a much more difficult task. In a way, this is also a learning experience because being still on the other side they receive advise from wise older brothers to cut their coat according to their cloth, but in their short-sightedness or self-righteous they ignore this advice.

There are also such students who can't understand their rights or the school's rules at all. Hence, they constantly act against the rules. Some even after they learn the school's rules still can't refrain from resistance or rebellion. This type of students stay in the earthly school the longest and through their actions they delay their entrance into true living in the higher worlds.

Earthly living is a school from which none of the students can drop out. Each has to go through their learning experience whether they want to or not. Life sometimes forces overly stubborn students in a special, but unpleasant way. I wrote about this in my book *In the Wheel of Life*, vol. IV.

Learning time and readiness to take more advanced exams is determined by each individual. If a soul is a wise and reasonable student, it understands what phase which it is going through now. In other words, attending school in the physical world is preparation for a life in the higher worlds; therefore it is the one path to the true goal. Hence, individuals try tirelessly to understand the laws ruling the universe and adjust their lives to them. This way the soul regains the light and is full of radiance (not only after physical death) when it enters the kingdom, meaning its true Home.

THE END OF LEARNING?

Each lesson that we are go through in human life is an experience that that makes us more like God. In this way we get closer to Him and at some point we can remain in our true Home forever. This is only possible when we pass all lessons, in other words we free ourselves from human desires not by denying them but through understanding them. When we abjure them, they become a starting point that pulls us back down to Earth.

I hope that this knowledge provides an explanation to many problems you have been struggling with, not knowing why they are in your life. It could also remove many difficulties you deal with daily. I hope that you will stop looking at the world as full of "injustices" because you will know that they are ostensible. When you fully assimilate this, you will see harmony rather than ostensible chaos in the present world. You will still see beings around you who are not equal, because each one of them carries a completely different baggage of experiences and have various talents, skills and energy that come from their various incarnations. On the other hand, dear reader, you will actually know that as souls we are all equal and that everyone is a student in the same school. We all have the same goal – to get to the level of enlightenment that allows us to pass the exam to the higher level. You will see quite clearly that despite all the differences, the path of each person is basically the same. In our physical state we all have to learn the same truths and imbibe them so that they become our second nature. Each lesson consists of the same factors for all people. However, there is such a great diversity of lessons that many people get lost in recognizing them. Through each visit on Earth we learn only a little of each of these virtues, because of their complexity we are unable to achieve excellence at once.

As you already know, each soul writes down a scenario for future incarnations before coming to the world, precisely outlining everything that will assist the soul in learning a desired lesson. One soul may plan to learn only one aspect of a lesson, for example: to learn patience and even that could turn out to be too hard to accomplish. Another soul may not have a bigger problem, but may have a difficulty, to for example: control its own fear or anger. It is like this with many things here, on Earth. Some person can play or sing beautifully, but perhaps don't have any manual skills. Another person may easily learn tough subjects at school, but have difficulties with speaking etc.

BODY

The physical body is a concentrated energy and reflection of your soul. It is in a way a vehicle, apartment, temple in which your soul fulfills a pre-established role. You can also think about your body as a gate through which you enter for co-existence with Earth. Your body allows you to become one with the planet because it is created from the same elements that exist on Earth.

Coming to Earth bonds a soul with the Earth's nucleus, the Earth's soul, so that we can learn through our strength of mind and learn love through debt. You are guilty and you pay a debt of love just as others are obliged to pay you. However, Earth is not the point of greatest power or spirituality. It is simply the right place to gain knowledge through love and sympathy or through suffering. Although the body is a reflection of the soul, it doesn't mean that an ugly, broken, stoop-shouldered body reflects an ugly, broken or stoop-shouldered soul. It simply means that the body reflects or shows the role a soul has undertaken to play during its journey on Earth, for a very specific time of its life.

To get to know a person's soul, one needs to take a look deep inside that person's eyes. Obviously, that doesn't mean that a blind people don't have a soul. It only means that they perceive the world through eyes different than the physical. By deducing analogically we will notice that smart, beautiful, wealthy person, based on Earth's standards, do not necessarily have a huge, amazing soul and sympathetic heart.

Often a lesson that we have to pass is hard for us to understand, for example: a woman who miscarriages many times would have a strong desire to conceive and give birth. At the same time, a man with whom she is in a happy relationship turns out to be infertile. She could have a child with any other man. Each choice will be wrong for her either she won't have a child or her beloved's love. This woman's lesson is finding happiness within and not finding happiness through a certain man or a child.

Feelings and matters of the heart are very important elements of life. In many universes feelings don't exist. Hence, many beings come to Earth to learn through feelings. This also explains why these sensations, among other things come from your body.

As you know we learn pain through our physical body. One of the first lessons that we go through in life is learning to feel. Fire, air, water and the Earth's elements which create your body (the same functioning elements of the Earth) are some of your teachers. They create your character, meaning your characteristics, which you have to learn or which you have to unlearn.

Your body is a boundary. Everything that exists on Earth has boundaries. Your heart for instance is a boundary inside your body's broader system. Boundaries are also our lessons. Eventually, we learn to reach out beyond the boundaries of our physical existence. However, in order to learn our lesson we must be completely honest (which is often related to the pain of discovering our own shortcomings or delusions) to ourselves and our soul in all situations that we encounter. In this way each lesson we experience through our body strengthens the significance of the direction chosen by our soul.

When your soul chooses a certain direction actions necessitated by this direction come to you in the form of thoughts. If you are meant to go in a certain direction, and you are not, you are acting against yourself and you will begin to suffer. When you are on Earth you learn life from it, so you have to conform to Earth's rules. To face up to that, you have to be disciplined. If you are not sowing and not reaping, not building and not continually balancing your mental state, you will fall on the mental level and the material level.

RELATIONSHIP WITH OTHERS

Each new lesson related to your individual path passed on Earth opens new internal channels of knowledge and wisdom, letting you to reach deeper and deeper into yourself as well as further into cosmos. Your individual energy combines then with the overall energy in an All Embracing Light. In order to allow you to learn, you became connected with the forces of the universe – truth, light and kindness. This universal movement of spherical forces is connected with the energy of each individual soul. Imagine it like a lit up spider web in in which each strand of the web is a person and everyone is connected with each other.

The soul is not a separate, isolated entity, and no learning (including the learning that takes place on Earth) would be possible if we had to accomplish it alone. This is why the people closest to us – friends as well as enemies – are helping us learn while we also participate in their learning experience. The physical body creates a feeling of isolation, but it's an illusion which needs to be quickly recognized.

Before we come to Earth, we all know where we will go and why. We agree to certain tasks and deadlines. We live together with a family or we leave them and we go on our own path. Either way, we play out our roles according to a pre-established scenario. Life is a stage of a theater on which we play out our roles. In this way we are learning.

Certainly, each person went through some tough patch in their life and asked themselves or God the question: "Why does life have to be so hard?" Think about it for a moment and answer yourself whether you would learn anything if your life was easy? Tough challenges offer the best opportunities to learn and quickly progress. As you know, pain is a teacher of knowledge on Earth (although this is not the only means to knowledge). In this way though, most of us are taught a lesson of knowledge and truth. With pain an individual grows.

Each soul is different and feels pain in a different way. You will never know another person's pain, because everyone needs a different kind of teacher. We can only empathize with someone else's pain through our own pain. The more developed a soul then the deeper the pain it feels, because it understands much more. It also means the greater awareness as an understanding heart, the greater the sympathy, and sometimes also the pain.

Delusive Goal of Life

On Earth we are taught that money, power, prestige, material wealth, tangible and things that provide earthly comfort are incredibly important, and even comprise the basic goal of life. This is obviously nonsense. In the end physical life is only a small part of our true life. Relying on the things that you can't take with you is like building sand castles. Does it mean that we should reject beautiful things and live in poverty? Not at all. God gives us all great, beautiful and wonderful things to be of use to us and use as much as we want. They should bring us happiness and fulfillment. At the same time it means that we are solely their users. We don't have a right to become attached to them, because they don't comprise our worth. All things (without any exceptions) we love and which we can't do without, belong to God and we have to be able to leave them behind when we leave for the next stage of our live.

In the spiritual world, behind the so called "death curtain" we will have everything returned by God (and a lot more):
the same things we had up until that point or better, once we
wish for them. In the Bible it is written, "Truly I tell you, it is
hard for someone who is rich to enter the kingdom of heaven.
Again, I tell you, it is easier for a camel to go through the eye of
a needle than for someone who is rich to enter the kingdom of
God". It is harder for a rich person, because it is not permissible
to take your wealth from the physical world to the spiritual, and
rich people are so attached to their wealth. There are in the spiritual world – if a person wants – the same things as in the physical world, but built from subtle spiritual matter vibrating on a
higher plane. Hence, most people are not able to notice these
things. Perhaps you are among them. Don't worry about it. If
you accept your death after leaving the physical world all those
things become as visible and tangible as material things do now.
By getting attached to physical things we become their slaves.
This also applies with attachments to people, knowledge, power,
respect, success and feelings of well-being etc.

On the other hand, complete rejection of physicality is as
bad as is an attachment to it. Rejection results from a person
subconsciously remembering that at some point he had to leave
what he was attached to. And because he suffered so much as a
result, he doesn't want to have physical attachments in his current life so as to avoid the painful feeling of loss. For many people this process is not conscious. Often they desire what others
have or what rich people have. Despite hard work they do not
achieve as much as they desire. When they realize that they once
rejected material goods and they allow themselves not only to
have them, but to use them, they can suddenly use everything
that God has to offer. One of the cardinal human mistakes is excessive concern about the consequences of our own actions. We

remain so absorbed with consequences that we forget to enjoy what we created. It stirs up in us anxiety and depression. Anxiety may cause concern about many things: how we will manage things, what will happen if the results we achieve don't meet our expectations, what will happen if we disappoint, what others will think about us. As a result instead of enjoying what we already have (meaning at the moment) we often judge ourselves severely.

Sometimes it is the other way around – we do nothing, because we are excessively afraid that if we don't succeed we will be rejected, hate ourselves or we will become lifelong victims or losers. We don't realize that we are already all of these. How is in your life, dear reader? Maybe instead of worrying about the results of your actions simply do your job, help others with joy in your heart and picture an increasingly better life for yourself.

In today's world we are being taught that we need the favor or respect of other people and such things as clothes and gadgets to find happiness. Meanwhile people come and go. We don't have any influence over how long they stay around, because each person has their own lessons to pass. At the same time we should realize the incontrovertible fact that we all, without exceptions have eternal, spiritual partners and spiritual families. We are immortal beings with an energy force that is never disconnected or separated from those we truly love and who love us. There will always exist somebody who loves and protects us. We are never alone. We are always protected by God and an army of spiritual beings who cherish us. They comprise our spiritual family. Therefore, let's always remember that in reality nobody or anything can hurt us because we are immortal beings and not just physical bodies.

Our own spiritual family is continually protecting us.

They are our non-stop spiritual guides. Each person who takes a deeper look inside their heart will discover that they are never alone. A sense of security does not come from people or material goods that are outside, but from the inner peace and knowledge of the true essence of The Highest Being we really are.

And because we all come from the same essence, there is no reason to worry. This truth is a secret to our sense of security and happiness. If we love each other, from the bottom of our hearts, we stop feeling fear, and the more and more we give, increasingly the more that comes back to us. If we would all finally understand that we are all spiritual beings, it would create a change not only in our hierarchy of values, but we would also finally achieve peace and happiness.

By forgetting this we focus our attention on external rather than internal matters. To no particular end, we look for things, chase after things and create external idols from things, people, money, sex etc. Seeking them becomes our only goal in life. This creates a constant internal frustration because we carve after it so much we are afraid to lose these things once we possess them. Meantime, life is continuously showing us that persons close to us can cheat, leave and die. The same applies regarding losing our position at work, or wealth due to robbery, catastrophe or fire. A sense of security comes solely from inside of us, and it has nothing to do with the amount of material goods we have. It is a spiritual characteristic; it is not material or earthly.

Money and all other material things belong to the physical Earth and we can't take them with us when we leave for the spiritual world. If our lesson consists of that or this is our destiny then we can lose everything in one night ... and afterwards regain everything in a short period of time. How we react to this loss will determine how fast and if at all, we regain what we valued.

When a truly wealthy person goes bankrupt, he doesn't break down but starts all over. After all, he has the knowledge and skills to create wealth anew. A person who earned money through scams and exploitation can't recreate that wealth after losing it. Despite achieving prosperity, from the beginning his consciousness is rooted in the sense of personal lacking and this sense is the reason for his fraud and loss of wealth.

A genuinely wealthy person knows that the universe is a storeroom for all prosperity. He is not afraid of loss, because he knows that he can always regain everything anew. Many so called wealthy people (with the consciousness of poverty) think that there is not enough wealth for everyone. Hence they think that in order to have something, it must take away "something" from others.

A genuinely wealthy person knows that it is not that a poor person doesn't want wealth; rather it is that he is unable to open himself to wealth because he is continuously thinking about the lack of wealth. If you want to be wealthy you should think about wealth. Analogically, someone who wants to be healthy must think about health, not illness. Health is to wealth what illness is to poverty.

Life is a school that seeks to teach us to avoid the negative results of our own attachments and the negative, harmful energies of other people. We learn not allow the false symbols of power such as money, sex and external idols shake our healthy sense of self-worth.

The key is understanding. Once you understand your own true nature and goal, meaning *Who You Are in Essence*, your life will be permanently changed in this world as well as in the other world. Then you will be able to transform not only your reality, but also the world around you, only if you wish to, obviously.

YOU AND GOD

Dear reader, I now want you think about your relationship with God. I realize this is a sensitive topic. However until you find the courage to do this, you won't move a step further. You can't avoid this topic forever. I am not talking about whether you are a so called believer, according to the Church or a nonbeliever. For you can stay away from church and still have God as close as your own breath, or your own hands and legs.

Unless you look at God from a broader perspective than what your religion says about Him, you won't understand your life or what I desire to convey to you. For everything that you experience in your life depends not so much on what kind of God you believe in, but whether you actually believe in Him, or even if it just seems to you that you believe in Him.

Writing these words I am obviously not trying to convince anyone about anything or pull anyone away from religion.

Just the opposite: I am trying, dear reader, to explain religion to you, helping you discover the deeper meaning of life the existence of which you might never have suspected. I would like to help you better understand your own religion and live better than before according to its tenets and in many cases bring back your lost faith, but on a higher level and with a broader perspective.

The matter of getting to know God is quite simple. It is based on bringing back an obliterated memory. You knew God before, because you were created by Him, and later you lived with Him for a very long time like a child with his beloved Father. I describe this in detail in the book *In the Wheel of Life*, vol III.

Obviously when I talk about God, I have in mind the Only and the Everything, in Everything, through Everything, for Everyone, in other words God as Absolute. I am not talking about Jesus or any other prophet who many people consider God. God can't be narrowed down to small human beings, for example: Jesus Christ or another Great Being of Light who believers of various religions call their God. God is Omnipresent, Omniscient and All-Powerful, therefore not Jesus Christ or Moses etc. However great they were, they weren't able to manifest His true greatness.

I am talking here about the idea of God as Absolute, God in whom you live, move and in whom you exist. God who is beyond all religions, God, who manifests in each person as an inborn instinct and unquenchable desire for something better, more beautiful and greater than what any person is or has.

All religions teach that there is one God therefore all of them confirm the same, basic truth that I am writing about. We could ask at this point, since there is one God, why have so many religions arisen with their followers fighting each other claiming that their religion is the only one and true religion? Are the bodies of followers of certain religion sick in various ways and in various ways they come back to health? Or perhaps they have experienced different emotions and psychological problems? Perhaps they might fear rejection, loss or treachery in different ways? Anger is after all equally poisonous for the body of a Muslim, Buddhist, as for a Christian. It is common for us to desire love. In terms of body and spirit we don't vary from each other at all. Therefore, why should religions make us different?

Dear reader, recall the Truth which you have in you, that you knew God earlier (as each one of us without exception knows this truth). When you began your descent in the direction of concentrated, physical activity, you still had complete, mindful memory of that fact. Only when your energy was permanently directed downwards, the curtain was placed in front of you and the amazing beauty of God's indescribable temple forgotten. You can also read about this in my book *In the Wheel of Life*, vol III.

You forgot about God, who He really is, but that doesn't mean that you are separated from Him or in a different place from Him at all. Your life is still a part of the great Divine's life, exactly the same as it was at some point. This is why no matter whether you are believer, atheist, so-called good person or recognized as a disgraceful person, you still have the Divine Spark inside of you and you are still his beloved son.

God that is above all religions appears in the form of inborn instinct in you. Otherwise you would never wonder about your life. Every time that you do this, it only means that God is sounding an alarm in you that something in your life is not right, that you distanced yourself from Him as from your Source.

That in-born instinct makes many people disagree with their own religion or another religion. Sometimes they argue with each other and sometimes it results in wars. Unconsciously they may not want to refer to such an immense power as a Christian's God, a Muslim's Allah, Buddhism's Buddha, or such because deep down they know that these terms don't completely reflect the perfection and the greatness of God's existence.

Religious people often describe God as The Highest Intelligence, The Universe, Everything, What Is, Inner Being, Spiritual Guide, Guardian Angel, The Being of "I Am". Whatever name or change of name he is given it does not change the immensity of His Power or the characteristics of Strength and Energy which He represents. All these names refer to the one and same God because God is one and is unity: "I am the Lord and there is no other; besides me there is no God" I myself prefer to use the word "God", because this is the only one of a kind word in the world that in all languages has the highest vibration.

Perhaps you are afraid of God, but you should know that He is your one true support. He acts as Divine Providence. He represents clarity of all ideas. This clarity is reflected in your consciousness and conscience. Usually you build your life according to these things exactly, although you often do this unconsciously.

God talks to each person in their heart. In order to be better understood he sends angels to people, or also other heavenly beings, such as Jesus. God talks to everyone, but still there are millions of people in the world who are lost, nonbelievers, or doubting because they are not aware of this. How to wake them up? They suffer and they do not even know why. They don't realize that when the signal from God appears they escape into conversations, work, TV viewing, computers, radios, addictions, or anything else that they find at their fingertips to deafen the warnings from God. They then get another signal and another signal until the required outcome is achieved.

If they wake up even for a moment and listen everything in their lives will get back on the right track. However when they don't want to slow down and listen to what God has to tell them, of necessity there are always different, drastic ways to encourage them to dive deeper into themselves. They could be stopped by some serious illness, a meltdown, an accident or some other misfortune from which it is harder to get out of. When you become immobilized in such a way, don't complain about your fate because through it you have the opportunity to think a little about what you are doing wrong in your life.

However, don't think that this is a punishment for bad deeds. God loves you very much and will try reaching you in this or some other way. Since you do not want to willingly hear Him, your Higher "I" has to somehow immobilize you for you to have an opportunity to listen to Him.

God doesn't talk to you because of His caprice. He knows that He gave you, and similarly each person, free will and He respects that. At the same time, He sees when you are wandering around and wants, though suggestions to direct you towards the truth. Only someone who knows the truth can understand the seriousness of his own position and by understanding it gets out from it effectively and forever.

Here Is Who You Are

You are a Self, a human being who manifests the highest creative energy called God. You emerged from a place of pure positive energy. Your soul wasn't born from a woman, only your physical body.

Your spirit and soul are your "self" that lives eternally. It cannot be hurt, burnt, drowned, killed, damaged by illness or damaged in any other way. You live eternally as God who created you is eternal and this is why you can stop being afraid of dying right now and abandon once and for all this crippling fear. If someone would like to do wrong by you, your soul and spirit would never die or suffer.

Perhaps the question comes to mind: "How come I won't die? Many times I attended a funeral and saw a dead person. Or somebody next to me, who I loved was dying and even though they tried hard to save him in the hospital, it didn't happen. Indeed, they didn't save the body, but I am talking about the soul. During so called "death" the soul discards the body like used, old clothing, because it isn't needed anymore. Free from the body's weight it is headed to the next journey. The direction in which the soul is headed depends solely on it, based on how it lived and what it believed in when it was still in a body.

You might ask why a person doesn't need a body when he could still live, with so much more to accomplish in life? This is looking at life from a very narrow perspective. Looking at life as a whole, meaning from a broader perspective, you would notice that the soul in such a body couldn't function anymore. The body's death is always a resignation from the current life when the soul recognizes that it is at a dead end from which it doesn't see any way out. It doesn't mean that from such situations there is no way out, it only means that the soul doesn't see any. This in a way is the soul saying to itself: "Oh no, I messed up everything, I picked incorrectly, I did this wrong. Things went so far in the wrong direction in this body and in this life I don't have any further chances for growth, only stagnation. This will result in a downfall, I absolutely don't want that, therefore I am letting go of this body and leaving." People are often not aware, but the soul knows perfectly well that it can't do anything else with that life. What can the soul do in a body damaged by old age, illness or various types of afflictions? It doesn't have any options and no matter what efforts it extends, it can't do anything else with such a body. It is the same situation when the soul feels completely powerless, when it went too far making wrong choices. It feels like a prisoner and doesn't see any way out from that situation. Any rationale for the soul leaving a body is a choice based on bad decisions it has made or a lack of choice. As a person it does result in "bad" after-effects. This is how it perceives it.

Every day on the job I hear how people vituperate God for punishing them with illness, pain, poverty or some other misfortune. They complain about how bad they have things, about how they have to suffer, but their problems are rooted in their narrow thinking. I described this topic broadly in my book *In the Wheel of Life*, vol III. Now I will just tell you, dear reader, that even the most serious illness is also a soul's choice. You may think that this as a "bad" choice, but this is the soul's own choice and it serves to teach the soul something which it previously decided to learn. Also death during an accident or a cataclysm is never God's punishment or bad fate, but the soul's choice. This confirms the fact that even in the most terrible cataclysm, collision or accident some people can come out without injury or even small scratches. The soul is never on its own. Each soul has a guardian angel, spiritual guide, and most of all its own higher Self.

Every second of each day, the soul is led and warned when there is a need, especially of cataclysms and accidents. They do occur however, because despite repeated warnings they are blind and deaf to these warnings. Sometimes only after death the soul sees what it could have avoided were it open to clues, or saw its bad decisions and mistakes. Whatever the reason for your loved one passing away, it was important enough for him (the soul that departed) to decide to abandon a body. For you it means that only his exterior covering "died", because your real loved one still lives on.

THE LIFE PLAN

Dear reader, before you came into this world as a soul you established a plan for your upcoming life. It considered various options that would position you to pass your life lessons in the most optimal way. This plan included the smallest details of your future existence, for example: places you would live, people you would go through your lessons with, your appearance and emergency options for ending life in the event your plan was too ambitious.

On the conscious level you obviously forgot about the moment of your birth, but on a deeper level the soul remembers everything. The soul also decides when and how to end its own incarnation. Even at the moment of death it has a choice about whether to remain in a physical body and try to solve its problem or to die. Death doesn't occur by itself automatically, the decision about when to die, where to go, and what direction to pick belongs to the soul. It has free will and nobody will decide for it.

Sometimes it overcomes the lessons comfortably and with happiness. However, the lessons are sometimes very hard and impossible to complete during just one lifetime. A great deal depends upon your soul's level of development and how fast it wants to learn its lessons. On the other side pervasive love dominates, everything is simple, easily realized, every moment is filled with great enthusiasm and the soul sees everything as easily managed. It doesn't realize that it has a different state of consciousness on Earth.

After coming to the world you forgot everything that happened before your birth. Your soul still knows everything; however your conscious mind doesn't remember it.

Each soul has its own tasks to accomplish on Earth, meaning lessons. They go through these lessons accompanied by other souls who are also learning at the same time. And the soul whose lesson is, for example to be a victim will find in its path a tormentor or tyrant. The soul whose lesson is to be a manipulator will find people that he can manipulate, while the soul whose lesson is to be a leader will find his subordinates and the soul who is learning to be a teacher will find students etc. Obviously the opposite also applies. Students will find teachers, tyrants will find victims. When for example a soul fulfills its role as a victim, it stops playing that role. It notices then that the tyrant is no longer part of its surroundings. If the tormentor, tyrant at the same time completes its own lesson then it stops being a tormentor. If he has not completed his lesson, he will look for another victim.

This is perfectly illustrated in the saying: "Until there is a victim, there is a tormentor. If there is no victim, there is also no tormentor". For one person a lesson might be easy while for somebody else the lesson may be very difficult and that person may have to go over that lesson through many incarnations. The role playing includes a task to make a person realize that he is the role's creator and remind him *Who He is in Essence*. This should make him realize that he is God's child. He has to understand that the role is teaching him sympathy and love for himself and faith in God and in himself. The role is also teaching him for example to forgive a tyrant and to forgive himself: for not standing up for himself, for allowing himself to get hurt (including mentally).

If a person is not aware of what he should learn from a given lesson and takes his role too seriously it could turn his life into a nightmare. When he feels he is in a noose with no way out, his soul can decide on death. Death then takes place at a very specific, previously established time. Before birth the soul determines a few times frames and possibilities for withdrawing from a lesson.

Usually there is no one date for death but rather a few possible times at different ages.

I am obviously not talking here about simply giving up on our own intentions at difficult moments, leading to suicide. We must be aware that suicides are caused most often by the presence of ghosts. The Transition to the Light earlier than the appointed date never takes place through suicide.

A person sometimes doesn't listen to his own intuition and makes decisions that take him away from the plan which his soul picked. He can blindly struggle with life and end up at a dead end from which he doesn't see a way out. At that point he can use one of the dates he set down before he come to the world to end his life. He can do that, but he doesn't have to at all.

He chooses the type of death that suits him best. This

could be an accident or quiet death during a simple medical pro-
cedure, but it could happen – although it is not always the case –
that having great feelings of guilt or hurt, death is preceded by a
long, serious illness as a way of seeking redemption for sins
(this is not the correct approach though, because feelings of guilt
doesn't have to be redeemed, but forgiven). Nothing happens by
accident. Everything is planned with precision. Sometimes the
soul thinks that it can't manage anymore and subconsciously
prepares for death, meanwhile it suddenly receives help from the
outside, receives additional incentive and literally revives. This
could happen when a soul goes through a certain lesson with
other souls that support it through its own development.

Death usually takes place when a soul has passed all the
lessons appointed for that life or when it is unable to rise to the
challenge of too ambitious tasks that it chose to accomplish. For
a soul this is not a big deal, it will simply go back to Source, rest
and full of renewed strength come back to Earth to finish its
own work with the same or different souls. In this context death
is not scary.

CONTACT WITH DEATH

When somebody from our surroundings dies, our subconscious is usually consumed with thoughts of our own death. It seems dreadful to us because we are afraid of it. We should be aware that we are the ones that give death this aura. Each soul knows perfectly well when it will die and how much time it has to complete its mission. Our fear is therefore completely unnecessary. We have to realize that our fear of death makes us live our life half-way. If we live life like that we won't have enough energy to accomplish our true goals. Fear will clip our wings and how can we live here without wings? We won't fly high enough because we will be fearful of falling.

It is different when we get used to the essence of death and stop fearing not only death, but also everything else; because once you are not afraid of death then you will realize you don't have to be afraid of anything else. With this realization we can elevate our plans above mediocrity. At that point we certain-ly know that we will accomplish them. We can then do every-thing effortlessly, lightly, and pleasantly, always having enough time and energy. Anything we undertake goes smoothly from that point.

When people know what happens after death they are less afraid, because they have a fuller picture of what will be happening with them. Unfortunately most dying people are not preparing for this important moment. Thinking about death while still alive seems too frightening. Usually we postpone such thoughts for when we are older. Very often we are already too old or sick then and in so much pain that we don't find enough strength for it. Long before death we receive anesthetics, and because of that we are not conscious of ourselves.

We should prepare for death in advance, at the earliest age in order to get used to it. Only then can we go through life fully relaxed and go to the next world without fear. Then will not be scary, and so called death so hard. Nothing bothers a per-son that is prepared for death at any moment of their life. This means that he can live almost indefinitely, meaning as long as he desires. If a person is afraid of something then he attracts that something to him. If he fears death so much that he runs away from even thinking about it then death will make itself known to him at the least expected moment. When that happens he will be completely stupefied and he won't know what is happening with him and what to do next.

ABOUT DEATH

As far as I can remember we never talked about death in my house. It was the same in my friends' homes. I wondered whether people weren't talking about death in front of kids or whether they thought that by not talking about death at all it would pass them by. Meanwhile death didn't want to give in to be forgotten. This was after a war and death was in our area often as a guest. Each time that it reached somebody from my area it struck like a bolt of lightning. I often heard then, no matter, the age of the person who died, comments such as: "What do we get out of life, the person hardly lived and already they are being put into the ground". Moments later, elders would comfort each other by saying: "Death is the only justice in this world. It comes no matter your status, merits, good or bad deeds. It touches everyone – the poor and wealthy, good and bad, healthy and sick."

How many times have I also heard: "Oh well, you only live once, why deny yourself anything". Consequently, many people around me indulged themselves. They needed to blow off some steam, drink, take drugs, get as much out of life as they could, so as to benefit as much as possible.

I assumed that people were behaving like this because they are abreacting horrible thoughts of the recent war. Although it had ended it was still taking its toll. Houses were demolished and walls collapsed, and there were missiles in the rubble which led to the demise of many people. Today, I see that I was mistaken. I am an adult now, but many people still think and behave in the exact same way.

Times have changed, but people still live in constant fear for their life. There isn't much positive information in the news. The events reported are primarily negative – accidents, catastrophes threatening us daily, global warming (the subtext being Earth's impending doom), AIDS, other serious illnesses, terrorism, and many other dangers. Many young people being fed this information every day don't believe will reach twenty years of age. The number of suicides and unsuccessful attempts to end life is constantly growing. This reflects the many stresses experienced globally in today's society. In such circumstances contemplations about death seem beyond the strength of most people. Understand, however, that we don't live in a peaceful world where death only comes at an old age after we have lived with dignity. Just the opposite – death seems to be around every corner. But shouldn't that be why we want to know more about it?

Just think dear reader. If we actually only live once, as some people claim, shouldn't each one of us respect our lives even more? Then, why don't people do this? The answer only came to me when I started dealing with exorcisms. By studying ghosts that possessed people, I realized that most people treat with this inadequately because of their lack of knowledge. Because they don't know anything about death, people are frightened by the thought that it may happen to them or even worse, surprise them. And, not only do they not want to know anything about death, they also don't want to know what happens to them after death and how to prepare for that circumstance. They wonder if it makes sense to think about death and contaminate their short period of life here, on Earth. And because they don't know what death is, they also don't know the basic laws of life. This is the source of their thoughtlessness, carelessness and stupidity.

How can you not want to know about something which is a basic fact of life and which it seems, nobody can avoid? Ultimately, this is as important as for example, daily hygiene. With full confidence I can state that knowledge of death is much more essential. As you read further in this book you will see there are serious consequences of a lack of knowledge in this area.

How Kids Look at Death

In many families – like it was once in my family when I was growing up – death is a taboo subject. Sometimes death is only mentioned when someone close to us passes away. If we did discuss it, then God forbid we did so in front of children. We think, quite wrongly, that they have enough time for such matters and until the time is right they should enjoy life. However, children are the ones most keenly interested about their (and our) existence. Children, not adults, ask most often: "How was I born?", "What will I do when I grow up?" And just as they ask about life, so too they ask about death: "How do we die" What will happen to me when I die?" Such questions are not only appropriate, but natural; it is just that adults don't like to bring up these topics. They fool themselves into thinking that talking about death brings it on and that by avoiding the topic they can somehow escape death. They put off their children so that they don't have to deal with this matter. If they did answer though, what would they say? They themselves know very little or nothing on this topic. However, when children are deeply bothered by something they are not easily satisfied with unclear answers. They start looking for answers themselves to cope with the emotions triggered by their concerns about death. The first answers they arrive at will dictate the nature of their future enquires on this topic.

If the answer satisfies them, they stop searching based on what they have heard. Other children though, keep searching, and where this will take them, only God knows. I know of instances where young people were so fascinated by death they had a desire to try it to see what it was like.

The history of those who unfortunately succeed, I often only find out about from their telling (as ghosts) while I am performing exorcisms. Many other cases I find out from the letters of potential juvenile suicide victims or from their school friends asking me to help their friends.

It is heart breaking when an eight year-old, nine year-old or ten year-old writes for help for himself or a friend. Why don't parents teach children about death? The answer I received from a little girl: "My parents don't know anything about death; they don't even want to read your book Mrs. Pratnicka" "Did you read my book?" – I asked surprised. "Everyone in my class read it" – she proudly answered. On the one hand her answer stunned me. I didn't address my book to such young readers (otherwise I would have written it differently). On the other hand however, I noticed how much this knowledge is needed, and especially, that parents isolate children from the topic of death.

Sometimes outraged parents call me because they caught their children reading my book *Possessed by Ghosts*. "Did I give it to him? Did I force him to read it?" – I ask. Only then they calm down. When I ask the respective parents whether they had already read the book, I always get the same answer. "No? Then please do it together with your child and help him understand it." – I advise. Then they back off. I think that when a child expresses an interest then something must be done about it, especially when it comes to very sensitive topics. You don't know how to conduct the conversation? Then let the child do it. Listen carefully to the subject of the questions. Sometimes you will find out that a child cares most of all about whether you will die, and if yes, what it would be like and what will happen to him. That question shows a fear of abandonment. Therefore, when asked the question "Mom, will you die?" you should answer: "Yes, someday I will die. Most likely it will be many years from now, when you are grown up and able to manage by yourself. But now I am with you". Create a warm, understanding, trusting and safe atmosphere while answering.

When posed with similar type questions we can answer with a sense of love and responsibility. I know that most adults didn't work through death themselves this is why they avoid this conversation with children. It is worth preparing ourselves, because the conversation will come up sooner or later.

Dear reader, children don't give up on a desire to know more about what interests them especially when it is perceived to be forbidden. In their minds questions and doubts arise. Everything that is unknown, kept quiet or hidden is terrifying, scary and misunderstood to them until they find some answer. Therefore when parents don't care to educate their children about these matters, their older friends will do it and, quite often in a vulgar and questionable manner. Is that what we want for our children?

Adults must realize that the fascination with death cannot be suppressed in any age group. It is only by understanding death will we grasp the essence of life and respect it. Some time ago, a mother called me asking for help for her only daughter. Three of her daughter's school friends had committed suicide within a few months of each other. The mother claimed that her daughter was behaving erratically and she was concerned that her daughter might harm herself. I cleansed the daughter of ghosts and thereafter she unilaterally threw away all her black clothing and metal and hard rock music. After many conversations with her mom, death stopped fascinating the daughter. This time the intervention was timely. Parents, please be observant and notice similar conditions in your children in a timely manner!

Other parents were less fortunate. The parents of a boy a few years old called and asked me to assist in finding their son. He had written a goodbye letter and run away from home. I asked his soul if it was alive, and he continually answered: "Of course, I am alive". Even after his body was pulled out of a lake, he continued telling me: "But I am alive!" For many days his soul was continually repeating to me in despair: "Tell my parents where I am. Tell them to take me home. I don't want to sit here. Why are they not coming? I wrote a letter saying that I want to kill myself. It is so horribly cold here". On and on he went. My remonstrations that it was too late, that he had drowned, that he didn't have a physical body anymore weren't working. He was screaming over and over: "But I only wanted to scare them, force them to love me more. I didn't want to kill myself". When I told his parents these messages, they were horrified. They continually asked themselves: "Was it necessary for this tragedy to occur for us to finally understand this?"

Dear parents, these are not unique cases. I have had

many such cases in my practice. Also similar cases are discussed in the media. These are a few headlines from newspapers front pages: "Polish teenagers are fascinated by death", "Death is trendy. It solves all problems", "Since 2001 the rate of teenage suicides has quadrupled", "In 2005, there was a six fold increase in the number of student suicides", "Suicides are no longer an adult issue", "Children from the same grade committed suicide", "In 2009, there was an eight fold increase in the number of suicides in middle schools", "This is the 39th suicide in the same town. Priests don't react". Children and teenagers often have psychological problems (which are primarily caused by ghosts), but they also want to know more about death at all costs.

Isn't it time to start the conversation about death at home with your children? Adults, especially those that have not worked through this issue themselves, are not ready to talk about the most intimate and at the same time the most natural event in a human's life. We are not at fault. The development of civilization resulted in us losing true contact with nature. We don't have the opportunity to observe nature's natural rhythm. The family model has also changed. We don't observe from up close anymore and don't see our grandparents and great grandparents growing older. That is why death is incomprehensible and scary to us. Despite that we should still talk about death. This cannot be a taboo subject. If you don't know anything about death, it is still worthwhile to properly prepare for death. When you start talking about it, it won't end with one conversation. A child is going to want to know more and more. In order to get a child used to the topic of death, it should be introduced gradually. How should we frame the conversation? Unfortunately, dear reader, there is no generic recipe, because each child is different, has different experiences, a different family history, is at a different age and at the same time is at a different level of understanding. A child up to three years old is unable to understand what death is. Preschoolers associate death with separation and a lack of movement. They think that if something doesn't move then it is not alive. Older children are able to understand what death is and also what caused death to occur. They are also capable of understanding that death is unavoidable and inevitable.

Therefore, we can tell a little child about nature, and explain that similar to plants which grow, bloom and later wither and die, the same process applies to each life, including human life. With older children we can use the same analogy but with animals unless somebody in the family had died.

If we missed an opportunity when a child asked us about death in the past, we can start the conversation about it during All Saints' Day as this is when most families recall memories of and talk about loved ones who have passed away. At this time children are also preparing for Halloween, which brings to the fore the topic of death in the media and on the streets. Children don't remain neutral on this topic. They don't ask about it at home? I daresay that's because they didn't receive an answer when they asked about it before. We need to have spontaneous conversations on this topic at home. I know how tough this topic is, for both adults and children, but we can't avoid it. I will repeat once more: what is unknown, kept quiet and hidden is terrifying, scary and incomprehensible for children. For most adults avoiding conversations about death (and this is a delusion) with children protects them from pain, suffering and fear. However, what is more terrifying for children are the many questions for which they are unable to find answers. Death thus gains the status of something scary, incomprehensible and at the same time as I mentioned above when it comes to suicide, something with a mysterious allure.

SUICIDE: WHAT CAUSES IT?

The reason people attempt suicide is possession by ghosts, and it is significant to note that ghosts are attracted to people with existing problems. On both sides of the equation, suicide can be effectively prevented. Would suicides occur on such a scale if we spoke about death in our homes? I am sure they wouldn't. In my book, *Possessed by Ghosts,* I discussed this topic extensively. I would like to remind you that the living is urged to commit suicide by ghosts that remain on this side of death's curtain. When a person doesn't know or learn anything about death during his lifetime, in most cases he doesn't go beyond death's curtain at the moment of death but instead wonders as a ghost without a goal in the netherworld. During such wanderings, it knowingly or sometimes unwittingly penetrates the body of someone still alive. More often than not, ghosts want to take over, meaning steal a body. This prospect is not always adequate or meets the requirements of the ghost. Before penetrating someone's body, ghosts are unsure whether it would be easier to get into someone's body, than to get out of it. For our consideration it really doesn't matter much either way or for that matter the reason ghosts choose to penetrate a human. I described them all in the book *Possessed by Ghosts*.

Here I will only describe the situation in which a human body doesn't meet a ghost's requirements and the ghost wants to demit the physical body which it possessed. It tries to achieve this in many ways, however without a positive result. A ghost feels imprisoned or even worse when this happens. Before penetrating a body it could move freely, but inside a body it feels like it is living in a tight cage. In this situation it only has two options. It can wait for the physical death of the possessed person and in this way free itself from the unwanted body or convince the person it has possessed to die. Ghosts don't see anything wrong with the latter option, because it understands that death doesn't exist as proven by its very existence. The kind of death obviously doesn't matter either. However to convince a person to commit suicide is a lot harder than it seems at first. Normal, healthy people have a strong desire to keep they physical body engrained in them. If someone wants to take your life away or you suddenly feel that you might lose your body, you find additional strength to save your life.

So how do ghosts successfully implement their plan? Firstly, by cutting the person off from his natural environment through isolation and secondly, by fully preoccupying his consciousness with its existence. Possessed people are more than likely unaware of their condition. If they were, they would defend themselves from the actions of the ghosts in every possible way. Of concern though, people often cooperate with ghosts to their own disadvantage. Unwittingly people shut themselves away and become unavailable to loved ones. With little effort the possessed person does only what he has to do and nothing more. A ghost also works on the person's surroundings. It aggressively pushes everyone away from the possessed person. How? By emitting strong negative emotions (like anger, fear, etc.) in the surroundings and as a result people feel uncomfortable in the company of the possessed person because the atmosphere is unpleasant. More and more, people would then avoid the possessed person and likewise he would avoid people. Further, the ghosts cause possessed people to act out naughtily (if a child) or aggressively towards the environment (if an adult). The possessed could be rebellious, annoyed with small things or even start arguments. Both possessed adults and children often feel so bad they start looking for an escape, in order to forget, even for a moment the nightmare they have found themselves in. They often find escape in alcohol, drugs, or constant work and kids, for example find it in computer games. Sometimes loved ones, friends and acquaintances don't want to intervene in the possessed person's life because they think what he is doing is his business and each person has a right to live their life as they choose. Sometimes it is like people are in a daze. However, quite often people are so absorbed with their own lives and obligations they don't even notice that the person next to them needs help. After long fights with a ghost in someone's body, acquaintances or family members, for example: will come to the conclusion that the possessed person bothered them so much with his bad behavior that they had had enough of him and the best thing for everyone would be for him to go away. This is obviously what the ghost wants – to have the possessed person all to itself. This is exactly what ghosts do to us; cause us to assign maliciousness to the possessed person. Meanwhile, the possessed person thinks exactly the same about us. We don't realize that between us and the possessed person there is a huge abyss which is filled by the ghost and from which it pulls all the strings, obviously not visible to the naked eyes. We turn away from a possessed person, and he turns away from us. The ghost gets rid of us, but the possessed person sinks even deeper into hopelessness and is a step away from the decision to commit suicide bringing the ghost closer to freeing itself from a body it finds inadequate. From that point the ghost starts persuading the possessed person that his entire life makes no sense. How?

It does this by constantly ruining everything in his life. Everything the possessed person does is wrong. This is not simply criticizing in order to point out mistakes that can be fixed. No! The ghost is intent on convincing the possessed person that he is zilch, garbage and worth nothing. "Look, nobody loves you, everybody turned their backs on you" – the ghost keeps saying. It is hardest for the ghost at the very beginning when a person still has a lot of self-awareness, when the person knows that he can achieve something, that he is loved, accepted etc. When a ghost finds the possessed weak spot or finds the possessed alone, it will use these as opportunities to immerse itself in the possessed. If despite the ghost's best efforts, a person still has strong support from family and/ or friends, the ghost would have huge problems convincing him to commit suicide.

When loved ones notice someone exhibiting symptoms such as locking themselves away or having a persistent sense of hopelessness, they should be aware that this is a warning signal and they should start seeking help. It is easy to miss this sign and later regret it for the rest of your life. All that is needed in these instances is to reach out to a good exorcist, like me. It is not necessary to visit me, all that is needed is to communicate with me by phone or by email and ask for assistance cleansing a possessed person remotely.

Many people told me that they ignored the above-mentioned symptoms. There have even been instances of a few suicides in a row in a family. Some people have experienced this horrific occurrence. A ghost convincing individual family members to commit suicide in order to convince the remaining family members to kill themselves later on is not unheard of. Could this be prevented from happening? Read next what happened to a family in England. The husband committed suicide. His wife's sorrow was similar to losing any other people but she had been fighting like cat and dog with her husband so she was not devastated too long by his passing. She actually felt some level of relief. For a long time before his suicide they didn't communicate with each other at all. After a few months their daughter also committed suicide. This loss affected the mother much more. She explained away the daughter's death as the strong emotional relationship she shared with her father. However, she started getting commands herself from an internal voice to commit suicide. At that point she realized the cause of the two previous deaths. She started to look for help until she found me. She understood that if she had been more careful, she could have saved both of her family members. In her case it was relatively easy to cleanse her and nobody else suffered in this family.

Here is another case. A woman called me and spoke in an anxious tone of voice. She asked me to help her husband because she suspected he was suicidal. I asked why she felt this way and whether her husband told her this. "He didn't say so, but this year we had four suicides in our home and my husband's behavior has started changing just like the other people who committed suicide" – she answered. I asked how he behaved, whether he drank, started fights, and locked off from people. "No, he doesn't drink. My father-in-law, brother, and brother–in-law often drank. Only my mother-in-law didn't drink. He behaves as strangely as they did. He seems absent and is always silent. We have four small children. Mrs. Pratnicka, please help me. What will happen to us if he also kills himself? I won't be able to manage" – she started to cry. I checked out this case and it turned out that her husband was in fact possessed by a murderous ghost. I struggled with the ghost for a year until it finally left. It was as vicious as anyone. Besides that, it filled the house with a disgusting smell. When the ghost was coming out of the husband it was tough to sit in the house because of the smell. They had replaced the floors and stucco on the walls a few times before I became involved and let them know that the cause of the unpleasant smell was the ghost. After it left, the danger was over. The smell was also gone.

Getting Accustomed to Death

Conversations about death are appropriate for any age and we should have them from time to time. But in cases where someone is closer to that time, (older or bedridden) talking about death is an obligation. This has nothing to do with a lack of decency, just the opposite, it is proof that we care deeply about that person. When we don't do this, we display great ignorance and a lack of respect for that person's biggest need. I am writing about this because it has become one of the greatest problems people struggle with presently. In the past we lived together as multigenerational families and we got sick and died at home. This meant we knew first-hand how to deal with these situations as we had a model. If we were overcome with grief and were unable to cope with our loved one's death, our neighbors, family and friends stepped in to fill the gap. Today's society is deprived of this basic knowledge. We don't know how to behave, because we don't have a model.

We are frightened by death and as such we are unable to talk about it, even when it's the right time to do so. In most cases, we don't know how to behave when somebody in our family is getting older, is seriously ill or is dying. We don't have an appropriate model anymore, of how to go through the various phases. We panic and fool ourselves into thinking that it's inappropriate to raise the topic of death as it may frighten sick or older persons. We think that this is not the way they should find out about their approaching death, and further that this type of conversation could hasten their death. This entire masquerade is absolutely unnecessary. The dying person's soul would already know that its present incarnation is coming to an end. This knowledge should also be shared with the dying's person consciousness.

I deal with this problem every day. People ask me what they should do when dealing with serious illness and whether to conceal the gravity of the situation from sick people. At the same time, seriously ill people often complain that they are aware they are dying, but nobody wants to talk to them about it. They often write: "Mrs. Pratnicka, why do they even come to visit me? I can't understand this comedy. My husband, my children, my friends are all collectively doing this to me. I am strong, but it would be a lot easier for me if they could help me prepare for death, instead of making it so much harder. I can't pretend in front of them that everything is ok because I know that I am dying. I can't continue talking about things that I am not interested in anymore. Fortunately I came across your books Mrs. Pratnicka. They are a substitute for my loved ones and fill the gap between us. On one side there is me, dying, and they are on the other side."

Obviously, there are cases, where elderly, bedridden persons don't want to know anything about death although they are already on their deathbed. This is because of ignorance based on a paralyzing fear of the unknown. A sick person who is afraid of death wouldn't want to accept that he is dying and s like an ostrich will hide his head in the sand, deluding himself that he is invisible. Now he has a chance to gradually prepare for death among friendly faces. Later, everything will surprise him and he will have to deal with death one on one. In such situations death surprises the dying and those left behind. They hurt each other for many years after, sometimes to the very end of their lives. And often, when a soul is surprised by death it doesn't leave at all. This happens when a soul is deceived into thinking that it is just sick. It wasn't told that it was dying. Therefore it is easy for the soul to be deluded into thinking that it is still alive on the physical plane, and as a result it remains among the living as a ghost. Later in this book I describe Margaret's case. Quite often, people deep in mourning don't want to allow the soul to leave. Such behavior has nothing to do with love or common sense. The place for deceased persons is on the other side of death's curtain. Both sides suffer when the soul doesn't get there. I describe the consequences of this in detail in the book *Possessed by Ghosts*.

When we know enough about death our loved one's passing goes smoothly and painlessly. When we resist this knowledge and rely blindly on fate then the transformation from material body to non-material, meaning from physical life to life after death is very traumatic and difficult for the soul because it is consumed with fear. It is also painful because death is forced to pull a soul out of a body. You will learn more about this in the chapter "Dying Unconsciously".

Therefore, everyone should think not only about life, but

also about the inevitability of our physical body's death. Our physical body breaks down, but we never die. We leave our body as if we are taking clothes off. Some people know this with a determined certainty; others only have a foggy sense of it. There are also some people who convince themselves that if they remove death from their consciousness it will never touch them. This large group of people denies death even when it is very close or has already occurred. Obviously the easiest and the surest way to change this is knowledge.

For the real human inside each one of us, death doesn't exist. It is neither the end of life nor the beginning of another one. It is all a continuation. I explain this in detail in the book *In the Wheel of Life*. The transition to the next stage of growth is a relatively normal process. Translating this into the physical realm – does lava in a cocoon die when it transforms into a butterfly? The butterfly emerges from the cocoon. And it can then rises high up in the sky where before it could only crawl on one or two leaves. When someone has a deep understanding of the principle of death, he will finally stop fearing this transitional phase. He also won't despair when his loved ones are going through this phase and not because he is neutral to it, but because he understands it. He will know that death came to him many times before and though it all he, as well as his loved one will be alive and do just fine. Moreover, instead of loss he will notice the benefits that he or his loved ones gain. Therefore, he will welcome death with calmness, without rebellion, even when the person departing is someone he loved very much. He certainly will feel sadness because of the parting, the same as is felt when a loved one travels far away. However, he will know that those who passed away are just as close as when they were alive and it's enough to discard the physical body during sleep to find oneself still next to them.

Be aware! The closeness that I describe here is completely different from what is felt during a possession. In the first case, both parties are free and independent, during a possession however, a ghost becomes an invader, a parasite preying on a person who is alive and sucking energy from them.

THE SOUL'S DECISION

It is important to understand that the soul unilaterally decides when and how to die. It can change that decision even at the moment of death and revive. Most often the decision to die occurs when a soul works through all the lessons it came to Earth to learn and decides to leave its earthly body. Each death, even those that seem the most accidental or resulting from a long illness is the soul's decision. The soul itself not only doesn't die, but after the body's death it is aware of everything happening around it.

My mom had cancer. Almost a year she lay in bed suffering. When I found out about her nearing death, I was pregnant, and shortly before her death I gave birth to my daughter. Death and birth came almost at the same moment? Astonishing! We both had lots of time getting used to the thought of her dying. When she wasn't able to get out of bed while I was feeding her, she suddenly started to choke and lost consciousness. I felt terrified and full of guilt. How could I be so careless? "God" – I called out – I contributed to the death of my own mother. If it wasn't for me, she would have lived at least a few more days". I don't quite remember what I was doing then, how I resuscitated her. I lost track of time.

Finally she opened her eyes. I was greatly surprised by her first words: "I came back, because you were in such a terrible state, I thought that you couldn't manage, but remember, I will die when you aren't around". Instead of rejoicing that mom was alive I stood shocked, with my mouth open. How could a dying person influence what was happening to them at the moment of death? And how come I wasn't the one that saved her, but rather she came back on her own? "Open the door for Sophia, because she has been standing behind the door for over hour and half" – my mom said a few moments after she woke up. "Who is Sophia? What are you talking about mom?" – I thought aloud. Mom, hearing me said: "Come to your senses girl. Suddenly you don't remember Sophia?" I realized that she must have been talking about her best friend.

I thought that mom was having hallucinations, but I didn't want to hurt her so I walked up to the door to pretend I was opening it for Sophia. There, at the door I was surprised by a tired Sophia. Upon entering our home she started saying: "I don't know what is happening to you, but I was standing there for hour and half and had no strength to either come in or leave. I can't feel my legs at all". I was shocked. How did my unconscious mother know what was happing behind the door? And as if that wasn't enough, mom said:"… and those people in the accident will all survive, after two weeks they will regain consciousness. Let their families know. They shouldn't worry…" What people? What accident? Mom had been taking psychotropic drugs for months and had hallucinated before, but now she sounded lucid, and she was not making objectionable comments, as in the past: "There" – she pointed at the window. We looked outside the window, at the intersection; under a trolley's wheels were two smashed cars. It was a horrible image, both cars were totaled, and here was mom saying not to worry because everyone would survive? She was also sharing other stories, for example: about what was happening with our neighbors who she had never even visited etc. It was hard to believe all of this, but everything she said that day was confirmed. Two weeks later she passed away. Today my daughter is thirty three years old.

In a short time span a breakthrough occurred in society's consciousness. This was during the era of socialism in Poland when nobody spoke or wrote about such things. Publications about near death experiences weren't readily available. I can give an example from my own family and friends to demonstrate how little information was available in this area. During that incident with my mom, there were seven people present at our home, but none of them wanted to believe her. Simply put, no one talked about this experience again and we all acted as though the entire thing never took place. However, fate wanted me to be a believer, because soon after my mom's death, while at my home outside the city, I met an acquaintance. Being concerned she started telling me about her own experience when her mother went through clinical death. She was terrified. "So embarrassing, so embarrassing" – she was mumbling. "Mrs. Pratnicka, if you only knew the nonsense she keeps saying. If this continues I will have to move out of the village, because everyone will be pointing at us, and they will send my mom to a mental institution". She was in such a state that if I didn't hear her out then she would have gotten a stroke or gone insane. I can't stand people who gossip. It seemed to me a huge waste of time and I don't let women who just want to talk stop me. However, this time I found the story so interesting I immediately invited her to my home. She was speaking erratically, but I remained patient and listened. I asked to meet with her mother who was very glad that someone was finally interested in her experiences. Her mother told me everything that she went through, and her story was almost identical to what my mother had said.

I stood up for that woman and authoritatively announced that there was no reason to deride her or lock her away in a mental institution. "She didn't make this up. She was talking about what happened to her during her clinical death" – I said. To prove it I told her my mother's story. She listened to me, but did she believe me? For a long time they had been pointing fingers at this woman, until the issue had died down. Over time I listened to her stories with bated breath. She spoke with great passion. Later, I will come back to the topic of clinical death.

Since then, not only have I personally experienced clinical death, but I have also met many people who also experienced it and saw what it was like on the other side. They understand that there is life after death and that in reality nothing changes. They even left their bodies and remembered it. They came back, because they wanted to come back. From the other side they noticed that they had left unfinished business and had a desire to complete it. Their loved ones were very desolate and they sympathized. Each one of these people spoke about different reasons for their return, but the fact is that they came to life because they themselves decided to do so. They were in euphoria because they discovered something extraordinary, something which changed them and their entire life from that point on. They remembered how being beyond their body they wanted to tell their loved ones that they are still alive, but nobody heard them. After their return they had a chance to share what they had experienced. They wanted other people to benefit from their experience; however their loved ones often didn't listen or didn't believe them.

Currently many books are being published on this topic, many doctors describe the experiences of their patients from borderline death, and also interviews on this topic are broadcast on radio and television. Still, in daily life people who have had these experiences are met with incomprehension, disbelief, and are sometimes considered, as in the past, maniacs, and even blasphemers.

FIGHTING FOR LIFE

Often we try saving people in the face of death. We tell ourselves that they have more to accomplish in life and should live a little longer. Perhaps this is a mistaken way of thinking. Age isn't an issue for a soul.

When a soul ultimately decides to leave, stopping it serves no purpose. It is good to encourage it to realize it's lifetime plan, but it shouldn't be stopped. We are capable of stopping a soul that decided to leave, but the soul and we will not benefit from that. I know of many cases where this became a curse for all the people involved. We don't take into account the soul's decision and the fact that the soul could have plans that are completely different from ours.

When we are fighting for a dying person's life, we are usually doing this for ourselves, to satisfy our own egoistical goals. For a variety of reasons we are afraid of being alone in the world. Many people ask me for help keeping someone alive. Sometimes these are in cases of serious illness, coma, clinical death, meaning those cases where the person is more unconscious than conscious. They would say to me: "Mrs. Pratnicka, please help us. It is such a pity that this young person has this illness and will not live longer". In their despair they would do anything to stop such a soul from leaving the body.

When I contact such a soul and ask what it thinks about the situation, it almost always answers that it wants to very much to leave, but sorrow towards its loved ones s ties it up like a chain and prevents it from leaving. Some are very determined though. They rebel and break the chains, but for many souls this is not easily accomplished. Sometimes a soul asks for an intercession with its family, to explain and convince them to let it go. Whenever I meet with persistent resistance while talking about it with a soul's loved ones it is usually the case that there is a lack of love in the family. However, where the dying soul has a loving family they always agree to let the soul leave. The soul would then leave immediately, not waiting for any goodbyes, as it is afraid that its family might still change their mind.

A friend who was a diplomat visited a European country. While there, he was invited to dinner at the home of a prominent person. During his visit he noticed that the host's daughter was behaving in a relatively strange way, as though she was not of this world, it was as though she was alive and dead at the same time. He called me to ask me what I thought and whether I could help. He said that she was a young, beautiful girl, and doctors couldn't diagnose any illness. I checked into her situation and what I saw not only surprised him, but also me. It turned out that in reality she is no longer alive. She was functioning only because her soul didn't have the courage to leave since it felt sorry for her parents. This information puzzled my friend so he talked a lot about the girl with her family. When he had a chance he also asked the girl more about herself and various aspects of her life, about her interests etc. She responded politely but with no enthusiasm. He was angry that I disappointed him. He thought that for some reason I didn't want to help him. It just so happened, that two weeks later while I was sitting with a large group of people, the phone rang and I received a message that the girl had fainted and fallen and since then had been hospitalized in a coma. They were even more insistent for my help at that point. I reaffirmed that she was no longer alive. Her soul asked me to convince her parents to let her leave. I agreed, although it seemed to me this would be tough to achieve. I repeated exactly what she asked me to say to them. At first they didn't want to hear anything, they wanted to forcefully keep her alive, as many parents do in such situations. However, after two weeks they agreed to let her leave. At the same moment her doctors pronounced her dead.

The issue of its family's sorrow is obviously a challenge for the soul (it is another lesson for it to work through). Each one of us has free will and is master of our own world. If its family's sorrow influences the soul, it means that somewhere inside it identifies with this sorrow. If it were capable of saying: "From this moment on I belong to God and nothing will stop me!", there would be no power that could influence its decision. It is worth noting this. Who knows, someday after our own death we might find ourselves in the same position as the soul that wants to leave, but can't.

If a soul didn't yet accomplish its plan or if there was even the slightest chance that it could still be accomplished, the soul won't leave. A person could be hopelessly sick with doctors giving up hope for recovery, but if it's meant for the soul to stay then that person will be miraculously healed.

I was once asked to help a businessman who had gone into a coma after a brutal beating. He was in a very serious condition. His doctors didn't give him much of chance of survival. His family was in despair. I made contact with him – let's call him Ron. I had a feeling that he would return to his physical life. My assistant informed his family of this. She explained to them that they needed to talk to Ron, to support him and encourage him to come back, to give him all the reasons for him to continue living. And they did this. His health significantly improved to the surprise of the doctors. After a month he woke up and a few days later returned home. This was quite a unique phenomenon for all the people involved. Many people spoke about the experience. It turned out that one of those people was his daughter's cousin who was also a very good friend of mine. Therefore, I was receiving information from three sides – from Ron's soul (mentally), his family and my friend. Ron's story is as follows:

He was assaulted and beaten by his two business partners with whom, until then he had been running a very successful company. After assaulting him, they took him to the forest and dumped him there. He lay there for few days until hunters with dogs found him. He was badly wounded, cold and had lost a great amount of blood. His partners, thinking that Ron was dead, went about embezzling the company's significant wealth. While recovering and still in the hospital, Ron told his daughter about this. However, he forbade her from talking to anyone about this because he was concerned for his family's safety. He knew that his partners were capable of anything. "What do you mean, what about justice?" – His daughter screamed – "they should be judged and sentenced, perhaps even get the death penalty". Then Ron answered her: "This is a fact. We must not move to quickly deprive anyone of life, especially if that person didn't live through his karma yet. I also didn't live through mine yet, that is why I had to come back. You are right. Many people kill, although they don't have any right to do so. They do this because of a lack of knowledge. They think that on Earth we live only once. If they knew what I know now, they would never dare take such a step. They would know that they will have to pay for everything in the future, but also that when they pass to another state, they will suffer greatly there. And if they come back to Earth they will have a very tough life. They will have to compensate everyone who they unjustly hurt. Therefore, don't worry about justice or revenge. Leave those matters to God". He said this with such a convincing tone of voice that his daughter understood and promised not to mention their conversation to anyone. Exactly what he told his daughter, he shared with me and asked me to watch over his daughter least she forgot what he told her. Therefore, only two people knew about the incident: his daughter physically and me mentally.

Ron also complained that he had no purpose for living. He was disappointed by everyone, without exception. While still in a coma he noticed that, in a way he deprived his family of freedom. He was giving them everything they needed, and they as a result had become passive, not doing anything with their lives. He once told me: "Nothing is bonding me to them. Constantly I heard from my family things like: "Please, come back to life, recover, we will take walks together on the beach, we will go away or we will buy this and that for ourselves. But nobody said (either my wife or children) that they love me, that they miss me, that they would like me to live for them, because they needed me". Then I told my friend this: "Talk to your family, let your cousin take care of her father, and your aunt her husband, let them talk from the bottom of their hearts, with love. If they won't do this, they will lose him". "What you mean lose him" – she asked surprised – "he is almost fully recovered, even you can't see any more bruises". "I know what I am saying. Please do what I am asking you" – I said. However nobody was able to awaken their love which they had buried deep inside for a long time. One day I heard from Ron: "It's time for me to leave this world. I took care of everything I needed to. I don't see any further sense in my living". He passed away the next day. It happened just as my intuition told me at the very beginning.

As you can see, dear reader, if a soul is convinced that there is nothing else to accomplish in its physical life then despite the achievements of today's medicine it will leave for a spiritual state. And vice versa: if a soul still has something to learn, then despite a condition considered critical in the eyes of medicine, it will return to its body, even if only for few moments or days, as in Ron's case.

SENSING OUR DEATH

People leaving the physical dimension sense when they are dying, and also see it. A few days before their expected death loved ones who passed away before gather around them along with spiritual guides who start cleaning the space necessary for making the transformation easier for the soul. This happens a few days before someone's expected death. This always happens, not just when we are laying on our deathbed.

For most people a sudden death is something which simply happens to people and the person who dies hasn't the slightest clue it was going to happen. This is not true. Most people who die suddenly informed the environment about their feelings of impending death months before their death. More often than not though, nobody wants to listen to them and they are confronted with comments like "Don't say stupid things. It just seems that way to you".

My uncle's case was quite similar. He was forty years old and a healthy, strong man, who half a year before his death had a feeling he would die. Because this was shortly after my mom's death, his beloved sister with whom he shared a close relationship, everybody thought, that he was being over-sensitive about death. As a consequence nobody wanted to listen to his feelings. They were running away from him as if from an intrusive mosquito. At the beginning he was frightened by these feelings. Multiple times I tried calming him down by explaining to him that there was nothing to be afraid of, the more so since his beloved sister was waiting for him.

With time he got used to that thought and got rid of his fear of death. This continued for half a year. The day before his death he came to me, and I suddenly felt that I was indeed seeing him for the last time. I wasn't alone in feeling this way. We talked about it for a relatively long time. We were even joking that since he had a need to die then he was certainly in a rush to be with his beloved sister. I said that I wouldn't dissuade him from that. He passed along to me all his matters (nobody else wanted to listen) and we said goodbye as though wouldn't see each other again. That night he died. Later I spoke to many people: his wife, his children and his friends. At first nobody was even aware that he continued talking about his death. Everyone was in conscious denial. With the passing of time they accepted his death and started to recall all those conversations. They felt guilty. They felt that if they had taken him seriously the last few months with him would have been spent differently.

Later on I analyzed many sudden deaths. In most confirmed cases there was a tendency for people to reject conversations about somebody's upcoming death and the fact that the person who is about to die knows long before their departure what will happen. This applies to any type of death that a person will experience – be it sudden or the result of an illness.

I am sure you are wondering why people are not trying or are unable to offer their loved ones a feeling of peace and hope. They do this, because they don't understand death and are afraid of it. However, this is a problem reflected in people who lead a superficial life. They don't perceive life as it really is. Otherwise they would understand and always remember that death is a transformation from one state to another and is a natural part of life. We would become more patient (without any effort) and would be able to more spontaneously show sympathy and love. If you know somebody who is suffering because they fear death or because they lost a loved one, take care of them, but don't send them expressions of sadness, because you will only burden them with additional heaviness and pain brought on by your own sadness. Instead, send them love and understanding.

After my mom's death many people who knew they would soon die or who had experienced a loved one's passing turned to me for help. Many of them weren't prepared to hear about life after death. Although they didn't have that specific knowledge, I felt, that I could still do a lot for them. Sometimes it was enough to have an appropriate tone of voice, heartfelt approach to the process they were going through or recognizing and understanding their concerns and feelings. Often a look, touch of the hand or a nice word was enough. Those who were ready to receive this I could tell more about death and dying. It was about reaching deep inside of them and moving an invisible string that will allow them to open up to understanding this process. Sometimes their reaction was incredible. It strengthened them spiritually and despite the great physical suffering of those who were sick, they had hope. A new spiritual energy entered them. Through their own intuition they became aware of what I spoke to them about. Their great terror disappeared from their faces and was replaced by a smile of gratitude as they agreed with their own fate. In most cases sick people know when the end is near and they are left alone with this important and difficult problem by themselves. After all, this could have happened completely different. I am writing about an era when we lacked books on this topic. Now you are in a much better position because you are holding such a book in your hand. You can read it, share it with someone or tell others about its content. This includes children, even those fairly young ones.

I know how painful it is to say good bye to a loved one. It is perhaps even harder for a person who is about to die, who has to face up to the unknown transformation called death for himself. If both sides knew more about death they would definitely approach it with greater calmness. It would still be sad for us though, however we wouldn't suffer as much as we do now. It would be like the departure of a loved one to somewhere abroad that is far away. In fact this person wouldn't be with us anymore, but we would know that they still exist. Maybe we would gain an awareness that in reality we never split up (separation is absolutely impossible) and the dying person just moves on to the next classroom. For the soul leaving a physical body, learning continues and takes places on higher planes, this being in essence on higher levels of consciousness. Admittedly, the dying person is no longer on the physical plane, but we are always connected on the spiritual plane and we can make contact with them after death through our love for them, through our heart. Love lasts eternally and if someone is truly loved then through that love you can have constant, non-stop contact with loved ones.

At this point, I would like to mention that souls in a spiritual form can always make contact with physical people if they want to. They do so only when it is something very important, or if they want to communicate something they think you should know. They never communicate when it is only you wanting the communication. I am obviously talking here about souls that have passed on to the other side of death's curtain. Souls that have remained amongst the living more often than not are not aware of their own death so any attempt to make contact with such ghosts can lead to possession by them.

BEFORE YOU DIE

You are in the Earth School and after ending your lessons you would already have taken off your physical body multiple times and came back Home. This is not frightening once we know enough about it. You just need to recall how in your youth when you ended each school year you welcomed the vacation with great happiness. It is exactly the same way your soul upon laying down its physical body is rejoicing that it has free time from learning ahead and it will be going back Home. While going through our earthly existence we don't realize how little we know about it. Only death and a glance at the beyond explain to us what life is about. Only people lacking knowledge about death, who are afraid of it, hang on to life and don't know what to do about themselves in the next phase. Therefore, talking about death is of great importance because it allows people to get used to the transition that is generally call "death, which is a further road we travel after our physical life. However, we must be able to handle this knowledge and accept it as part of our daily lives. Many things are now being presented to us from a broader perspective. Until now it seemed death was the end of everything. But in reality, it is a continuation of our existence. In order for the transition from one plane to another to occur without disruption, we should know as much as possible about it. Then we will approach life differently and it will actually boil down to a very simple formula.

We come to the physical world mainly to care about each other on Earth. Before and also during our earthy journey we receive everything we need to work on the development of our own soul. Those are our gifts. When a soul touches the Earth, it can't leave Earth until the moment it has fulfilled all of its obligations. During our physical life on Earth we undertake many tasks and all of them should be accomplished before our physical life ends. If someone for some reason is unsure that they will live long enough to accomplish their tasks, they shouldn't undertake them or they should find the right person to assist them in accomplishing these tasks. This is because nobody can die with uncompleted tasks. Otherwise that person would leave some part of himself on Earth and won't be able to leave in peace. In every case the person knows when the time to leave has arrived and he has to leave this world because he can't accomplish anything else in his current incarnation.

If one of us discovers, or we get an intuitive feeling that the moment of death of our physical body is coming, we should perform a "ceremony" in which our tasks are passed on to someone who agrees to complete them for us. Each person leaving this world should clean up their life this way. We are obliged to apologize to people who we have wronged, give and receive love, demonstrate our gratitude for time spent with loved one,

and pass on our social and family obligations to someone. Each
one of us should do this on an ongoing basis. But how many
people actually do this? If someone has a backlog, because he
has never done this before, then he should do it at least symbolically in spirit. Society today does not consciously allow for this.
People will instantly hear: "Don't be stupid, you will still be
alive". Earlier I described what my uncle went through. He told
everyone around him, but nobody listened to him. Ultimately
though, how others react, is up to them.

The task of someone who is leaving is to free himself
from anything that could disturb him as he journeys on. That also includes passing all things, even private things on to loved
ones. Obviously, while he is still alive he doesn't get rid of them
physically, only symbolically. It would be wonderful if people
accepted that person's tasks (initially symbolically) in order to
release that person from all of his obligations. It's about his
soul's tasks being accomplished. That is necessary for someone
to peacefully leave this world. His energy will be completely
clean. Thanks to that, his soul will be able to continue its journey on its individual path.

Often the person who is dying is unable to perform such
a ceremony, because his loved ones don't allow him to. An alternative is to write down a will (even secretly). People leaving
this world should be aware that even the poorest person has
something that others could find useful. If all of us knew that,
life would be simpler, and death would be received completely
different: in peace and with understanding. Remember that the
person's ultimate goal, therefore and yours as well is to broaden
the sense of freedom. This is done by developing our sense of
dignity, love, kindness and respect for oneself. Only when you
achieve this, will you gain love, respect, knowledge, kindness,
and understanding towards others, even towards all humanity. If

you will try to achieve this the other way around and first think about others and not about yourself, then you won't achieve the goal for which you came to this world. You will die unfulfilled.

You should know that the timing of any death is not accidental: even the death which seems rather sudden and unexpected for the physically living. It has to come at the right moment for the transition, just as occurred at birth.

Despite each soul having its own tasks to accomplish, it has a close link to the entire universe's life force. Each life, that touches Earth, has its own schedule to follow. The departure of each soul cannot be ad hoc. It has to be synchronized with the remaining souls because a general plan exists that includes all streams of the universe.

That plan involves not only those who are leaving this world, but also those who remain, meaning us, the physically alive. When a soul is leaving its body, many powers, including angels and spiritual guides, help to bring a balance of energy to all of the people who were in some way connected to the deceased. Therefore, it is not easy to leave a material body, because it has to accomplish everything that the soul undertook to do while on Earth.

FATAL ILLNESS

For young and healthy people, illness and death seems to be incredibly distant and unreal. They delude themselves into thinking that illness and death will never touch them. They don't accept the fact that illness, and even death come unexpectedly at times and that sooner or later they will have to confront illness, old age and even death; if not theirs then that of their loved ones. But illness and death don't have to be linked with old age at all.

Most people, especially young people, take life too lightly. Only news of an incurable illness makes them realize how precious their life or someone else' life really is. No matter whether this happens to them personally or to a loved one, it strikes like lightning.

Each serious illness, ours or someone else's, creates a personal crisis that makes us reflect on how we live our life. Until then everything seems more or less okay (we close our eyes to certain anomalies in life), however illness shows us the trivial experiences in our daily lives. Probably because it gives us pause and makes us think about our own life.

When the time comes to die people become bitter and resigned. In a manner of speaking they lived, but they didn't leave any trace of themselves. I once heard someone say "If I could squeeze my life into my head, there would be nothing left over. I am leaving this world empty handed". This was said by someone with a beautiful house, wonderful family, who also ran a large business where he worked very hard. I answered him this way: "It is not important what you achieved and what you didn't. What you experienced, it has already happened and you have no influence over it anymore. Now think about why you attracted illness to yourself, what you can learn from that. Now, presently, while you are sick, you can gain more than you did during your entire life. If you don't like what you created for yourself up to this point, accept that, forgive yourself for whatever you have to forgive yourself and begin to create anew. Obviously you can give up, but know that there will come a time to experience the same thing anew, but in much worse conditions. You can use this occasion to heal this or not. Everything depends of you". At the beginning he wasn't doing anything for himself. He had one surgery after another. When the next surgery was scheduled during a short space of time, he stopped to reflect. He began to work intensively on himself. He was a completely new and healthy person, but not such a long time before he had been given zero chance of survival.

Dear reader, I would like to present the subject of serious, fatal illnesses from all sides, because illness not only touches the sick person, but also impacts all family members and throws their lives into serious disarray. It doesn't bypass children as they witness its effects and are greatly affected by it.

I will also show you how children approach their own illnesses – even very serious illnesses. They play even as their health worsens daily. At first it would seem that they are carefree because they are too young to understand the implications of their illnesses. This is only a delusion. They know perfectly well, that before their illnesses they were strong, they could run, jump, and now they are unable to get out of bed and soon they would probably die. They are happy and spontaneous, because they weren't hypnotized yet by adults and know perfectly well *Who They Are in Essence* and why they came into this world. They still have a childlike trust in God. Everything, that He gives them is good, even their illness. Unfortunately, adults forgot about this over time. They forget *Who They Are in Essence* and what the goal of their life is, even of their illness. That is why it is a lot harder for them to part with life than it is for children (You can read more about *Who You Are in Essence* in my book *In the Wheel of Life*).

ARE YOU ILL?

Dear reader, perhaps you once got news of an incurable illness and lamented that medicine could not do anything in your situation. I understand that this was and still is the worst moment of your life. Perhaps, you are experiencing shock, especially if the symptoms showed up suddenly. Perhaps you are in denial over the diagnosis, thinking that it is not true as things can't be that bad or your doctor made a mistake. Maybe you are rebelling against this diagnosis and constantly asking yourself: "Why did this happen to me?" Perhaps you are unable to accept your new condition and the many things you won't be able to do anymore. Maybe you have accepted your illness won't just disappear and you are learning how to live with that fact? Perhaps you are at the resignation stage. Instead of taking charge of your situation, you lie in bed defiantly and full of despair saying: "There is no point to getting up, because I will die anyway…"

Dear reader, don't give up. Don't think that all is lost, that it's the end of the road; nothing can be done about it anymore. Each serious, fatal illness, no matter what it is, it is accepted that it cannot be healed from the outside (meaning by doctors, medications, procedures). However always remember, that it can be healed from the inside.

I will come back to this topic later, but before I do it, I would like to tell you that many illnesses, even very serious ones, which medical science tells us are fatal, are caused by ghosts (people who died and instead of going to the other side attached themselves to living people). Such ghosts could be a beloved granny, grandpa, friends from school, neighbors, parents; meaning someone who was very close to us and with whom we shared a strong emotional bond. It could also be unknown ghosts, but that happens less often.

Illnesses caused by ghosts are the easiest to observe through their incarnations as various forms of cancer (because they are relatively easily to diagnose) when a sick person has a visible tumor or growth. Then, when the ghost or ghosts are led away, the tumor or growth immediately disappears, and the sick person returns to health. With harder to detect illnesses this recovery has to be confirmed by a doctor. Often we feel so much better that inwardly we know that we are returning to health (this happens in most cases). Hundreds, if not thousands of my clients experienced this. During an exorcism ghosts are always led away. Unfortunately, ghosts sometimes return. It doesn't matter if it's because of its attachment to the previously possessed or because it is attracted back by the previously possessed who finds it hard to part with the ghost. This is a separate, broad topic. I would like to mention though, that when a ghost returns tumors or growths appear. Not necessarily in the same place which proves that a ghost is the cause of the illness.

Cancer doesn't disappear by itself to reappear some time later in an advanced stage. Therefore, removing the cause, meaning the ghost or ghosts, almost immediately removes the result of the possession, that is, the illness. Many of my clients avoided dangerous surgery in this way. I broadly describe this issue in my book *Possessed by Ghosts*.

However, we can't always handle these matters by the above-mentioned process. At this point I need to clearly state that not every living person's illness is caused by ghosts. Many people are sick due to their own, unresolved psychological burdens (although ghosts could be attached to them). Therefore, even after leading the ghost away the sickness will still be present. In such cases, ghosts are not the cause of the illness; although they are attached to the sick person and are using their sickness induced weakness (it is much easier for them to possess the person). Ghosts are not usually attracted in such cases to illness, but to the psychological problems that caused the illness. It is a matter of vibrations – the ghost and the sick person vibrate at the same, low level. Obviously ghosts are not attached to every sick person. However, in most cases where people reach out . to me, the seriously ill person also has ghosts. For such people it is twice as hard. Healthy people who are under the influence of ghosts could feel weak as a result of the ghost's presence, it is even worse for sick people. However I will repeat – there is no guarantee that when ghosts are led away an illness will go away at the same time. In many cases it does in fact happen this way, however not in all cases. People shouldn't feel frustrated or disappointed if their illness does not go away at the same time, but rather they should enjoy their freedom. When ghosts are led away, people are a lot more energetic and they find it a lot easier to work on their own person.

Now I will return to illnesses. If you are sick and no external methods are helping then you have to look for internal causes of your illness. Sicknesses will go away if you work on them. However you need to accomplish this on your own. No external party can do this for you. Just as one person cannot swim for another person, one person cannot tackle another person's life lessons for them. Someone external to you can help you, however without your own internal intervention aimed at your life and health nobody can heal or save you, not even the Almighty God himself. He doesn't have anything to do with your illness. You attracted it to yourself and you have the power and potential to free yourself from it. You just have to decide whether you want to perform this task or not.

When you get to the cause of your illness and you treat with it, you will be amazed at how simple it is as a task and how effectively you can undertake it. However when posed with the problem it seemed challenging. What is required to overcome this is not just effort, but assertiveness and determination and adherence to the rule: "Whatever it is, I will free myself from these shackles". Before you start, know that your suffering is not a form of punishment, but rather a type of learning experience. Many people can't learn any other way but through suffering. If this is also your case, decide what you want and determine to learn in a different way. Many people are able to do that, I believe therefore, that you will be able to do it also. Essentially, everything depends of how badly you want to free yourself from the cause of your illness so that you won't have to suffer anymore.

HOW OUR SUBCONSCIOUS WORKS?

Dear reader, do you realize that the state of your health or relationship with yourself comes from a coded picture of the world that you have in your mind. Every activity from your past: all events, relationships, thoughts, ideas and beliefs influence your body's function. It is all stored in your subconscious. It is all stored deep inside your thoughts as though in a deposit box and like a program steers your life (I write more extensively on this later on). Obviously, one-time, random thoughts don't have creative power compared to thoughts that are constantly repeated or deep beliefs. Do you know that whether or not you love and accept yourself and also whether or not you have respect for and trust yourself depends on your feelings of well-being and it all directly depends upon your health? When you send signals of suffering to your body, its cells shirk in fear causing physical illness. And when you send signals of happiness they become a source of happiness for you. You are here to live a full, happy life and express your capabilities in the most perfect way. To put it differently, your purpose here is to lead a prosperous life full of happiness and beauty. Have you realized these expectations yet? If not, you shouldn't be surprised if you have health issues. But you can fix this any time you want to. The power to change this is already in you. Therefore, forgive yourself and begin to express more and more happiness and beauty.

Also you must have a complete realization that it is God's intention for you to be always fulfilled and healthy. Perfect health and a fulfilled life are your right. Do you make use of this? Not completely? Surely it because, you don't realize that deep inside you, you have one more body (it is not physical, but spiritual), which is always young, beautiful and healthy. Our physical body doesn't live by itself. Life comes from our spiritual body. If you only had a physical body without a spiritual body, you wouldn't be able to in any way act, think, move, speak, feel, see, hear, breath, or in other words live in general (I will expand further on this topic later in this book when I discuss the concept of death). Your life comes from your spiritual body which is inhabited by God Himself and it is always young, always beautiful and always healthy. If you don't reflect these characteristics it is because, at some point you introduced the wrong beliefs to your physical body. It doesn't matter if these beliefs came directly from you or from other people.

It is God's intention that the physical body be a faithful copy of the spiritual body and fully displays its characteristics. This is a basic truth that you should always remember. You, this great indestructible You, on a deeper level is always healthy, beautiful and young. However, you forgot this fact, because you give faith to your mistaken beliefs. This is why your body reflects them instead of the truth. The examples presented shortly will help you better understand what I am referencing here.

For now, I can tell you that all of my clients who returned to health (from very serious illnesses, even fatal illnesses) discovered that they did something shameful in the past themselves or others hurt them. When they grasped the cause of their illnesses, they had to face these tough experiences and heal them. We are not talking here about treating the illnesses, only its causes.

Firstly, we have to understand that we ourselves administer punishment in the form of illnesses and it doesn't come from the outside, from bad fate or God. We create it ourselves as a consequence of our own behavior. Perhaps you would ask: "How is that possible? Are sick people masochists?" Well, dear reader, in each case our subconscious determines the punishment. We depend on its judgment. It categorizes our deeds and considers them as good and right or bad and wrong. If it thinks that we committed a violation it begins to feel guilty and as a consequence creates a punishment. Obviously, we don't realize consciously that this is how it works. The greater the violation according to our subconscious' belief, the greater is the punishment. It could take the form of serious illness, an accident, misfortune or prison. This process unfolds while our thoughts are wandering and we are not aware of ourselves (in other words, unaware of own subconscious feelings in regards to own deeds, and even thoughts). Unfortunately, this problem presently applies to most living people. They run away from themselves by embracing addictions, gossip, television viewing, computers, so that they can avoid delving deeper into themselves.

On the other hand, when we are in a state of full consciousness, nothing ever threatens us. At those times we are fully aware of ourselves and have an opportunity to verify how our subconscious receives and accepts deeds and thoughts. Assuredly, you have already experienced moments when after some important event you had a mental conversation with yourself, you analyzed whether you should have behaved differently or explained to yourself why you behaved how you did. Perhaps your subconscious was feeling guilty and this is why you were discussing it with yourself. Sometimes we are so busy with other, "more important" matters, that we don't want to engage with our subconscious' reaction or we even run away from trying to understand what we have done or what someone else has done to us. The more traumatic the experience the greater the temptation to run away from what is unpleasant. We are not aware of our subconscious and we don't know how it classifies any event. If the event is considered bad and shameful then in the future we may have to endure serious consequences as a result, as occurred in John's case which I present momentarily.

What is a completely normal occurrence for one person's subconscious, even trivial, could be a serious wrongdoing for another person's subconscious. This explains why one person steals, cheats, betrays and doesn't get punished while another person thinks about it and punishes himself. In order for you to better understand what I want to communicate here; I present below a situation in which I was personally involved.

A neighbor I was close to, an older gentleman – let's call him John – had heart disease almost his entire life. He had two strokes and he was close to having another. I was asked to help. However his family came up with the idea, and he wasn't eager or against it himself. He was however feeling miserable enough that without enthusiasm, he decided to participate in the therapy. At some point he began to talk about how he saw himself as a young boy who hit his friend's leg so hard that the friend fell and couldn't get up by himself. He later realized that he had broken his friend's leg because he saw him walking with his leg wrapped in bandage. After we finished the session John ascertained that since he didn't remember that event then it is was just his imagination. I had a different opinion because I had many such sessions and I am able to differentiate when a given story is true and when it isn't. I asked whether his friend was still alive. He said yes and he lived nearby, but they don't talk to each other. I asked John's family for help organizing a meeting between these two gentlemen. I will describe in detail how the meeting transpired, because it is relatively essential. "You know Francis, I would like to apologize for that leg" – said John. "What leg are you talking about John?" his former friend responded. "You know, Francis, when I hit you with a stick and I broke it". "John, but I never had a leg broken. You must be mistaking me with someone else?". "No Francis, it was definitely you. I remember it as clearly as if it was taking place right now". "Seriously, it wasn't me". "Then why did you stop talking to me?". "I thought that you stopped talking to me. When I tried talking to you, you turned away from me". They were bantering like this for a relatively long time. I said that it didn't matter what happened half a century ago. What was important now was for them to forgive each other. They willingly did that and talked all evening recalling their youthful years. A few days after that meeting John's doctor called with information that there was an open spot at a clinic. He claimed that John's condition was serious and asked John to come to the hospital as fast as he could. John was against it, because he was already feeling better, but his explanations didn't work.

At the clinic they performed tests, and later more and more tests. They performed many because they thought that there was a mistake. The tests showed that the patient, John was fully recovered. The third stroke never happened, on the pictures there was no trace of the two previous strokes. The doctors

didn't really want to believe it, but the patient from the very beginning was under the care of the head of the hospital department. The past pictures of the patient's heart explicitly showed
traces of the two previous strokes. Since then that elderly man
had been rejuvenated by a few years and managed to travel half
way around the globe. Now from time to time he tells his acquaintances about a person that destroyed his life by punishing
him for something that most likely never took place. He proved
to himself that people involved in some events remember it in
various ways. One group punishes themselves from that reason;
the other group has no idea about it.

Now let's think about the possibility of John's subconscious picking up those false images which so intensely influenced his life. Well, the subconscious arranges each event in its
storage memory as vibrations and creates from it a matrix, in
other words a pattern which informs the physical body. This
process takes place in every human. If an event was rationalized,
meaning if the conscious mind illuminates to the subconscious
what really happened, then we keep that influence on our life,
because we shape the event according to our desires and needs.
However, each event that is not rationalized causes that subconscious to judge it for itself. And, based on how the subconscious
classifies it (as good or bad), will determine what kind of future
it will create for us. This happened in John's case. Negative (and
of course subjective) vibrations of that event comprised words,
images and thought forms, that were not only recorded in his
subconscious, but it also created a matrix, meaning a pattern to
which his body later conformed.

If the subconscious classifies something once (accepts a
pattern) it will reproduce it like an automatic stamp, because it
has the ability to replicate. As a result it will apply this pattern
repeatedly, accepting it as an authentic subconscious pattern. As

a consequence each similar event, heard or seen, we have will be taken as real, as our truth, because our subconscious believes it to be so.

Let's discuss another case, Caroline's, whose mother repeated to her from a very young age: "Never let boys kiss you, because they only want one thing". This sentence got deeply coded into her daughter's psyche. As a result it left a burdened mark on the girl's subconscious. When Caroline was fourteen years old she went to her friend's birthday party where she was offered a glass of champagne. This small amount of alcohol was enough for someone that young. Her friend's parents made sure that she was taken home by a boy slightly older than her. When they were already in front of her house, the boy not only tried to kiss her, but also put his hand under her dress and touched her womb. She escaped and ran into her home.

Later she grew up, got married and forgot about her mom's past warnings. A few years later the most serious type of cancer appeared on her womb. A date for her surgery was set, but the doctors claimed that her condition was hopeless. Caroline wanted very much to live and a few days before the operation contacted me. She was brought to me by a common friend. We didn't have high hopes, but we tried to face the problem. First, I had to explain to Caroline the rules of how the subconscious mind functions. When she fully understood them, I asked her to dig deep inside herself and see in what way and for what reason her body deteriorated. She started to think about it and at the same time we slowly regressed into her past. Meanwhile she was trying to understand where and what event, thoughts and words was pushing her into sickness and failure. She was presented with various situations; however none of them was the right one. Finally she reached the cause which she had completely forgotten about. It turned out that her subconscious had accepted the incident with the boy as such a huge offence to-ward her and her mother that it had punished itself by creating a cancer. Imagine dear reader that it had the shape and size of male's hand.

"If you want to recover" – I said to Caroline – "you have most of all to remove what causes your illness. To that end you must forgive yourself as well as all people that were involved in that incident. This is an absolute necessity, a requirement with-out which you won't achieve health and well-being. In order to completely cure and prevent this illness from recurring, you have to truly forgive, from your heart. After, forget about it and walk away from your existing life, your thoughts and that entire experience. Thereafter maintain yourself in that forgiving and forgetting way until any leftovers of those experiences are com-pletely wiped away from your subconscious thoughts. Besides that, stop worrying about yourself, stop treating yourself with condemnation and excessive criticism, and also stop condemn-ing others. Forgive yourself and others". Caroline went back home and continued working on herself intensively because she wanted very much to live. She understood that no matter what happened in the past, what was important now was what she thought and how her subconscious reacted to that.

Many times she was sure that she had convinced her subconscious and had completely forgiven the people involved in that event, and then it turned out that deep inside she still con-sidered herself a bad and unworthy woman. When she went deeper into those feelings, memories came back, very clearly. Being with me, when she looked at them for the first time, she saw them blurry, in the distance and foggy. It could even be said that she felt them more than saw them. Later, when she reached them, they showed themselves to her very clearly. She under-stood fully how bad the little girl she was felt and she saw in detail the entire scene of how she almost let that boy kiss her. She also saw the hand that was under her skirt. Therefore she was continuously forgiving anew. At some point during this eager forgiving (herself and her mother) she felt with all her being that the worst was behind her. Later, she was able to easily forgive the boy, and most of all forgive God against whom she had held grudges for He had punished her with the illness. Consequently she discovered to her surprise that it was now easier for her to love and accept herself. Up to that point she had worked on herself using the following affirmation: "I, Caroline, love and accept myself", however it hadn't changed her life for the better. She was repeating it anew; however she felt that affirmation was yielding no results. Nothing changed in her life; it only bounced back with an empty echo. Later, everything changed. As she forgave the aforementioned, the affirmation began to work. She also started to respect and trust herself more. She was incredibly surprised by it.

She went to the hospital; however they didn't operate on her because the doctors noticed that the cancer was regressing. With time it was becoming smaller and smaller until it had completely disappeared. When Caroline changed her thoughts, it also changed her beliefs on a deeper subconscious level, so her body started to recover on its own. Each body is able to recover, including yours. When Caroline put aside her subconscious hostility towards men, she grew closer to her husband which was mutually rewarding. Today they are a loving, married couple and they are making up for lost years.

Such sudden recoveries are not singular, isolated cases. I could go on for some time listing those I experienced personally. Most disorders which I took care of directly or indirectly are very similar to each other. Their pattern is as follows: some time ago we did something which our subconscious accepted as wrong and punishable. It punished itself by creating an illness, accident or misfortune the nature and strength of which depends on how it classified this event. The greater the violation – in a subjective sense –then the greater is the punishment. When, years later we discover the cause of our feelings of guilt, it may seem trivial to us, inconsequential, or even funny, however at the moment of inception it was judged to be a significant wrongdoing against our value system by our subconscious. In such situations ghosts often come along to intensify our suffering.

At first it always seems incredibly difficult to reach the cause of the subconscious' problems. This is because hidden deeply in our subconscious is the "wound" that has had a great emotional influence on us. When we understand how the subconscious interpreted a given past event, everything returns to normal. We feel as though we are reborn. In a dark place of our being, a little bit of light starts to come in and it heals everything. What seemed to be terrifying for the subconscious mind, now, understood and forgiven, gives way. It is possible that during our life we did much worse to others than that which causes us problems. We were however conscious of the reaction of our subconscious in those situations. Therefore, those things didn't have any influence over us. It is different when we are deeply shaken by some event and we had neither the strength nor the occasion to interpret it. The subconscious then judges it by itself, and how it classifies it dictates how it will impact us later on.

What John and Caroline worked through with my help, they could also have done on their own. Many people do. Many of my clients call or write letters to my office asking for help; however they only receive instructions from us. Later they are forced to work on their problems by themselves, in their home or in hospital. How long they have to work on it? Until they achieve their goal.

Real problems for those people actually only start when they don't want to recognize their problems and forgive what they should. Many of them were a step away from death. After working through old sickness causing traumas they recovered in body and in soul. If they die without forgiving themselves, they would join the groups of wandering souls, because as "sinners", they wouldn't have the courage to go to The Light. Until that time, through most of their life they feel miserable, dirty and sinful subconsciously. Their subconscious recognized that one or another violation required punishment. So their life became one great torment. However when the process of recognizing the real cause of the subconscious' problems starts and forgiveness begins, they will experience great change.

As you can see, dear reader, John and Caroline (as well as many of my other clients) took care of their salvation. This only happens when we understand, that nobody else, but we ourselves brought these negative conditions upon us. Therefore we have all the power to free ourselves from this by changing our own thoughts. A person should take a look at the problem, explain to the subconscious where it made a mistake (meaning tell it the truth), and the subconscious by itself will release us from the negative conditions that have afflicted us. John and Caroline became convinced on their own that the only way to change their wrong beliefs was absolute forgiveness. This simple process can also transform failure into success, and illness into health. In order to achieve that you would have to substitute present thoughts about: sickness, failure, despair, limitations and unfairness with new thoughts about: health, courage, power, inspiration and harmony. When they become permanently rooted in you, your physical tissues will undergo a change and you will start looking at life in a new light. Old matters will drift away; everything will start being created anew as though you were re-born, obviously not physically, but spiritually. Your life will take on new meaning; you will be rejuvenated, overflowing with happiness, confidence, hope and energy. New possibilities will open up for you to gain health and success, which until now you were unable to notice, or which didn't make any sense or had any meaning to you.

BENEFITS OF BEING SICK

There are other issues associated with being sick. After analyzing most of the cases that I dealt with over the past forty years I know that illness always offers some benefits to the sick person. If it only caused suffering, it would be easier to free ourselves from it. It would be enough to take a look inside our subconscious mind, reprogram the traumatic experience and right away we would be free. Unfortunately, the benefits that come from being sick often make it harder to recover. It's like a person standing at the crossroads, crippled in a way by an inner conflict, like a split personality. He would want the benefits that the illness gives him, but at the same time he would want to be healthy and not suffer.

Often I ask my clients to take a sheet of paper and on one side write down all the advantages that they get from being sick and on the other side the disadvantages. When one of my assistants offers them the paper to do this, we always hear: "Excuse me, but what kind of benefits can I get from being sick?!" However when they think about it for a while, they find advantages, sometimes quite a few. They are often surprised by the fact that the number of advantages is always greater than disadvantages.

To illustrate this, I will use the example of a student, Marianna, a very sickly girl whose father reached out to me for help. She had a serious, incurable illness, but at the same time she was possessed by a few ghosts. At the beginning it was hard to determine whether the ghosts were attracted to the illness or were causing it. We didn't have any contact with Marianna initially, because her father was afraid of how she would react. In my practice people often ask for help for someone else but want to "protect" the sick person from this knowledge that could heal them right away. That is what happened in this case.

When healing from a distance wasn't yielding any results, I asked my assistant to have the father tell his daughter to call. I recognized that it wouldn't make sense for him to call, because it would waste our time and his money. By his tone of voice you could hear that something inside him was agitating against this, however he must had given it some thought, because a few days later his daughter called. She had prepared in advance for the conversation as though for an exam. She was so talkative; she didn't even let me speak. She said at the very beginning that she knew she was possessed by ghosts, because she had read my book. She understood from it why her sister committed suicide. However she was very sick and the doctors don't give her any chance of living much longer. She told me how many well-known doctors had already treated her without any success and how many therapy sessions she had gone through with the best psychologists and even psychiatrists, including one professor. When I was finally able to interrupt her monologue, I told her that, I would take care of leading the ghosts away, how-ever in order for the therapy to be successful she had to cooper-ate with me and my assistant. I said that I would ask her ques-tions and she would have to answer them. "Of course, I already went to many therapists. I know how this works" – she joyfully answered. I suggested to her at the beginning to think about what benefits she got from being sick and to list them. "How can I have benefits from being sick? I am really sick. Various medi-cal tests confirm that – she screamed. "But I don't deny that, I just want, together with you to find the cause of your illness." – I said – "This is why it's necessary for you to search inside yourself for the advantages you get from your illness and the disadvantages. We will take care of the disadvantages later, but first tell me what advantages you get: Attention from your par-ents, the ability to feel sorry for yourself, sympathy from your friends? Search, what else?" She understood what I meant and she started to count them out. We counted twenty seven various benefits. Here are some of them: "I don't really like my college, because my parents picked it. That is why I go to lectures when I want and to which ones I want. My parents allow me to sleep in even when they know that I will be late to lectures. When I get on the bad side of a professor I always have an explanation that I was feeling bad, because I am so sick". "So how do you manage with exams since you are almost never at school?" – I asked. "Oh, because I am sick it also works for exams. I always get some sort of credit. If that doesn't work out then I take a year off. As a result of my illness I have already taken a few years off and nobody holds it against me that I am a permanent student. ". "And what else?" – I asked. "Well, I don't have to get married, have children, work; and all my peers are already on their own. I don't have to help at home or do anything for my-self, meaning do laundry, cook or clean. On the other hand I can meet with friends when I want and for as long as I want. If I am not in the mood, then I can stand them up, because no matter what nobody will hold it against me."

She was counting the advantages out like this for a few more minutes, and when she was done, she was very proud that she had found so many reasons for being sick. It looked as though she was expecting me to praise her. She was surprised because instead of praising her I said to her: " I will not be able to do anything for you until your benefits from being sick are no longer greater than the disadvantages. You, yourself, have to want to change something in your life; I can only assist you with that. You have to understand, that neither me, nor both your parents, or anyone else can live your life for you. Since you think that your time is slowly coming to an end, then think about whether you still want to senselessly waste it and additionally expose yourself to ghosts that are with you which will hinder you after death. You are sick because you told your subconscious mind that you obtain benefits from it, but each one of us, including you, came to this world to act, and not to figure out how to cleverly to slink away from acting. If you don't want to study, then don't study. The world won't come to an end because of that. Or start studying something that you like, what you feel passionate about. If you don't want to get married and have children, then don't. You can live however you like and nobody, including your parents, can forbid you from doing that, because this is your life and you are solely responsible for it. You have a right to try, to change, to create, and what do you do? Instead of standing up to your parents you run away into illness and it seems you see this as the easy way out. However your cleverness will end at the moment of your death, which you think is soon. If you die right now you would go to the other world without any goods, empty handed. Is that what your soul desires? In the face of death everything that now seems attractive you will have to leave behind, otherwise that "something" will hold you here and you will suffer because of that "something". You have ghosts inside you, but this is not an accident, because ghosts most often possess people that are just like them, because in the other world like attracts like. When you change then the ghosts that possess you will stop being attracted to you and it will be easier for them to leave when I lead them away and they won't come back again. The cause is not in the ghosts, but in you, that they are attracted to you like a magnet, and you allow them to hold on and not want to let go. Even though I lead ghosts away every day, they have the right to come back. They have free will and can use it. However you also have free will and it is your responsibility to not attract them back when I lead them away. Even if they don't want to leave, your task is to ensure they do not possess you again". When she hung up the phone she was deep in thought, in a way far away. I resigned myself after that conversation. I realized that no matter how hard I tried to cleanse her non-stop day and night, there was nothing or very little I could do, if she didn't want to be healthy herself. After a little while her father called with questions, because his daughter didn't say anything to him. I told him that my conversation with his daughter only confirmed what I already knew. The girl didn't call again and I wouldn't have known what was happening with her except for her father's curiosity.

After some time he called again asking what I did because his daughter was changing literally in front of his eyes. I answered that lately beyond checking on her I had done very little work with her because ghosts were no longer around her. I said that the changes were certainly the result of her finding the inner strength to change her life and all I did was direct her along that path.

He was amazed and couldn't understand how it was possible for one conversation to influence so many positive changes, since many persons had already tried talking to his daughter. I replied that apparently she finally grew up to face life whereas before she wasn't ready to do that. In those circumstances one conversation is enough; otherwise you could have thousands of conversations without any results.

It may seem that the case that I described here is atypical, perhaps even extreme. However the subconscious would create an incurable illness for merely one or two advantages. Most people who are sick, would like to be sick and benefit from it (as in the example above), and at the same time be healthy enough to not suffer. This obviously can't be done. To recover, we have to find the benefits that the sickness brings and find in good health the benefits that would equally satisfy us.

Dear reader, here is another aspect to being sick. Perhaps after you reach the hidden cause of your sickness in your subconscious, you are still unable to heal that hurtful experience. Instead of forgiving yourself and others, you will be frustrated, rebel or feel sorry for yourself. Perhaps the role of a victim works well for you and you don't want to change anything. Look around. Many people are willing to withstand agony and die rather than change their lives. They don't want to let go of feelings of anger towards somebody who supposedly hurt them. They live with the delusion that such anger gives them strength, or even dominance over their executioner. They want to manipulate that person by making them feel guilty for example, applying the principle "I want forgive him. But let him see how I suffer, and perhaps I will even die". Others only want to feel sorry for themselves. Feeling pity becomes the focal point of their lives – they mistake this negative emotion with love. Others attract sickness with their pity or the attention of other people for example, based on the principle "Until now I have been a lonely person, and now I have many people around me". What is it like in your case? As many people as there are, there are reasons this is why you have to discover them for yourself. Yet others can't understand the simple truth, that the cause of their suffering is inside them and they have all the power to free themselves from it.

Perhaps, dear reader, you are thinking that each case is different and your case wouldn't work according to the principles described above. You are mistaken and the faster you awaken then the faster you will be able to change what you don't like. You can change anything. You will find out how to do this in the following parts of this book.

YOU ARE NOT YOUR BODY

Working on you is obviously not a simple task. It is probably the hardest task. By going deep into ourselves, we realize that we don't have anyone to blame for our problems and limitations. We start understanding that it's not God or bad fate that brought illness or some suffering upon us, but ourselves. Each person assuredly did it for a completely different reason. Some got sick because they didn't love themselves; others meanwhile live with constant hurt and can't forgive themselves or others. In order to recover they need to take full responsibility for themselves and change that.

If the cause of an illness is lack of love for oneself, or non-acceptance of your own body or life then you won't recover until you start loving yourself. Dear reader, for you, the most important person in the world is you. There is no more important person, thing or matter. People mistake such an attitude as being egotistical. They do that because they only consider the physical part of a human, disregarding the whole being. If someone loves only his ego, his petty personality then he is really egotistical. On the other hand, when talking about the whole person, I also have in mind your soul which lives eternally.

You are a beloved child of God, and your soul wasn't born out of a women. Your mom only gave existence to your physical body. Your real body is neither mortal nor prone to suffering and illness. If you believe that then you are living with a delusion. What you consider your body is your concentrated thoughts. Inside you resides your real body. It is of a spiritual nature. It's imperishable, eternally young, beautiful and healthy. This is the real, great, imperishable You. You can't be hurt, burnt, drowned or damaged by illness or damaged in any other way. You live eternally, as eternal as God who created you.

Therefore stop being fearful once and for all about everything and leave behind the crippling fear that you will get hurt, experience loss and die. You will never die or get hurt. You are sick, because instead of identifying with your spiritual body you identify yourself with your burdened, illusion-filled physical body. You are not feeling your spiritual body? Perhaps you do not love and accept yourself entirely, you don't know your own true self-worth and you are not the most important person to yourself. I am not talking here about the small human who people most consider themselves to be, but about the great, Divine "I", who you are in reality. When talking about your self-worth I don't have in mind moments when you compare yourself with others. All people are equal and important to God. He who exalts himself and puts others down is a person whose small ego overtook him and that person doesn't realize that he is living a delusion. It is the same with a person that demeans himself; consider himself zero, someone not worth anything, and perhaps sees others as great, important people in his life. In both cases delusion doesn't let such people recognize their true self-worth. Nobody is better or worse than any other person, because all people are equally important. Each person is the most important person to himself and other important people come after. Do you approach life that way? If you are sick, then most likely you don't. Therefore you need to discover in yourself that unique being that you are and start to value your worth.

Issues and people come and go, and you always remain with yourself. If you are sick, it's perhaps because your life ran out of love. It may seem to you that you love others; however you certainly don't love yourself. Who knows, maybe you always ran after someone or something. You drifted so far away from your true "I, your body revolted and slowly became dilapidated. Perhaps it lacks balance and it's hard for your soul to function in it? Perhaps there is the same chaos in your body as there is in your life?

I will try to explain this. The body of each human consists of an uncountable amount of individual, independent, fully intelligent cells (their amount is so great it's even hard to imagine). Together they create a body, and it bonds them together as a whole like a magnetic power of love. Each organ is a separate, independent concentration of the same cells. All the cells that combined to create an organ work towards its well-being, and at the same time for the well-being of the entire body. This is how it is in each healthy body. However, if you don't love yourself and you don't like your body then you lack love and your cells, instead of focusing on the organ that they belong to, will wander around the entire body as they want. This is why some cell joins organs other than their maternal organs. One cell working in such a way won't damage us although it is foreign and vibrates with a slight difference. If the emotional instability occurs often and lasts too long then more and more cells will be attached to non-maternal organs and create illness.

However, no illness is accidental. Each part of the body symbolizes different areas of life and is connected with its eventual problems. Illnesses of a given part of the body points out, with great accuracy what you can't manage, neglected, or went too far with. We have forgotten that the physical body is perfect on its own. There is no laboratory in the world that could achieve the results produced by the physical body. It functions even though we didn't create one iota of the incredibly complicated processes which it performs, for example: we consume food and it is transformed into life by itself.

So, when your body hurts in certain areas, instead of fighting the pain, think about what problem you need to deal with. Each problem appears in a different, specific part of the body; however it is the same part of the body for everyone. So if someone has heart disease then it's obvious that he gave away his entire happiness for his professional life or other "obligations". He never slows down, rests and is continually on the run, not surprisingly he eventually experiences a heart attack. If a woman has breast cancer then she surely mothers everyone, cares about everyone, but not herself. But if she has anal cancer then this means that she postpones all matters for later, that her drawers and dressers are full of junk. Looking from the sidelines it could be noticed that she is greedy, if not towards others then certainly towards herself. Each part of the body can be analyzed in this way, because each part– even our individual fingers – corresponds to a different problem in our person's life.

If you are unstable emotionally it is because you don't live or didn't live according to your heart but rather according to the false beliefs of others. You inherited these beliefs from your loved ones – from your mom, dad, grandma, grandpa or strangers, for example: neighbors, friends, teachers, priests in church, from books, radio, television, and computer games. Either way, you accepted them as your own. Don't blame your loved ones because they also inherited them from their loved ones at some point, and they from blasphemers, cheaters, ignorant people, people looking to make a profit and people who consciously misinformed people. Hiding the truth, they falsely claimed that the body is weak, sinful, imperfect, prone to illness, subject to decay and death, conceived vilely, and born out of sin. This type of indoctrination started from time immemorial. It is not surprising that most people are born, grow up, eat, sleep and work, get married, even laugh and are relatively happy. At the next phase though they become unhappy, sick and then die. When these people depart all that remains is their children who will do just as they did. They don't leave any mark behind so it is as though they never lived, because they are children of circumstance, a creation of their environment. Their life is subordinated to the customs and habits of other people. They are using other people's thoughts non-stop and copy the actions of those they meet by accident. Don't think that it is any different now from the past, for example in the Dark or Middle Ages. Still you are being persuaded by untruths – those are thoughts that only an immoral person can come up with. Don't you think? Take a look at commercials on television or listen to what the Church says.

Not surprisingly like others you wrongly belief that your body was conceived and born in sin and that you will have to suffer greatly in life, because you are marked by Original Sin. Didn't you hear those lies during your very early childhood? You heard those and many other terrifying things until you finally started to believe in them (otherwise you would always be healthy and never get sick). No wonder you feel unworthy of

God and view your body as sinful, imperfect, weak, prone to sickness and in slow decay from old age. Why would you care about your body which, sooner or later gets old, disabled and dies?

We cannot accomplish much (fulfilling our dreams and goals) believing that external conditions, people, circumstances or events limit our capabilities or preempt them. People who believe that don't even know what a huge mistake they are making. They rob themselves, because they don't believe in the possibilities that prayer or avowal gives them. Many people make gods out of other people and as a result they think unfairly of themselves. They think a given set of circumstances or some people excel at God's Power and that is obviously absurd. Personally more than once I was coming out of a situation that it seemed impossible to overcome. However I gave that challenge to God and with all my heart believed that He would take care of this taking into consideration the well-being of all involved. I placed everything in God's hands without stopping to think about it and treating the problem as though it did not even exist. I wasn't worrying about how this matter would be taken care of. I simply believed, period. Even when the world around me was against me and thought I was insane, I wasn't changing my mind, I was just vigorously trusting that God would redeem me. And that is what always happened. When you also believe that God lives inside you, you will become for yourself your own redeemer.

Now think for a second, if-you had never heard, learned about or believed in the above-mentioned lies, and they were not part of your vocabulary, would you accept them as an adult? I am sure that you wouldn't. Therefore examine yourself and recognize why and for what reason your body underwent decay. Perhaps you will remember the words or events which guided you to those causes.

Therefore, stop blaming your mother, father, sister brother, employer, government, the weather or a rock in the road. Admit to yourself that you allowed other people's negative thoughts to influence you and disturb your peace. Know that you are responsible for yourself and not for what other people think of you. Your true enemies are not people or circumstances, but your own negative thoughts and emotions which create discomfort and sometimes tragedies. They are stored somewhere inside you and they include among other things fear, superstition and ignorance, feelings of guilt, jealousy, hatred, self-condemnation and hostility.

They create illnesses, suffering and personal limitations. Since the enemy is within, isn't it about time to say to yourself: I forgive myself, I birthed those thoughts and from now on I radiate love, peace and goodwill towards all people".

Until now you thought that you were just a body so it is no wonder you didn't love or accept yourself. Do you understand now why you are sick and why you didn't accept your illness that you created)? You need to realize that you attracted it to you. Accept this fact. Accept also that you obviously can die, however, never let go of the thought that in spite of everything you can live continually.

By not accepting your illness, you are constantly fighting with it. And he, who fights loses. Say to yourself: "I, John, am accepting my illness and also know that I attracted it to myself by my false beliefs". Also, think about and go back through your past to understand where and what faulty knowledge, thoughts and words pushed you into illness and any other misfortunes. Remain steadfast in your conviction that since you brought these negative conditions upon yourself only you can change your thoughts to free yourself from them. There is a chance that you will recognize those beliefs on the first try. If so, that's great, but if not, there will be time to do so later. Only when you fully accept your illness will you be able to take the next step and ask yourself: "What can I do to get rid of this sickness and why do I need to do it? Perhaps your body will show you how you should use it. Whether you see it right away or not, you need to forgive yourself the fact that you created the illness. Understand that your past already happened and there is nothing you can do about it. All you can do right now is forgive yourself in order to forget your past as soon as possible. And what does this mean for your future? You are creating it at this moment. That is why what is happening right now is so important, what you are thinking, feeling and the desires you now have all depends on the reality you create for your future.

You create your future through your moods, and your moods are created by your reactions to events, experiences and the news that each day brings. Therefore it doesn't matter what happens to you, it's only important what you think about it and how you react to it.

You need to start observing what you introduce your mind to, especially in the evening. Your conscious mood before sleeping penetrates to your subconscious and the subconscious independently makes it reality whether it is beneficial to you or not. Your reaction to today's sensations therefore influences your future. When you focus on thoughts about illness, deficiencies or failure and fall asleep with such images, your subconscious mind will recreate it the next day and next the day, etc. during sleep and as a result in the future you will experience exactly the same image in the material world.

If you would love only who you are currently and accept your illness, then you would suddenly start noticing the benefits that being fully healthy gives you and... you will begin to re-cover. If everyone accomplishes this then all of humanity would stop being sick. How is that possible, you might ask? Well, in the physical body new cells are constantly being produced that are tasked with replacing the old ones (every seven years each cell is substituted in your body). If each of us lived accordingly to our true beliefs we would never get sick or old. We would always be full of power to transform any emerging abnormali-ties in our body. I will write more about how to accomplish that momentarily.

You need to recognize that while you have false beliefs a devastating process is damaging your body. Instead of the old and sick, the new cells die, stillborn. This is why you get old and infirm; it is because new cells don't substitute old, used ones. I now hope that you better understand how changing your false beliefs to true ones allows you to aim achieve perfect health. Your body would be able to renew itself. It has the potential to completely rebuild itself with new cells within one year, and during seven years you can transform into a completely new person. To achieve this, you have to find the benefits of being healthy and eliminate those that make you sick.

ANSWERED PRAYERS – HOW TO
REPROGRAM YOUR SUBCONSCIOUS

Dear reader, God is a reality for everyone. He expresses Himself through perfect health, beauty and youth. Those attributes are given to you forever and they are kept in your spiritual body, which is always healthy, never feels pain and is never sick. How is that possible? Well, you are God's child, you were created in His image, you resemblance Him and it is His intention for you to be always fulfilled and healthy.

Perhaps you are not aware of that because your external senses tell you otherwise. According to your senses you have already lost your health (if you are sick), youth (if you see personal signs of aging) and wealth (if you have financial problems). If you believe what your senses are telling you, know that you are making a huge mistake. You have this mistaken belief because you don't realize the presence of God in you as expressed through everlasting health, beauty and perfection. That presence was not born and will never die; therefore its attributes will never stop existing in you. They were given to you by God and will remain with you forever. In His world nothing will ever be lost. Everything is God's energy, and as you know from physics class energy never perishes, it only changes its form. Therefore you don't have to acquire health anew, you just need to come back to the state which you had at the beginning of your existence.

You feel ill, because your mistaken beliefs made you lower your own vibrations. In other words, you descended to a lower state of consciousness. This happened to you because of fear or because of your other negative emotions, such as anger, rage, hatred, jealousy, etc. Either way, you allowed your vitality to be lowered and as a result of that also your state of health. In order to recover you need to turn to God again and begin to identify mentally and spiritually with His Everlasting Healing Presence and its unchangeable attributes. Call on it to bring back your health and revive your entire being. Be confident, that it will positively respond to your true beliefs the same way it once answered to the untrue ones.

To talk with God we must use true, scientific prayer also called affirmation or decree. It's not a begging prayer. All prayers in the Bible are decrees confirming long-wished states (meaning its existence is already acknowledged at the moment of praying), and not begging prayers. I will say this differently: prayers affirming health are nothing more than focusing on attributes and characteristics of God that already exist in you. They were always in you, they are there and always will be. Hence, contemplating God's Healing Power and His guidance is nothing more than turning away from unwanted images – from illness, old age and poverty.

Dear reader, you have the power inside you to heal yourself. You don't have to attain it, because it's already an integral part of who you are. Illness came to you from nowhere and it will return there (it came into being by mistake, in God's view a mistake is nothing). It is God's intention that you are always completely healthy. Nobody else, just Him is the real source of our health and our resources. If you want to be always healthy then you need to firmly claim: "At this moment God is already healing me. He is the Source of my health and my resources. His wealth freely circulates in my life and always exists in divine excess." In saying this, realize that you are already under God's care at this moment and what you are decreeing already came true. If you stick with this positive truth, the circumstances of your life will change for the better. Believe in it and accept it, because according to your faith, "thy will be done".

Your affirmation, decree or prayer should be repeated every morning, after waking up and in the evening before going to sleep, and even during the day, preferably out loud (but it can also be done quietly), firmly trusting that deep truth of prayer, that it would reach your subconscious and become the new matrix by which your subconscious starts creating a new reality. You have to implicitly trust that your subconscious would accept what your consciousness trusts in. Let the words that you speak become your daily prayer. Therefore, be aware of what you say and think about going forward.

Obviously God also answers the prayers of atheists' despite their claims that He doesn't exist. People living with joyful expectation of the best have true faith and are not really atheists, even if they don't go to church. True atheists are people who doubt love, happiness and Infinite miracles. They are people who constantly worry, condemn others, criticize themselves and others and are unable to forgive themselves and others.

As you can see, the transformation from illness to health

can only happen when you reprogram your subconscious. By going deep into your subconscious you will discover what mistaken belief caused your illness and this will be a first step to recovery. That belief could be anything: events from the distant past as well as from the present. Perhaps you recognized at some point that you were hurt, cheated on or left out etc. Currently that mistaken belief causes you to be sick.

Perhaps you don't want to notice the connection between your illness and your feelings of powerlessness and dissatisfaction with your work. Who knows, maybe you want to become who you are not, maybe you live somewhere that is not right for you, or live with a person not right for you. Illness can also be taken over from other people, meaning you believe in their perceptions. Many commercials are constructed this way to encourage your subconscious to assume an illness or cause it to occur; as a result you would need the advertised medication. If you don't allow yourself to be influenced by the commercial the company that advertised the product would quickly go bankrupt, because there wouldn't be any people interested in their products. People who create commercials know the laws that rule universe perfectly well and know that you attract to your life what you fear. Hence, it's enough that the commercial gets you scared. Like a sheep you would join the flock of other sheep and give in to the action of the collective mind. But, you can also decide to think independently and then no commercial or news about a flu epidemic would have the smallest influence over you.

You can be a vegetarian, exercise, meditate and practice yoga throughout your entire life, but if you are in a toxic relationship, hate your job, wonder about illnesses (someone else's or your own) or constantly fight with your family then you will always lose your energy and power. And, as a result illnesses will appear or you will slow down the process of your healing. If however you are acting in a balanced way and changing your negative beliefs to positive then you may have nothing and eat, for example: animal food or garbage, but you will be healthy and happy.

Therefore, dear reader, seek out the causes of your illness. You can't change other people. You can only change yourself. When you forgive yourself after a traumatic event (and obviously all people that were involved in it) then your health will improve without any intervention, because there won't be any snag in you, that inflammation which caused your illness.

It's possible you won't discover what causes your illness because your subconscious won't show you. Don't worry too much about that. You can still work on yourself, but in the dark, with the help of affirmations, meaning prayers. It's about removing the old and damaging for you programming and substituting it with a new system of valued beliefs. This will allow you to achieve your desired result which is full health. In order to realize this you need to convince your subconscious with the help of affirmations to get rid of any doubts and objections. It is essential that you believe in affirmations with your entire being. When you accept this on the physical level it will be easier to transfer it internally so that you can feel it with every cell of your body. Perhaps you think that it is easier to say this than to do it, because you affirmed something many times before and nothing came out of it. And, because of that your critical mind denied affirmation and persuaded you that it's not true. This is why you have to avoid critical censorship of your mind, in order for the affirmation, your new truth to be retained in your subconscious mind. How do you do this? Well, talk to your subconscious and tell it what you desire, as though affirmation was already accomplished. Ultimately inside your, in other words, on your spiritual level, you are healthy. Hence, become an actor, be aware of your role and begin to function as if you were already healthy, happy and fulfilled just as you would already have listed in your positive affirmation characteristics. Your subconscious will accept this image and will begin to recreate it. You will start to get used to a new role, and your old beliefs would undergo a positive transformation. You would be like a magnet attracting more and more of what you desire to your life. Know however that only a small benefit results from momentary positive thinking through affirmation, and later to wondering about illnesses and allowing old negative thoughts and attitudes to return for the rest of the day. Desire has to be immovable. You have to want to recover with your entire being, and not just through reason.

Therefore, say the affirmation to your own body trying at the same time to get through to your subconscious (you have to make contact with it). Keep checking, whether you consider the affirmation an absolute truth and whether you believe in its fulfillment. You can say to yourself for example: "I, Martin, I am absolutely healthy. At this moment God's Intelligence heals me". Let those words become your daily prayer. Repeat them aloud and quietly in the morning, in the evening and during the day, whenever you remember. Trust implicitly that this truth reached your subconscious and awakens latent powers in it. If you believe in what you say consciously then your subconscious will also believe in it. If however, you continuously repeat that you are healthy, wealthy and happy and you are doing well, but in reality you don't feel like that at all then you won't gain anything.

The subconscious will recognize this as you showing off (as some people like to do) or putting on a mask in front of people.

Therefore, you won't achieve anything in the external world that you don't deeply feel to be true internally. You won't succeed if in your heart you don't feel that it's true. All you will achieve is robbing yourself of energy. Words are not enough. Many people demand success, health or wealth, but their subconscious in reality only believes in financial restrictions, illness, failure and limitations. Such demands are fantasy and empty words. It should be proclaimed and felt that we are already in that desired situation just like an actor who lives and assumes the personality of someone in a role. Most people forget that God is the only Source of wealth, health, peace and everything that exists.

As you can see wealth and poverty, health and sickness are nothing else but a state of mind. Everything comes from the mind; however the essential difference is whether it comes from the Mind of the Almighty or a human's mind. You always receive what you believe in because your subconscious takes in your strongest beliefs. Remember, your attitude always counts and your deep beliefs always show. Therefore stop making excuses. When you truly pray and affirm, your health comes back to you quickly. Relief of pain and symptoms speak for themselves. If after some time your condition is not changing for the better this means that you are lying to yourself. How long should we wait for our prayers to be answered? Everything depends on your faith. The seeds sowed in your subconscious are the same as any other seeds. Each grows at the appropriate time. Your subconscious decides when to answer your conscious mind. For one person this could happen very quickly and for another very slowly. Everything depends on whether you allow anything else to influence your mind over the power of Almighty God. The power of the Almighty God always acts for your well-being, however quite often it is disturbed by you. Often it is unable to break through your disbelief. Your faith can be disturbed or undermined by the people around you. You need to decide that they don't have any influence over your deep feelings and thoughts. Be certain that each image carried in your mind permanently becomes reality. You already have proof today of that – your subconscious accepted your strongest beliefs and created your reality. With equal simplicity and will power it can also accept your conscious wishes.

I will repeat something that is very important: be certain what you tell your body is true. You can't pretend in front of yourself that you are strong, healthy, and full of life while you are sick and could barely walk. You subconscious won't believe it. It's like calling the color black, white and white, black. However your bad state of being won't cancel everything out, because as you probably know, nothing lasts forever, even your serious illnesses.

You now know the laws of the mind and the spirit thanks to which you can overcome your illnesses. You don't believe that? Well, inside you resides the perfect archetype in the form of your spiritual body. God gave it to you among other things so you can return to health in case you got lost by your false beliefs and fell sick. Therefore, call on your spiritual body and draw from its strength and inspiration. All you have to do is to belief with your entire being and bring over what exists on the spiritual plane to the physical plane. Even if some part of your body was amputated they can be reborn again, reconstructed, because it has its spiritual equivalent, in other words archetype, in an untouched state.

When I was a child, I met an older forest ranger during summer camp who had a thumb grow back after he cut it off with an axe during war. I didn't believe that was possible. I constantly visited him and asked how he did it. At the beginning he didn't want to talk about it, however he knew how much I cared about it and he finally answered me. He said that he didn't know how his thumb grew back. He only knew that he never allowed himself to think that he was missing a finger. He still felt he had it. I believed that because many amputees feel the same. My neighbor didn't have legs, but he still felt them and wanted to scratch them at times. After some time, the forest ranger noticed to his surprise that his thumb began reappearing. Every day it seemed a bit longer to him. He even began to believe that he had cut off less of his finger than he realized. He only accepted the change when his thumb began to grow a nail.

This knowledge gained from my childhood came in handy later. Once while I was working with a huge saw I cut off my index finger. All my workers passed out, however I didn't lose consciousness. I didn't get scared, didn't despair and didn't get angry at myself; I just picked up my finger from the floor, cleaned it, placed it on my hand, wrapped it in bandage and quickly went to the hospital. The doctors thought I was a hysterical woman who had just hurt her finger and was screaming that I had cut it off. They got ready for a small treatment without the right preparation. It was only while cleaning the supposed "wound" that the finger fell off and they started to run and scream that I had really cut it off. After long preparations they started to sew my finger back on my hand. Today this is a normal surgery, but back then they couldn't do that type of surgery yet. I forced them to do it and thank God I still have all my fingers, and the doctors learned something new from my case. Just like the forest ranger, I didn't allow myself to think that I would lose my own finger. I couldn't imagine how I would function without it. I forgave myself that I attracted such an experience to myself, but I wasn't able to discover what the cause was. As a result of that my finger didn't want to heal. It kept hurting, abscessing, falling off and was rejected. Finally I discovered the cause for this situation and forgave myself and those problems immediately went away. It healed so perfectly there is no mark from that incident. The doctors didn't hide their fascination and surprise.

My thoughts on that incident while writing about it made me realize that my finger would not have fully recovered if I didn't love myself. A person that doesn't love themselves doesn't care for their well-being. They agree to various sufferings and uncomfortable things and to have bad things happen in their life. If you don't love yourself and don't accept yourself as you are then you won't have any respect and trust for yourself, you won't know what you desire nor would it be possible to achieve all that you deserve. Besides that, you need to have a deep understanding that negative events weren't sent to you by bad fate or by God, but you attracted them yourself for your experience. Therefore, don't ever feel like a victim, even during the toughest experiences. Circumstances in your life are a reflection of your inner world. You fell sick, because assuredly you noticed deficiencies imperfections or limitations in yourself. Therefore don't be surprised if you are currently experiencing such circumstances.

This knowledge gives you great power. If you channel the emotions which you tried to ignore earlier (because they weren't pleasant) you can recognize your problem and tackle it. Recall how many times God through abnormalities appeared in your body and tried to make you aware of the need to tackle a certain problem. Instead of doing what intuition suggested to you, you hid anger and hurt which with time manifested into pain. I am assuming that like most people you tried to not think of the problem hoping it would disappear so you quickly reached for, a pain killer for example. You fell sick because it turns out that dealing with that experience like that negatively impacted your health.

However, the fact that you are sick isn't the end of the world. Don't worry about it. Since you attracted this experience because of your mistaken beliefs, then you can also free yourself from it. Forgive yourself and all the people involved in that experience and change your beliefs to support your true beliefs. When you forgive yourself for this, you will gain a great chance for transformation and a return to good health, as happened in John and Caroline's respective cases.

CREATING NEW HABITS

Dear reader, if you want to achieve a better state of health, you can't desire it half-heartedly, only when your small personal self wants it. Your desire has to come from your entire being – from your soul, your mind and from your true, divine identity. Only then will the willingness to build a perfect, healthy body be true, because it will come from the entire person.

You can achieve everything you want, however in order to do that, you have to mold your brain anew as it is the communication medium with your body (and not only with your body). If you experience varying degrees of discomfort then it is clear records about this exist in your brain. You have to stop expressing yourself through these records and create new records, expressing perfect health.

However in order to do that you can't reject old habits, such actions as the rejection of old habits don't exist. People constantly try quitting old habits and almost never succeed. There is a different way to do it. Instead of fighting with the old habits – mental or physical – create new ones. You don't have to fight with the place in own brain where you recorded thoughts that generated old, negative habits. Simply record opposing thoughts in a different place in your brain and start expressing yourself only through these new thoughts.

Let's say that at some point you created a record in own brain that you were small, weak, sickly, and afraid of your own shadow and early death. Well, with such a record people doesn't live comfortably. If you don't want these records to create "truths" about you from one moment to the next, you have to record something else in a different part of own brain, for example: a record that you are healthy, strong, brave, and that you can live as long as you want. Once you create that new record, from that moment on you need to start expressing yourself only from that place, and never again from the previous place. Therefore you have to truly forgive yourself, forget about the old images and walk away from your current life, thoughts, emotions, acts and your entire previous experience. Keep yourself in that forgiving and forgetting mode long enough for all reminders of the old experiences to be erased from your subconscious thoughts.

Perhaps, at the beginning it will be hard for you to shift to a different course. But with time it will be a lot easier to reach that new place as the old one will begin fading more and more until it doesn't have any influence over you. Continuously keep in mind the fact that since you were able to learn lies, believe in them, and allow them to create their own life, well then you are also fully capable of walking away from them.

If old thoughts keep coming back to you or are being repeated to you by your subconscious mind then demand they leave you, every time they come to you. Tell them: "I forgive you completely. Leave me alone". Tell your subconscious mind also: "Erase all untrue thoughts and models. Don't accept any other records, besides the truths which now I am approving".

If you don't stay with this scheme persistently and don't accept it as an absolute truth, in other words as fait accompli, you will lose the essence of your own existence and instead of a full recover you will get sick again. It's not enough to just desire good health; you must make a determined statement that you are already healthy. Know that nothing good comes out of recording a wish to be healthy in your brain. Admittedly, you are not recording thoughts about illness anymore, however you are making thought after thought saying that you are sick, and as a result illness will be expressed by your body. Therefore, record new thoughts that you are healthy and it will be manifested in your body.

It would seem to you that you are lying to yourself by telling yourself you are healthy. This is an illusion however. Right now you are lying to yourself thinking that you are sick. By seeing yourself absolutely healthy you are not imagining untrue things at all, nor creating false beliefs. You are saying the most truthful truth. How is that possible, you might ask? Well, deep down you have a cheerful, spiritual body, always young, beautiful and healthy. Every kind of energy comes from that body, and not from your physical body. The physical body doesn't have life at all; that is why I refer to it as clothing.

Therefore, even if they will cut out your physical organs during surgery, you will have inside you the perfect archetype with which you can rebuild your physical body. This is possible, because the spiritual body is never out of balance. Illness and a negative emotional state have no influence over it, because it stands above those states.

This facilitates the conclusion that sickness is an untruth, and your newly formulated health corresponds to truths. You are sick because you have false beliefs, so with their departure your illness will also disappear. Realize this truth, the great "You" is forever healthy, forever young, and forever beautiful. Your sickness only happened as a result of false recordings in your brain. It doesn't matter if you created it yourself or you got it from other people, because at any moment you can erase such recordings. You brain and its thoughts are like play dough which you can shape as you wish.

If you are sick, but you want to be healthy, you just have to make a recording that consists of new images (those that you want to experience), and the subconscious will read them and create a corresponding recording to make them reality. It is absolutely assured that you can achieve this, although it might take some time and will power. Know that there are cases that occur often, where people achieved such medical transformations literally within a second and experienced an immediate improvement in health.

They started to experience good health right away. They saw it, felt it, heard it, knew it and adored it. They displayed it with thought, word and action. Acting like they had imprinted those thoughts and images on their subconscious, their subconscious reproduced it for them. If you did the same thing you would soon be convinced that the subconscious reproduces truthful images with the same willingness as it reproduces those that harm us.

Not all people are able to use this method. They still have to learn it. This process could be compared to, in some sense, learning how to walk – a child falls, gets up, until it finally begins to understand what the process is. If you belong to the latter group, don't give up, just realize that you are going through the learning process. This is a very different kind of process to what you were using to date. You need to realize that until now you were using the language of illness and everything that was involved with it. In order to transition to a state of good health you have to learn a completely new vocabulary (similar to learning a foreign language). Even if you already know what some word mean, you still need some time to get used to it, for your subconscious to accept it, and for it to become your second nature, your new life. For one person working on returning to health it is sometimes incredibly strenuous. It requires continuously repeating, recalling the new images with determination, while for other person it's not hard at all. A lot depends on will power. Each recording performed on the brain's board must be engraved with desire and our own efforts which often require patience, endurance and a long time. It is easier to use focused will power and feelings of certainty of results, when your desire is strong. If your new desire is weak then you need to continuously fuel it anew, strengthen it, because with time you would run out of the willpower needed to focus on your goals and you would return to the old, unwanted rut, in other words to sickness.

If you want to learn something new, you have to pay a lot of attention to it, until the desired skill is permanently recorded on your brain. Learning how to return to health is no different from learning how to drive a car or play the piano. However, you can't get into a car or sit down by a piano and wonder what pedal or key to press. Right away you would feel negative consequences about your lack of the required skills. For a long time you practiced your faith, repeating and accepting untruths, therefore you have to spend the right amount of time to unlearn all of that now.

Therefore, make the desire to be healthy the same as any other desire. When you desire something strong enough, you will certainly achieve it. You have unlimited, Divine capabilities at your disposal. You can develop each capability or skill and become whoever you want to be. If you want to become someone new, you have to record it in your brain, that you are already that person, not that you are becoming that person, and then start expressing yourself through that new form of thought.

WORKING ON YOURSELF

In order to return to the best of health, the deciding factor among the above-mentioned is forgiveness, to yourself as well as to the people that hurt you. It may be (as in John's case) that you would have to ask for forgiveness, because you hurt someone and you are feeling guilty, although you may not realize that at all. Consciously you might not remember that, but your subconscious remembers it and created punishment in the form of an illness.

Most likely you will say that you have nobody to forgive. My assistants and I hear such statements from clients non-stop. I propose then that you make a list of people you are mad at and the causes of that anger. You should obviously also include yourself on it. Are you surprised? Well, you should forgive yourself first and foremost, for instance that you allowed yourself to get hurt, didn't take care of yourself and your well-being, you didn't love yourself at all or not enough and that you fell sick, etc. When you focus on it I am sure that you will create quite a long list. Don't throw it away, because this is the same list which will tell you who you should forgive and for what. You are not capable of forgiving someone if you didn't forgive yourself first though. You carry on your shoulders a great weight of which you are not even aware. Perhaps it will surprise you that most people are not able to forgive themselves. They are more willing to forgive others, but not themselves. If this is how it is in your case, then you have to try until you succeed. I guarantee you now that you can't imagine how much lighter and healthier you will become when you free yourself from that great feeling of guilt, anger, and hatred.

It could be that you know who are you mad at, however forgiving that person could turn out to be an incredibly hard task. That's how it was with me once. I was forgiving everything and everyone, but I couldn't forgive my dad. I felt that I had to forgive him as well, but when I got around to it, I felt a strange, unfounded fear. On the one hand the desire to forgive was growing within me, but on the other hand a greater resistance arose within me. I knew that forgiveness was necessary, that without it I wouldn't be able to grow, but that feeling was stronger than me. I found myself in a trap that was squeezing in from all sides. At some point I felt incapacitated by that fear, because I had never experienced anything like that before. I was even afraid that I would discover something frightening that I won't be able to forgive him. In my head there were many black scenarios I didn't remember regarding ways in which my dad could have hurt me in the past.

Finally, I decided that I couldn't go on like that any longer; I had to do something about it, even face it. One time when I was home alone, I took sheets of paper and decided that I would write as long as it took to get to the bottom of the problem. I wanted to write down that I was mad at him and wanted to forgive him, but instead I wrote: "Dad, you bastard, dad...I love you". Dear reader, you can't imagine what happened to me at that moment. Most of all, I was so surprised that I opened my mouth, because I had never used such words before with regard to him. I felt as though an entire weight had fallen off of me, as though I had found myself in a different, better world. I was full of love and felt that I had nothing to forgive him for anymore. I was looking at the sheets of paper and laughed at myself, but also to myself. Finally I was free. When I cooled down, I was still wondering why I had waited so long to forgive him since it turned out to be so easy. I had suffered unnecessarily because I had postponed facing that anger for quite a long time (a few decades). Your case could be the same. It is mainly about a willingness to forgive and the rest would happen by itself.

Many people don't want to forgive, because the fight with their "enemy" became, over the years, their entire life. To forgive they would have to let go and they are afraid to, in a sense, lose the meaning to their life. They don't realize that they do this for themselves, not for their "enemy". People who are in a fight often ask me for help. Time and time again our explanations regarding the necessity to forgive don't work. Lately, it's a bit easier for us, because in my book *In the Wheel of Life,* Vol. III I described this topic in detail. I often receive messages like: "Mrs. Pratnicka, Thanks to your book, *In the Wheel of Life,* Vol. III I now understood what forgiveness is about. Thanks to that I freed myself of a great burden and became a better person. Thank you Mrs. Pratnicka, from the bottom of my heart."

Forgiveness should be approached diligently. This means that we have to forgive with our entire heart and soul, not half-way or logically. Among my clients there are people who approach forgiveness too lightly and shallowly, just to get rid of this issue. Then they forgive and forgive and nothing changes in their situation.

They don't understand that to fully recover from illness and prevent it, the cause must be removed. The forgiveness of oneself as well as to others serves this purpose. It is an absolute necessity, a requirement without which we won't achieve health and well-being. Often I am asked how to recognize if we have forgiven. When this happens, we stop having negative emotions when we see or think about a person that hurt us. If you don't feel even the smallest sting when mentioning this person, then you would know that you have forgiven him and forgotten about everything. Try, if you are able, to see a person who hurt you as a happy, harmonious, cheerful person. If not, that means that you didn't forgive them, that you didn't let him off the hook. Sometimes it seems that we have already forgiven everything and suddenly we find out that the person who hurt us is doing very well. We then begin to feel angry. Deep in our subconscious mind there is still hurt and antipathy. The past hurtful memories didn't fizzle out completely, but is in hiding smoldering and it poisons our body which could be the cause of our illness. Not recognizing this consciously we return to the old issue and unconsciously scratch on the not yet healed wounds.

In order, dear reader, to make this topic clearer I will use an example. One of my clients called me complaining that he had been working on himself for many months, constantly forgiving himself, but it hadn't helped him at all. Because my assistants couldn't manage this case anymore, they transferred him to me. I knew that his mistake must lie in the way he forgave, and not in the method. Too often I had witnessed its perfect results for others and me. I asked him to describe how he does it. "Mrs. Pratnicka, I forgive a thousand times a day and nothing changes.

I am still sick and I still have ghosts in me" – he said at the beginning. "Why do you have to forgive so many times? And how do you know that you did it a thousand times?" – I asked puzzled. "I know, because I count every time. I simply say the word forgive and count on my fingers, and when I reach ten, I write it down on a piece on paper". "I don't understand" – I said. "Well, normally" – he said impatiently – "in my head I think the number one and word forgive, later two and the word forgive and so on until I reach one thousand. In the past I was constantly making mistakes and had to start over from the beginning" – he said in a triumphant tone of voice. "Did this become automatic for you?" – I asked. He affirmed. "Do you do anything else while you are counting?" – I asked. "Usually I watch television, a movie or a game" – he answered. I said: "Martin, but then only your head is forgiving, forgiveness most of all must come from the heart. Didn't you ever think to forgive once and sufficiently, right from the soul, instead of a thousand times ineffectively? Are you forgiving only because it was recommended you to do it or to lessen your suffering?" – I asked "After repeating in your thoughts the word forgive you don't even know who you forgave and for what. You are sick because you don't love yourself or accept yourself". "Oh yes, that's true" – he exclaimed. "Therefore in order for you to recover you have to begin to love yourself the way you are, with all your good and bad qualities". – I said. "Then what's next? Am I supposed to accept my sickness?" – He asked angrily. "Yes exactly. First you have to take responsibility for attracting sickness to yourself because only then can you consider how to free yourself from it. You also have inside you a hidden need to be sick, feel sorry for yourself as well as to be a victim. Perhaps there are other negative needs inside you as well, but those are the most visible to me and from those you need to free yourself first. In fact, you were supposed to repeat the affirmation many times on a daily basis, so as to re-iterative internally – »I, Martin, love myself and accept myself«, and »I, Martin, free myself from the need to be sick, I, Martin, free myself from the need to pity myself«, or »I, Martin, free myself from the need to be a victim«. Do you now understand where the mistake lies?". "Yes" – he said thoughtfully – "instead of forgiving myself, I was just doing it because your assistant recommended it. Oh my God, at school I also studied from my teacher, but never for myself. He ordered us to do homework, so I politely did my homework, but I didn't receive any benefit from it. Mrs. Pratnicka, I will try to change this". I answered: "Don't try, just do it. If you just try, then you have excuses such as "But I was trying, and nothing came of it". Decide on it and do it no matter what the situation". At the end he said determinedly: "Mrs. Pratnicka, I will do it".

And he did it. Now he is a healthy and changed person. After some time he sent me an email to thank me: "Mrs. Pratnicka, when I worked through this I noticed that I started to truly look at people, not just glancing at them stealthily. I understand them better, I am more empathic, it's easier to forgive, but most importantly, it's easier for me to say the word sorry". Everyone should do what I recommended to Martin, not just the seriously ill. It would be much easier for people to live in this world. Perhaps, you recognize that there is a lot of work ahead for you, but it's worth doing it because it can work wonders, if it is done with a truthful heart.

ANSWERED PRAYER

Dear reader, many people send prayers to God constantly; however nothing changes in their life. They then begin to doubt the power of prayer and ask themselves; and often me as well, what is prayer if it doesn't work?

Because this topic is not for everyone and is not fully understood, I will expand on it here. There is no other way to return to health or achieve anything else, than by sharing our own desires (in other words affirmations) with God, our Father. It doesn't matter what you call Him, because everything is One anyway. Therefore you can make your request, that is, prayer or affirmation directly to your higher "I", your Existence "I AM", The Eternal Spirit, The Highest Mind, The Highest Intelligence, Jesus Christ, Allah, Buddha, or your other Great Master or to the Cosmic Consciousness. They are one and the same Omnipresent, Almighty Intelligence and Energy, the same one "Presence" of Life. It is important however to direct your affirmation to what is higher. Don't imagine God as an all-powerful monarchy that sits on a great throne, who you would have to beg for mercy, but as a loving Father who will give you everything that you ask for. At this point, I have to quite clearly emphasize that under no circumstances are you to pray to a deceased grandma (or other ghost) and ask her for help for yourself or for some other family member, because instead of receiving one, you will also be possessed by your grandma's ghosts (or someone else's). I dealt with thousands of cases of people who prayed to deceased loved ones for help and ended up suffering.

A deceased person is not a saint and – as you will become convinced in further parts of this book – death in no way makes that person greater than you or gives them any additional powers.

If however you pray to God or a being that is greater than you, you can in your prayer ask for anything. It doesn't matter if your request is regarding who you desire to become or what you desire to have, know, see, experience or to learn. You can use prayer for all your daily activities. Therefore, use this Great Energy consciously and know that you use It in order to achieve things that you desire, because "all things for which you pray and ask, believe that you can receive them, and they will be granted to you".

Perhaps you already direct your requests to God, but you don't receive any reply. This could be because you live separate from Him and not in unity with Him. Perhaps you view God as someone who resides far away, someone unreachable, almost foreign, living in an unknown heaven who you have no access to. You could say that this is how religion taught you to think. Oh well… What if you lived in unity with God, would you need religion for anything then? Would you then desire an intermediary in the form of a church and priest? I think that you would trust God, and not religion. The church very well knows that humans have an inferiority complex or rejection complex and won't take advantage of The Highest Power or Wisdom which resides within them. Isn't there confirmation of that complex within religion orders when you hit yourself on the chest and say: "Lord, I am not worthy to receive you..."? After such a statement are you going to look for help, safety and support in God, who – as you claim yourself – you are not worthy of? I don't think so. What you are looking for outside of yourself, in church, you can find in God who resides within you. That is also why you don't have the courage to do anything, because you are too afraid of Him. This is obviously a mistake caused by a lack of understanding. What are you looking outside for? God is within everything that exists – visible as well as in invisible. His Presence and Power is within everything, above everything, penetrates everything. It is omnipresent; therefore it is within you as well. You cannot reside beyond the all-pervading Presence of God. Contact with that Presence and Power takes place through your thoughts and feelings. Free yourself from your mistaken thinking and you will notice God as an almighty power already present deep within you and then allow Him (if you obviously believe in Him) to perform true miracles.

The church (it doesn't matter what it is named) knows that you would have everything you needed to fulfill your life if you were in unity with God. What do you think; would the church allow for that? I do not think so, because what would the church be without followers? That is why in their eyes they put God far away from you. They describe Him so that you fear Him, don't trust Him and don't ask Him for anything.

In writing this I don't claim that religion is bad or unnecessary. I am only showing how destructive a lack of knowledge can be when we are unaware or perceive matters in the wrong light. If you had the courage to go beyond the religious dogmas, you would have an opportunity to broaden your consciousness. You would realize that you already live in God, move in Him and your well-being is in Him, and it is not that you will only achieve these things after you die.

How is that possible, you might ask? Recall what you were told in religious class or in church about God's omnipresence. Since He is everywhere then He is also within you, and you are within Him. If you recognize this deep down, God would be as close to you as your own breath, as your own body, and everything that you ask of Him you would receive, because there wouldn't be anything standing between you and Him. I didn't come up with this. The Holy Bible talks about it, but does your religion present it that way? Someone knowledgeable in Church's studies would say yes. I however would say that this image is presented in an incomprehensible manner, and as a result, the average follower (who is in the majority) is unable to understand it.

In all religions of the world you will find these Great Truths, because they are common to all of them and are foundational. However these Truths are covered by thick layers of rituals, ceremonies, symbols, liturgies and various interpretations. In the midst of all of that, religions forget that there only exists one Truth and that is that God is this Truth, and that was the case yesterday, today and tomorrow and it will always be the that way. Unfortunately these eternal Truths of Life are lost in dogmatized beliefs.

Dear reader, if you feel lost, terrified or uncomfortable after reading what I wrote; then know that I am not trying to change your perceptions or religious beliefs. I am not forcing you into anything with my words and I am not urging you to do anything. You can apply this knowledge when you are ready to accept it. You can also never apply it. If what you believe in makes you happy, pleased, and fulfilled or it is for you a source of comfort then don't change your perceptions. If that is not the case though, then think about what I wrote. By knowing the laws of the mind you have a chance to benefit from power based on this knowledge, because everything is a matter of your consciousness.

When you are conscious of God you pray differently. You trust Him with your entire heart as one trusts a beloved father, otherwise you would be afraid of Him, you would consider Him to be a harsh, punishing God. By being fully aware, you are dedicated to Him with your entire being and there would be no time to think about Him without love. When you lack His consciousness, you only think about Him from time to time or forget about Him completely.

Being aware of Him you turn to Him like your own Father in the same way a child turns to his beloved father. There is no child that wouldn't believe his beloved dad has everything that is needed for him in life. He knows with his entire being that his beloved dad loves him so much he would never decline any of his requests. This is also why he receives everything from him.

When you are not aware of God on a daily basis you don't reach out to Him at all or you only do so from time to time. Throughout most of your life you felt very resourceful and thought that you would be able to manage every situation on your own. It is only when you are unable to manage something anymore or everything is going down, you recall that God exists and you are willing to ask Him for something. If you ask God with the same confidence as the trusting child did, He would immediately answer your call and deliver everything you need to you. Why would it be any different given that you and the Father in such instances have Unity? A state of conscious Unity is achieved through constant seeking. By trusting God you are allowing Him to act through you, to always protect you, support you, and provide everything that is needed for you to live. This approach is a completely normal and everyday thing and you should view it as such. But, you would only be able to think this way when you are fully aware that you are His beloved Son and you can have everything that your beloved Father has.

You don't achieve such unity spontaneously however. First you have to attune to the vibrations of your own soul. Only when you are fully united with it can you consciously connect it with God. This is not a hard task. The moment you think about that great vibrating and pulsing Law, which is God, you realize it and gain from It immediate access through your own internal make up. This requires from you a constant, mental effort; in order for you to live consistently in a state of widened consciousness.

Only in such a state does the effort put into connecting with the spirit become a prayer. True prayer is an effort of your mind aimed at getting to know God. It's not an effort intended to create a new relationship, but rather to fully understand and recognize an already existing relationship. Therefore, the state of unity depends on your level of consciousness.

By being conscious of your unity with God, your Father, you will also be conscious of everything else, because everything else already contains that consciousness. The true and the only goal of prayer is a conscious, purposeful union with the Spirit. All other goals are already contained in it.

Therefore, you shouldn't pray to live in health, peace,

strength and wealth. Prayer serves the purpose of maintaining your connection with God. When you are united with Him, you are healthy, live in a state of peace and harmony and have strength and wealth, because everything is contained in that unity. Those qualities appear naturally, by themselves when you live in their consciousness. You don't have to ask or solicit them in any special way.

In such a union you have to believe with your entire being. You don't have to repeat a prayer twice, because your request at the moment of first verbalizing it becomes an affirmation (decree), and not a prayer like you used to use until now. You were asking about something by praying, but now by affirming (decreeing) you are actually stating a fact to materialize a matter at your request. When you believe with your entire being, you stop asking. Since you have absolute trust – which appears when you are aware of your connection with God – then you know that you have already received. Therefore, all that remains is for you to be thankful.

This also confirms the Holy Bible. All of its great paragraphs or prayers are not requests, but affirmations, also called decrees. Let's take for example "The Lord's Prayer". When you are saying "...thy will be done on earth, as it is in heaven. Give us this day our daily bread and forgive us our trespasses..." are you asking for something, or begging? No! In the case of a begging prayer, instead you would say, for example: "Could I get a little bit of food", "Could you forgive me God my sins". Affirmation confirms that what you are saying has to happen. However, the effectiveness of prayer depends on how strongly you believe that it will happen.

You will receive everything, when your faith is true, deep, and not superficial, as probably obtained up to this point. It can't just seem to you that you believe in what you affirm while somewhere on a deeper level of your subconscious you have doubts and fear lurking.

What I am writing here is a great Truth. By practicing it you would know that you can't lose. For that reason with intense and cheerful determination hold on to this, to receive or achieve what you chose for yourself by your own desire. Never doubt and never give up. Be conscious that each desire, each expectation comprises energy fields, which like magnets, attract what you desire to you. Never, ever allow your mind to imagine bad things which could eventually happen to you. That is also a prayer which on physical plane creates things which you really don't want.

Doubts would only appear when it seems to you that you are separated from God's Power. It is only in a state of separated consciousness you would feel fear. When you truly believe, you and God, your Father, are connected in Unity, your prayer at the moment of speaking becomes an accomplished affirmation.

Wish for others only what you would wish for yourself. Always remember that what you send out from yourself, returns to you. Carefully ensure that you don't send out thoughts, emotions, words and actions which you wouldn't want returned to you.

Never think negatively. Always be conscious that deep acceptance with fear (in other words imagining) of negative conditions is in essence a mentally attraction of them.

WHEN A SOUL DESIRES TO LEAVE

Dear reader, it is possible your soul wants to leave, despite you having worked on yourself intensely. Don't feel despaired or disappointed because of that. Don't think that you could have done something more or better. You did everything you were capable of doing at that level of your development. Accept that and get ready for the next stage of your life. Acknowledge the truth that death doesn't exist. You simply take off your body like old, unwanted clothing and you as the essence of your being move forward. The more conscious you are of this truth, the less you would fear death. Death doesn't end your life. You will live on in your spiritual body instead of your physical body. Your spiritual body is a true copy of your physical body. It never falls sick and is eternally young and beautiful. Each day I receive proof of how true that statement is and during my years of practicing I have gathered tens of thousands examples of this.

As I wrote previously, Life is a school. And as it is in any school, those who work diligently go to a higher grade and the stubborn ones repeat the same grade. As a result if a person works on himself and changes his false perceptions to new, true ones then even if he dies he would live a better, more perfect life than he did up until that point. On the other hand, the person who doesn't make an effort to work on himself will lead the same life, or perhaps an even worse life. Why? That is because his false perceptions (manifested through illness, life difficulties, or tragedies for instance) would decide his journey onwards. However, whatever the circumstances in your case, don't be afraid. Whatever you decided is good. You are on this world to collect experiences and learn from them. The life you have chosen to date (even if you suffer because of it), you have a right to it. Someday you would get bored of it and desire something new, different and better.

Do you want to know if you are following the right path? Just ask yourself: "Do I desire the life that I am leading presently?" Your answer will determine what you decide to do. It is obvious that if you want to live a better life you have to change something. Life won't change by itself.

For a change to happen, consciousness and decision is needed.

That is why you should realize that if you are sick it was brought about by your own perceptions. Isn't it about time you recognized this and changed your perceptions to new ones? Nobody else, but you are the creator of your life. You are responsible for everything that happens to you in your life, whether you want to accept this fact or run away from recognizing it. You are continuously creating perceptions, always anew, even during your sickness. If you are becoming even sicker, it's only because you are continuously thinking about pain and sickness instead of health. Who knows, perhaps you are continually feeling sorry for yourself. In that case, life will be helping you by creating circumstances in which you would be able to experience more and more pity for yourself. What better way to make this happen than through the intensification of the symptoms of your illness and suffering?

Isn't it about time you forgave yourself for everything that you created so far and started thinking in a new, creative way? Create your life anew. Desire to live better, healthier, happier than ever before, and you would certainly realize that, if not in this life (if there is little time left for you), then in next one, after you take off your physical body.

If your physical body dies, that doesn't mean, that you lost, you are worse off or that you did something wrong. None of those things are true. Your work on yourself is not going to waste. If you forgive everyone everything, including yourself, and fall in love with yourself then you would lead a completely different, better life, without illness and suffering in your upcoming, spiritual life as well as in next incarnation. This is what I wish for you from the bottom of my heart.

Perhaps you are leaving because your soul has finished its tasks for this incarnation, as that is the case with sick children (you shall read about that in a moment). Or perhaps you have worked through your challenges and you could successfully live on, but you have a physical body very damaged by illness, and as a result your soul is not able to take on more challenges? Either way, your soul would discard this body with happiness. But do you also want to discard it? No? This is surely because you are still afraid of death. You identify yourself with your personality instead of with your soul. Only a frightened personality holds on tightly to physical life, but not your soul. If your soul wanted to stay with physical life, then it would remain despite everything. If however only your personality wanted to live, then you have no chance of that happening. Let's say that somehow your body was saved. Without a plan for this incarnation you would live with no purpose, instead in great frustration. Therefore, never go with the needs of your personality, but only your soul's. Your Personality is physicality, but you are neither one of them. Your soul lives eternally. Trust it. It has completely different, more powerful plans than your personality, which dies with your body.

DO WE HAVE TO DIE?

Dear reader, do you believe that civilizations which lived eternally once existed on Earth? They didn't go through a transformation called death of the physical body (I described this topic broadly in *In the Wheel of Life*, Vol. III. People in that epoch lived as long as they desired. The Holy Bible merely mentions a few people, descendants of that great ancient civilization. They include figures that lived a thousand years and more. Noah who built an ark died when he was nine hundred and fifty years old. At more or less the same age Methuselah, Jerod, Kenan, Adam, Set and others died. You can read about them in The Book of Genesis 5,3-32 and 9, 28-29. Since someone can live to one thousand years then you will certainly agree with me that he may as well live eternally.

However to live eternally, you have to act perfectly. Otherwise what would be the point of the life we currently lead as a civilization? Do you agree with me? Members of ancient civilizations lived perfectly for eons. Unfortunately not everyone was capable of living in such a perfect state. In each civilization there were people who give in to negative emotions. Perhaps they did this due to glut or boredom initially. The facts, however are that their behavior infected others, the same way rotten apples ruin other apples in a box. With every passing day more and more people allowed themselves to accept negative emotions until an "epidemic" of negative emotions engulfed almost the entire civilization. In Earth's history there were many such civilizations and each failed in an identical fashion.

How did death enter the lives of those ancient people? Well, when they lived perfectly, they had a solid base and were able to live eternally. Their lives weren't subjected to any shocks. When negative emotions started to burst into their daily lives their bodies became subjected to great, intense vibrations. Unfortunately, no substance is able to withstand constant shocks and remain untouched. Take a look at what happens to a solid building during an earthquake. If they don't fall apart immediately, then cracks, leaks and slips will eventually appear. It is the same with the physical body. If it is continuously under pressure from various huge shocks, then sooner or later it would fall apart.

You also live in a sphere subjected to a great intensity of shocks. This causes strong trembling in yours and other people's emotions. It is not surprising that your physical existence has to end with death. Recall how many times in your life you were boiling with anger from negative emotions. Certainly, it happened many times. Therefore don't be surprised if you are currently sick and that you started to think about yourself as getting older, falling apart and dying. You could say that not all people fall sick. That's true. However everyone is falling apart in some way. You would notice that by their aging.

There are also many people, who despite everything don't give in to negative emotions. I am not talking here about people that deny they have negative emotions. They simply suppress them. I am talking here about those people who are fully conscious of their negative emotions, but don't give in to them. Not because they are strong, but because they understand Life. And you can also reverse the state that you are currently living in. You can realize that your illness is not from God, and that He has nothing to do with it. It is also not given to you from the outside. You have free will and you can't be influenced or broken in any way, if you won't allow for that. You draw sickness upon yourself and now you have to find out how you did it. If you decide to be healthy, you would recall how you did it or it would be shown to you. You would recall at the same time, *Who You Are in Essence*. You would begin to see yourself from the standpoint of eternal Life. You are not only a body with blood and bones, but mainly a spiritual body, eternally young, eternally beautiful and eternally healthy. What you consider today to be your body is mostly a concentration of materialized negative emotions and thoughts. Some are full of anxiety, others hatred, perhaps also jealousy, rebellion, aggression etc.

Like most people you forgot that you are a soul that came to Earth to learn something. For a soul it is not so important what it is learning because everything it experiences are lessons.

What do you think about that? Perhaps you approached your life too seriously and judged yourself too harshly. Do you realize that you are just learning? Since you are, then you have the right to make mistakes. It is the same for people around you. Therefore, don't judge them too harshly. I assume that if you understand this on the deep level of Self and henceforth you would live in an absolutely different way. I think most of the time you would be immovable, no matter what was happening around you. Then your body wouldn't lose its radiance and you would be as God planned for you to be from the beginning – forever young, forever beautiful, and forever healthy. Perhaps it's hard for you to believe what I write about here. You will receive proof of that, at the latest after the death of your physical body.

THE ILLNESS AND DEATH OF CHILDREN

Validation of my statements is sick children. Admittedly, they could be just as sick as adults; however they approach illness as well as death completely different. That is because they haven't forgotten *Who They Are in Essence*. So why are they sick? It's because their souls planned it that way. They came to this world not to live in the body of an adult person, but to finish a lesson. To complete their task they sometimes need a short life, after which they leave. This explains why some small children and young people die.

Sick children know perfectly well that they would pass away and sense the moment at which it would happen. In this regard, it could be said that children are more "grown up" than adults. Usually they are the ones who cheer up their parents, never the other way around. Continually they ask them not to worry. They assure them that no matter what happens it would be ok. They convince them to have faith in God. They encourage them to believe in Him, and He would take care of the rest.

Unfortunately parents don't readily accept this and are unable to talk to children about it. They don't discuss the topic of illness or death. Some would say that it is awkward to have such conversations in a hospital or hospice, because places like that are depressing, intimidating and perplexing. This is just an excuse however. Even when parents of a seriously ill child spend entire days at home with him, they only bring up current issues such as food, shopping and cleaning, and they are closed off to serious topics.

The situation does not change much when a child's death is fast approaching. Many parents don't realize that their child would die in emotional isolation and wouldn't have the smallest chance to share his feelings with his own parents. Sometimes the gap could be filled by others such as a friend, aunt, uncle, doctor, nurse or even a random passer-by. However, this very rarely happens. How often does a child have the opportunity to meet with someone one-on-one and even for a moment to talk to them? With an adult he couldn't, because the adult would impatiently interrupt such a conversation or would get very saddened by it. A child, in a meantime, doesn't want to make his parents even sadder.

When a child doesn't have the opportunity to express his suffering, then suppressed fear, doubt, sorrow and the feeling of losing his parents are often transferred to the child, and as a result, he starts feeling these emotions. It's not always like that. When a child sees that parents can't deal with his illness emotionally, he tries to pick up the pieces himself.

Dear reader, know that all terminally ill children are aware that they are dying. They treat the topic of death as they would any other. When a child has someone to talk to openly, without inhabitations, he would talk about own condition. All you have to do is take a closer look at the behavior of children at hospitals or hospices. There, children speak loudly to each other about their illnesses and death, however only when their parents are not around.

A child has a small body, but he is not stupid and basically it's very hard to deceive him. He knows perfectly well what medicine and for what he is being given. He also knows when his condition worsens, realizes that earlier he was stronger, able to run and jump, and now he is unable to get up from bed and he would die soon. In such situations, to persuade him that everything is ok with him, only worsens the situation, because within him would arise the fear which the adults carry within them. That is why what will happen on the other side should be explained to a child. To do that however, we have to know something about that topic ourselves. In order to comfort him, we have to get used to these issues and not be afraid of them.

I witnessed many instances where parents avoided bringing up the topic of their child's death until the very end, and towards the end of his life, in horror they broke off and limited contact with him. I asked why they were doing that and each time they answered in the same way: "Mrs. Pratnicka, I don't have the strength to talk about it or look at how he dies. After all he is in a hospital and surly he knows that is what awaits him. Certainly, the doctors and nurses have told him about it..."

Parents pass on this obligation to the hospital or hospice's personnel, but do they always have time for that? After all, there are many other children who need support. Will a busy nurse approach a child with the same love as a parent?

To adults, children give the impression that they don't know they would be dying soon. They seem unconcerned and spontaneous, but that is just a pretense. More often than not, they don't talk about their health because they don't want to sadden their parents. Children, despite an illness are spontaneous to the very end. When adults are ready to face up to the death of a beloved child, it always turns out, that the child knew he was dying and he was calm and resigned with fate. It would seem that a short period of time on Earth forced them to develop faster – intellectually as well as spiritually. However the truth is that they came on Earth for a short period of time. Their soul planned such a scenario, and they saved this plan in their conscious memory. They didn't forget like adults do. Obviously, I only have in mind only those children whose illness allowed for normal brain function and not those with various brain disabilities.

The fact that a child knows about his condition could easily be noticed by observing how he prepares for his departure. Long before death he shows his parents that he is dying. He often gives away belongings which are especially important to him, and in analyzing his life closes old matters, makes peace with friends or siblings and plans what will happen next. Because there is no life on Earth in his plans, he plans in detail how his funeral should look, what he would be dressed in while resting in the coffin and even what his mother and father should wear. That way he prepares his parents and himself for his departure.

Children talk about death in their own way – they start talking about heaven, angels and they begin drawing their family and themselves as angels. Even very small children do this, three or four year olds. However parents don't want to notice or hear this, because they would have to talk directly with the child about death. Besides, they want to keep their child alive at all costs, even though the child continuously makes them aware that he is dying. This is why they don't listen to him and don't see messages sent by the child. On rare occasions though, parents miraculously mobilize their strength and face up to the challenge. Not only are they next to a child at a moment he passes away, but they help with transition by comforting the child as best they can.

Children always leave in peace, resigned to death and the world. A child never dies screaming, fighting off death with all his strength, as adults often do. It is different with parents. Most parents don't let a child leave. Parents shake their child, scream, not letting him die. They order a departing child to stay and withstand death to the end. They scream continuously that he is everything to them, and without him they won't be able to live, they order him to stay with them. They don't recognize that such behavior only increases his suffering and denies him energy and comfort. Instead of helping they disturb him at this important moment. Sometimes a child mobilizes his strength to meet his parents' expectations; however he breaks down eventually because he cannot beat death. Most parents are not prepared to provide companionship to a dying child. They run away leaving them alone and without saying goodbye.

In extremely rare cases parents allow their child to leave. They provide companionship to the end, making death gentle, safe and painless. Such parents prepare themselves and their child for the transition long before. On receiving the news of terminal illness they react with agitation, bitterness, sadness and shock initially. However they later mobilize themselves and after first questioning: "Why did this happen to me?" transition to: "What best can I do for my child in this situation?" This gives them additional strength. And while in a sense they still don't understand the illness and suffering of their child, they don't cry because of it, and if they do, they do it secretly. They know that they are needed by their child and they still have a lot to do for him. They make a conscious decision to be happy and they change from within. They look for the most beautiful things and enjoy each moment, even the shortest moment, for example: they show their child a butterfly, the sunshine coming through a window, the petals of a flower. They want to make him aware of everything and show him as much as possible. They stop thinking that life is slipping away.

The unpleasant feeling that caring for a terminally ill child is one of the toughest experiences that could have happened to them also goes away. It transforms into something incredibly deep and really beautiful. They begin having an intense yearning for life. With their child they get in touch with eternity and at the same time they understand the truth about their own life. The child teaches them how to respect life the way it is and shows them how priceless it really is. The sick child is a huge gift for mature and responsible parents, and not a scourge from God as many people think.

It might seem that such parents accept the death of their child because they believe in God, and as a result it is easier for them to accept death. Nothing could be further from the truth. They simply know what death is, got used to it and don't fear it anymore. These are not always people who believe in God, because this knowledge has little in common with religion. A person could be a practicing believer and paranoid about death or so called not practicing and have tremendous knowledge on this topic. For believers it is obviously easier to accept the death of your own child, however only for those who deeply believe in meeting the child once again after death. Unfortunately this rarely ever happens. From my practice I know that being a part of a religious group doesn't automatically help you accept death. Quite the opposite, most so called believers hold tremendous grudges and anger towards God for taking away a beloved one. They stay in a state of rebellion and aggression for many months, years, and sometimes even until the end of their lives. Their grudge and frustration they aim at God, doctors that they didn't take better care of their child and at themselves, thinking that they were also at fault. They suffer, because they don't understand that their child's soul came to the world only to finish up some lesson and he only needed a few years of life. This is the only explanation as to why small children and young people die.

Perhaps your child is seriously ill or dying, because you needed this suffering to release love from within you. Perhaps your child's soul loved you so much that it came to this world to help you learn this lesson. And maybe you will learn to love and your heart would only open when something precious is taken away from you? This is why medical science is consistently helpless at saving small children. Doctors and parents unnecessarily blame themselves. Some children even die without being sick. They simply depart. Other children have to pass some lesson through illness. There are two scenarios possible here: after passing a lesson they depart or become healthy even if the illness seemed to be incurable. Those who die didn't come to this world to learn any further lessons and this is why they immediately leave after finishing the task which they undertook. They don't have any future plans for an existence on earth and any reason to remain on this physical plane.

It is another matter when children die as fetuses. Sometimes they are still not ready to come to Earth, and sometimes their parents are not ready to have a child. They turn back and wait for the right time. It's not unusual that the future parents are experiencing changes that would enable a child to complete his lessons. The child would then wait until everything is back to normal or choose different parents.

CARING FOR A TERMINALLY ILL CHILD

All parents react with rebellion, bitterness, sadness and shock upon receiving the news about their terminally ill child. And all parents want their children to be healthy and happy, to learn how to walk, speak, to attend school, etc. Parents' adapt to a child's illness in progressive stages, and these stages sometimes intersect. Parents go through a tough time not only because of the child's condition, but also because their own tiredness, lack of sleep, sadness and lack of hope.

With time, the parents of terminally ill children begin noticing not only negative side effects of their child's illness, but also those positive ones. They realize how much they gain because of their child's illness. They notice how much their sensitivity changes. They learn to dismiss negligible matters and recognize what really matters in their family. They often tell me, for example "Before nothing was working out for me, and now that I am able to manage (work, school, life) it's because of my ill child, John". They talk about how their family relationships were strengthened. Before the parents fought about unimportant things, and after they would stop talking to each other. Now, it's a waste of time. Thanks to the child's illness they learned to enjoy the small things. They understood each other without words. They learned to better manage time. Many parents who asked me for help said: "Mrs. Pratnicka, I understand that life is a great secret. There are enormous opportunities in that little human (my child) although he is sick. Even though his life is crippled and he has had only a few experiences (for example, he doesn't walk, run or play like other children), his spiritual life is much richer than healthy kids who goof around and get lost in life. This aspect of his life is not limited by the few square meters in which he lives. The most important thing in his life is love and happiness. My sick child doesn't display the signs of boredom or frustration which often appear in my other, healthy children".

At this point it should also be mentioned that many serious illnesses children go through are caused by ghosts. I was able to restore the health of children with various illnesses which medicine and alternative medicine couldn't help, including children who had laid in beds like vegetables from birth. In such cases I only help when (and I do it only at distance) I know that the child is sick because of a ghost. Therefore, I don't treat his illness, but rather lead away ghosts, which often enough (but certainly not in each case) are the cause of the illness. When the ghosts go away, the illness also goes away and the child "miraculously" returns to health. It is the same in almost every case of autism. It is obvious that a child then has to make up for the time lost when he was occupied by ghosts, however this usually happens at a very fast pace, and as a result he catches up quickly to healthy kids developmentally.

Many years ago I helped an eight year old child, let's call him Marc, who had always been sick. Despite his eight years of age, he couldn't turn around in bed by himself, not to mention do other things. He was functioning like a so called "vegetable". He couldn't talk, so they communicated with him by blinking eyes. He had a few ghosts inside him. When I started to work on him, the ghosts left almost immediately, this very rarely happens. In such cases this process is usually long, because ghosts constantly leave and return.

This however case was different. Marc started being active immediately, meaning he started to move, which didn't happen before at all. His activeness was growing with each moment, obviously as much as his very poorly developed muscles allowed. His parents were extremely happy! They called me every day and thanked me for even the smallest progress in their child's development. One day, Marc sat down and soon after let his legs hang off the edge of his bed when his parents were not next to him and almost fell off of it. He didn't want to just lie down anymore, he wanted to walk, but obviously he didn't know how to. He had to be taught how to walk, just like a baby, from the beginning. It was like this with everything –eating on his own, personal hygiene, going to a bathroom (until now he always wore a diaper). When he had learned all these things, his father called, but this time he was very frustrated. He was yelling on the phone that he had a disabled child, that it would have been better if Marc still lay in bed as he did in the past. From his wife I knew that everything was alright with Marc, that he walked better and better and even ran and jumped around the apartment. Also he was managing well with other things so I couldn't understand what the problem was. "Did the ghosts return and we have to start over?" – I thought. When he calmed down I started to ask questions. It turned out that Marc still had not spoken. He behaved as if he was hearing, but he didn't react to it. "So how do you communicate with him?" – I asked. "That is exactly the point! In the past it was easy, because he just lay in bed and we communicated by blinking eyes. Now he is everywhere, everything interests him and I have no idea what to do about it, how to reach him..." – said the disappointed father. "Didn't you teach him how to talk?" – I asked "You need to teach him the basics of speech first. Normally, a small child does this spontaneously. First they make sounds, later they repeat something they hear adults say, and then they constantly asks for something. It will be the same with Marc. First he has to learn how to make sounds, later he should be taught how to pronounce certain words, and only then how to build sentences. This requires a commitment of time and a speech therapist. For Marc, the time for spontaneous learning has already passed, and besides that he got used to another kind of communication. Did you see a doctor to check Marc's hearing? Does a psychotherapist work with him so that he would have a chance to make up for lost time?" It turned out that they had done none of these things. Hence, I said: "Marc had an entire eight years taken from his life. You can't expect miracles from him now; you have to teach him what every other normal developing child would have learned during that time. His peers were learning for eight years what he learned in half a year. Therefore he is no worse off than them nor does he have any psychological disorders, he only needs time and your help". He answered: "I will never go to a speech therapist or psychotherapist with my child, what I would say to them? That my child was possessed? Never, ever would I do that. Besides, almost nobody in my community knew that we had a sick child, and now everyone is asking about noises coming from our apartment. We have been able to explain it so far, but how long would we be able to manage this? Soon it would be the end of winter and we would have to take him outside. What would we tell people then? That he is not normal or he is deaf?" So while mom and grandparents were happy about Marc's progress, dad was wondering whether it wouldn't be better if Marc returned to his original state. He lied calmly then, now there was a lot of work, trouble and commotion around him.

Half a year later dad no longer thought like that anymore, he was just overwhelmed by the rapid changes he wasn't yet ready for. He had to get used to them and with the passing of time he got better and better. Marc had graduated from high school and passed the entrance exams to attend a polytechnic institute. During that time a kind speech therapist, who cared for him worked with him until he wrote his SAT exams.

Dear reader, don't think that this scenario is unique. I have dealt with many such cases in my practice. Some parents desire their child's health, even the smallest change for that matter, however when it happens, they often prefer the child be returned to his former state. There are many reasons for this. Besides the ones already mentioned, most frequently they are afraid that their sickness benefits (allowances) would be taken away, others desire steadiness, meaning, for the status quo to be maintained.

This also happens when a child is sick and possessed by ghosts, but the ghosts are not the cause of the illness. Cleansing from ghosts offers a lot, because the child would feel a lot better and have a lot more of the energy needed to deal with the challenges which caused the sickness.

How to Take Care of Seriously Ill People?

The appearance of a serious, terminal illness in a family affects not only the sick person, but also his family and friends. Usually they all panic. They don't know how to behave, what to do. The sick person doesn't know whether to talk about his condition with his family or hide it. The family is similarly affected. Family members wonder whether the sick person knows about his actual condition, whether to tell him the truth, or if should they pretend that everything is alright. They ask themselves questions about whether to talk openly or not interfere in his personal matters. Such things should be sensed. If a sick person has a desire to, then we should certainly talk to him about his illness.

Dear reader, almost every person confronted with situations like that wants to talk about his illness, and also about the fact that he could die soon. He desires to express his feelings.

This pertains even to a person who is withdrawn. He is just afraid to raise this topic of discussion. It's worthwhile in that case to quietly initiate the conversation. In such situations be ready to listen, and nothing more. Only listen and be quiet. It is extremely important to let the sick person speak freely about what concerns him. Therefore don't interrupt him, don't judge him, and don't neglect his concerns. This would give him a chance to express his sadness, perhaps also his despair because of the approaching end of his physical life. You would probably hear how frustrated he feels because he wouldn't have a chance to achieve various personal goals.

Those goals could be anything – from traveling to seeing own children or grandchildren. Perhaps you would find out how overwhelmed he is by the fear of suffering, losing control over his own bodily functions or a lonely death where his family members and friends turn away from him due to their inhibitions over his situation. This is the best way for you to learn about his real feelings and understand what he desires, what he fears and what he expects. While talking to a sick person you have to continuously remind yourself that he now lives in a completely different reality to you, a healthy person. Assuredly, among his feelings you would find pity due to his losing his physical body. Know that this occurs in almost all cases of dying people no matter what their age. An elderly person is equally strong as a young person when holding on to life. What is important is how the dying person lived his life, whether he understands death and if he made time to get used to it, or whether he is scared about it because he doesn't know anything about it.

For every sick person the transition from life to death is considerably easier when his loved ones understand what death is.

Many sick people tell me that admittedly they are not

afraid of death anymore, but it irritates and saddens them that their loved ones are so worried about their health and want to keep them alive at all costs. They especially don't like that they don't have an opportunity to talk with their family about death. The sick person avoids this conversation because he sees his loved ones are living with tension over this topic. He would wait for the right opportunity to have this conversation; however the right time never arises because as stated before, his family and friends avoid serious discussions on death. What does this silence and avoidance lead to? It takes away the strength everyone could have used for a mutual exchange of thoughts on this topic. Not only would the sick person have a chance to talk about what is bothering him and bring up important personal matters, but also those close to him would have an opportunity to collectively face sickness and dying; whereas everyone is dealing with it alone now.

Often, an ill person doesn't have an opportunity to bring up the conversation of his sickness and his concerns regarding it. Most people are unable to handle seeing the suffering and also the humiliating consequences of illness. They worry that they won't know what to say or do during the last hours of a sick person's life. If this is how it is in your case, don't beat yourself up. That is quite normal. You are overwhelmed by the serious illness of your loved one and you are not in control of your emotions when you see his suffering. I was also shocked by the terminal illness of my mom and for a long time couldn't accept it. I became more and more sad, weak, and unable to live as time went by. This lasted as long as I focused on the crippling, disfiguring consequences of illness. Love won out though. From that moment on I started to focus on my mom, not on her illness and amazingly I returned to being a strong person. I started to handle her sickness and slowly got used to thinking of her death.

This approach obviously requires composure and determination, however it's possible for anyone to achieve. As you can see, dear reader, suffering and illness provides us with challenges and teach us how to go beyond our normal limits. During sickness you have an opportunity to learn about yourself from a perspective that you didn't know before now, you didn't even suspect that this perspective existed. I discovered it and you can too.

Praying for a Sick Person

God is a reality for each person and because of that each one of us has the power within us to heal ourselves as well as others. However few people are aware of this opportunity given to us from God. Most decline to, or rather it could be said, idly say prayers, and as a result nothing changes in their lives. They can't help themselves or help their loves ones, as they do not know the rules of prayer as described earlier in this book. Obviously each prayer is a conversation with God, therefore it's an individual matter and each person can pray as he wishes.

It is quite different when it comes to the prayer for healing or changing one's life circumstances. That prayer has to be performed correctly and scientifically otherwise it won't be heard. All the requests I have for assistance include this area as it is an area people have problems with. We constantly hear complains (whether we want to or not) along the lines of: "Mrs.

Pratnicka, I say the Ave Maria and Litanies non-stop and my health does not improve, or it even gets worse" or "Mrs. Pratnicka how many times have I prayed already and given money for a holy mass, and even paid for an entire year of Gregorian masses and I don't see any results". In the voices of these people we always hear great concern and a complete lack of faith in prayer.

They don't know that prayer is not about constantly saying Ave Maria or Litanies. It's about clearly stating what you want from God and deeply believing that you would receive it. By constantly repeating litanies we don't live up to that rule – we don't tell God what we desire and we don't believe that God would answer our prayers. Besides that, by repeating prayers frequently and worrying about their health or whether they would receive what they asked for, people create the opposite results to what they desire.

So how should we pray for a beloved person's or best friend's healing? Most of all get interested in the beloved sick person's fate. Be willing to help, but don't harbor any concerns. Approach this without becoming too attached to the results – as to whether you can help him or not. Understand that in reality it's not you who is healing him, but it is being done through God, because everything is in His Presence's hands. If you approach this critically or with concern, you will achieve nothing, and you may even intensify the illness. Certainly you would ask: "how is it possible that by being concerned about the health of someone I can make them even more ill?" Well, know that within a moment of praying for someone you judge him. If you perceive him as a sick person and hope that thanks to your prayer he would get even a little better then you judge him incorrectly. However, when you see him in perfect health, full of energy, full of enthusiasm then you judge him properly, because you perceive him the way he should be according to the Divine plan provided for each person. When you see him in your imagination as healthy and strong, you give him strength and the willingness to return to health, and when you see him sick you take away that strength and willingness. Your interest in a sick person is your own decision; however how you judge him would determine the effect of your affirmation. You can't focus on the illness and hope that despite everything your loved one will recover.

Each prayer, especially prayers for healing someone, is thinking (or contemplating) about attributes, in other words God's qualities. Recognize and accept that God's Presence is inside that person, meaning his health, energy and well-being. Realize that this Presence is already inside him (and not that it would be), so he already have its vital forces, health, power, intelligence, peace and harmony. You would see in your imagination how the Divine Presence penetrates his whole being, how it works inside him and through him, how he is already under God's care and at exactly that moment healed. You must feel immovable confidence that your affirmation reaches the subconscious of the sick person you pray for, because implicit power is inside each person. It would help your loved one's subconscious to fully realize its own healing power and according to the law of the mind actualize and solidified what is within him. So instead of powerlessness and sickness inside of him strength and health would appear. Accept this with your entire being. Believe in the power of your prayer, meaning affirmation.

State with full belief, for example that Grandma Ann (always say exactly who it is about and call that person's name) is already healed. Not that she would be healed at some point, but that she is being healed at the moment you are sending the prayer. Feel the presence of God and realize how Grandma, in that very moment would be feeling health, vitality, power, and the intelligence of the Almighty Spirit on the outside. Request that Infinite Intelligence guide the doctors or nurses who take care of her. Or contemplate peace, harmony, health, vitality and Infinite life flowing through grandma and bringing her back to health and physical excellence. Pray in this way until you get a feeling of peace and contentment. Relax and accept, in other words believe in what you affirm and also in your prayer bringing miracles, and then stop completely to think about it.

Never say to yourself "For now that is enough. I will pray more later on", because that neutralizes your prayer. In reality it shows that you don't believe in your prayer as the prime mover and immediate healer of your grandma. Decide that your prayer is already working at that very moment and forget about it. And when you recall grandma, start everything from the beginning again, meaning pray as though you had not yet prayed for her at all.

When praying for someone never be impatient. The healing process could happen incredibly fast or be very slow. Everything depends upon how strong your faith is in what you are doing. A lot also depends upon what the sick person believes in and how much that person expresses agreement with the healing on the outside. It should always be taken into consideration how the treated person perceives his own problems and the difficulties that he is struggling with. However don't be worried beforehand, just be confident that the image carried in your mind would be actualized.

PREPARING FOR THE TRANSFORMATION KNOWN AS DEATH

When someone close to our heart falls terminally sick we are often afraid to even think that something terrifying would happen. Usually it's about the fear of death. We are not prepared for it and we don't know how to deal with it. We wonder whether we should tell the sick person that they could die any day.

Among loved ones, we constantly ask ourselves these questions. When it is proposed that we tell the sick person about their condition, everyone panics. Ultimately, most people don't discuss this topic. I would clearly state: "If there is no chance of recovery for the person dying we should talk openly". That is a necessity and there is no exemption. It doesn't matter whether the person close to you is dying because of serious illness, accident or old age. In any case it shouldn't be concealed from him that he would die. Thanks to this, the sick person would have the chance to make the most practical steps. He would have the chance to not only say goodbye to his life, but also to adequately prepare for death. The farewell as well as the preparation would lessen the anxiety that he neglected something. And if he died consciously then he would transition to the other side of death's curtain in peace. If we don't inform him about his condition and don't help to confront this reality, he would only have a slim chance in the future (after the death of his physical body) to free himself from that feeling of guilt. He would feel guilty and won't have the courage to go further (beyond death's curtain), because his serious sin (in his subjective view obviously) won't allow him to do so.

Dear reader, don't wait until the last moment to inform a sick a person. Perhaps you may not find the right moment at all. Even if you are afraid of that conversation and you are not prepared for it, find the courage to have it. However don't be abrupt and cold-blooded. These kinds of conversations need to be approached very gently and with love in your heart.

The sick person should be asked what would happen if his sickness turned out to be incurable, terminal and whether he ever wondered about what awaits him after death, whether he is afraid of it and whether he is prepared for it. Then he would have an opportunity to realize how important the approaching time is for him to adequately prepare for the transition to so called "death". There is a chance that it would form part of a heartfelt conversation, which would create a unique occasion to reveal his deepest feelings. The dying person could want to bury old misunderstandings, express grudges or ask for forgiveness. You also have an opportunity to do that too.

We should talk about death like we talk about everything else: directly and with peace. If the dying person doesn't know this topic then it needs to be explained to him that after death he would still live just as he did until now. If he isn't aware of this fact, then after the death of his physical body he would be greatly surprised. He could then mistakenly – which creates a lot of problems – assume that he were still alive, that he didn't die after all. Not being aware that he is a spirit he could want to return to his old life (as well as to ours) and live like he did up until now. How tragic the effects of that often are as I described in the book *Possessed by Ghosts*.

It certainly could be the case that sick the person desires to hold on at all costs, to delusion that this is not the end and he would recover. He should be comforted and told that what he wants could certainly happen (we wish that for him from the bottom of our hearts), but it wouldn't hurt for him to work on himself, forgive whom he should, and most of all forgive himself. If he is religious and practicing, I think it is also proper to confess his sins and reconcile with God. However we should constantly make him aware of his condition. Most likely the sick person won't accept this at first, but the possibility he would accept his condition improves with each new attempt to talk to him. Be persistent, but certainly not intrusive and try until you achieve success.

It's hard to predict how your loved one would behave, because during illnesses that ends with death, many, sometimes very deeply hidden, personality traits are very vividly revealed. These include traits such as egoism, egocentrism, or foolishness. A sick person however could absorb new knowledge with simplicity, openness and hope; as a result he would be greatly thankful that he was given a chance to understand his upcoming transformation (death of his physical body) and change of his fate. Don't be perturbed or disappointed if he is self-absorbed and at loggerheads with his surroundings to the end. Any attempts to get closer to him then would be rejected with aggression and distrust. He would loudly express that you are speaking nonsense and demand you feel sorry for him, meaning that instead you take pity on his suffering, as a means of sympathizing with him. He could also curse to the very end and deny that he was dying. He could call on you to save him, and not discuss death. And even though there is basically no room in this phase for complaints such as "Why has God punished me like this", this is exactly what you would hear constantly. Be aware of the fact that he wouldn't want to accept this knowledge about death, because he is panic-stricken and afraid of it. You have to learn to deal with this obstacle and help him eliminate this great, completely unnecessary fear. However, to do this effectively you also need to get used to the reality of death and not be afraid of it. Then, it's a lot easier to address these topics.

I would like to mention here again, that in extreme situations where the dying person finds his inner thoughts exposed, it would show what he had accumulated during his life. Therefore you would have a chance to see the beauty of his soul or its ugliness. If you see ugliness, realize that such an attitude is the result of his feeling a lack purpose in his life up until now. He would see that very clearly. Therefore, don't be astonished that each of your attempts to help him (to make him aware of the nature of death) is explicitly rejected. However don't get discouraged. This is also a means of calling for help, even though it is being done in a very unlovable manner.

WHAT IS IT LIKE IN PRACTICE?

Most families up until the very last moment deny obvious facts and pretend that everything is alright. They have a strong desire to delude themselves into thinking that there is nothing to worry about, that the sick person would recover and everything would be as it was in the past. I know cases – and they are not rare – where loved ones, up until the very last moment deceived the sick person, convincing him that the medicine he was given was just to strengthen his body. However, more than one sick person had this to say on this topic: "They are trying to convince me that those meds are vitamins. I am strong, and it would be much easier if we spoke openly about my condition. I want to talk about death, my suffering and concerns involving dying, and here I am with nobody to talk to".

George had more luck than most sick people. When he was dying of a malignant cancer, his wife Christina was 28 years old. This is what she wrote to me: "Mrs. Pratnicka, during my husband's illness there were some terrible moments where I thought of speeding and crashing my car into a tree but what saved me was the thought that I would orphan my three children. I couldn't eat, sleep or talk to my children. I dried out like hay, even on the inside, and my heart shrank. When I was on the edge of despair, somehow by coincidence I got hold of your book *Possessed by Ghosts*.

I didn't have the strength for anything, but I read your book in one breath. I understood the concept of death, and I realized that basically there was no death; and full of trust I talked to God to help George get through this. Until that moment we never spoke about his condition. After reading your book we started to talk openly not only about his current condition, but also about his possible death. Then, not only did I calm down and become quiet, but also George, who became so serene and somehow accepting of this tragedy. A few days after our first conversation about this he told me that he had already taken care of everything, that he had said goodbye to us, that death didn't terrify him anymore and he was ready for his departure. He asked me not to despair, because it would be a lot harder for him to go through this. And then I finally understood that instead of so much despair I should tell George how much I loved him. I realized that love was the only thing that I really gave to George during this tough time. And this was the only thing I would later regret– that I didn't tell him about my feelings.

When I understood this, death, George's departure, my separation from him, became easier to handle. When he died, right away I let him leave. I didn't suffer as much as I used to when I thought that death was the end of everything. I was wondering how I would have gotten through this if it wasn't for your book Mrs. Pratnicka. Certainly, in my despair I wouldn't have

let George leave and I would have forced him to suffer and vegetate. Thank you, Mrs. Pratnicka. Much appreciate. Christina".

Because the sick person's family often conceals the fact
until the last moment about his approaching death, they don't allow him enough time to prepare for death. It is as though they
don't care about what would happen to their beloved one later
on, when he isn't here anymore. His family and friends don't
care enough to allow him to reconcile with circumstances in his
life up to that point so he could go further. But, it's enough to
tell him about it. A religious person would ask for a priest himself, and a non-believer would start going over his life and reconciling life events. Therefore, find the courage, because after
your loved one's death it would be too late for sorrow and explaining the reason for such shortsightedness. It's obviously not
about blaming yourself. If you feel guilty then forgive yourself
and ask the deceased person for forgiveness. Whatever happened, it happened. I am writing this so you would know what
to do in the future, so you wouldn't experience this type of unpleasant situation.

And here are few words of bitter truth. If after what I
wrote there are still people who don't want to tell a sick person
about his condition then this probably means only one thing –
they should wonder why they take care of him, because I can
say with full confidence they are not interested in his fate. I assume that they never thought about what would happen to this
sick person (as well as what would happen to them), when he is
no longer among the physically living. Insincere loved ones
would do better if they threw the terminally ill person out on the
streets and stop taking care of him. By concealing the truth from
him, they have already abandoned him, and at the time when he
needs them the most. So go away, leave him, save yourself the
time and effort. Don't pretend that you are interested in him.

The truth is that such persons are only interested in themselves. Therefore I propose to these people, have the courage and show a sick person your true colors. It would benefit him and you, because the sick person put in that situation would have a chance to reflect and take care for himself. Currently he would rely on insincere loved ones and this takes away his strength and common sense.

Such people are taking care of the sick person, but they are only focusing on his physical body. When he abandons the body (and they bury it), he would go further. He is certainly something more than physicality and needs more than just procedures on his physical body. Because we never die, our further existence is dependent on us reconciling with things that happened in our life up to the point of death. What chance would a sick person have to reconcile if he doesn't know that is dying? Being a religious person, would he go further (behind death's curtain) if he had sins on his consciousness? And being a nonbeliever won't he be stopped in his physicality by various unfinished matters? Either way, such a person would die unconscious that he was dying. Such behavior with regards to a sick person carries a great feeling of guilt felt by those who don't inform their loved ones about death. If you belong to this group, realize that it might not be easy to forgive yourself such feelings of guilt later on in life.

THE PARTICIPATION OF CHILDREN DURING A SERIOUS ILLNESS

Serious illness is hard for adults to accept, and even more so for children. Children are usually left alone with their thoughts and feelings. However I am not saying to protect them from the prevailing pain and sadness in a family, but instead make it easier for them to handle this situation by going though it gently so that it doesn't remain like an unhealed wound inside of them for the rest of their life.

The hardest situation to accept is a child not knowing that someone very close to him is seriously sick. The child would suffer a lot, because he would witness a great, slow loss and he wouldn't understand the cause of it. I am not just talking about the worsening of the relationship with the person close to him, but also the loss of his own sense of security. A child would need stability in his surroundings and the reality of that would be completely disturbed. That is why we should talk about illness and death with even the youngest child when it occurs, after that, the right moment is lost forever. Dear reader, don't be afraid that you won't know how to initiate this conversation that the child won't understand you, or you won't know what to talk to him about, because illness and death are foreign to him. Be ready for the conversation, bring it up and the conversation would evolve on its own.

The child would ask questions in his own way, and you would answer them. Know that a child is the perfect observer of reality. He is interested in the world from birth and through his exuberance would know what to ask. However in answering his questions don't shower him with excess information. Rather share it in parts, in other words give it to him moderately as the sickness progresses. Don't lie, but also don't be brutally honest. It's important to explain to a child that sickness is not a punishment and it could happen to anyone and most importantly that it's not the result of the child's bad behavior (children take on responsibility for everything, a feeling of guilt). Give him information which would become a guide for his future behavior, for example: what he could do for the sick person, what must not be done. Remember that your child essentially wants to be a participant, not just a bystander.

He needs to be next to the beloved sick person, care for him and his needs, as much as his parents do. He still wants to talk to his beloved for example: he would want to fix his grandpa's pillow, give him tea or the newspaper or change the channel on the television for him. If you had relieved him of these activities, it's worth re-engaging him with them. This way the child sees the gradual changes in his grandpa and gets used to them. Even when the sick person's health significantly worsens and it is known that he is dying, it's good to allow children and teenagers (if they want) to participate at that moment. If they don't want to see that, they shouldn't be forced to.

In families where a member suffered chronic or serious illness young children are protected by making sure that they know nothing about the illness, to "ensure that such an unfortunate thing doesn't also happen to them". This leads to the children finding out about the suffering and death at home from others, often getting a completely false impression of the truth and as a result they suffer more. Dear reader, death and sickness will never avoid children even when you as an adult try protecting them by avoiding this topic.

Most adults don't realize that children intuitively feel the pain, sadness and concern that prevail at home. Therefore, it does not make sense to conceal the truth from a child and force a fake smile. Such a child would subconsciously feel the deceit, and as a result lose trust in us and feel abandoned. He would completely stop trusting us and it would be difficult to make contact with him in the future.

What should we do in such a difficult situation? It is better to share with your child your sadness and helplessness in caring for a seriously ill loved one, than to hide it from him. This will free the child from feelings of guilt and fear that "grandpa died, because I was naughty", or "mom is in a hospital because I beat up my brother".

Also, when we are crying we should explain the reason. So that the child would understand that the sight of tears is neither good nor bad, but only brings relief to our suffering, as a result the child would stop being afraid of crying.

Sometimes when a loved one is sick our full attention is focused on that person. Our time is filled with caring for the sick person, but we also have to go to work, do home chores: for instance grocery shopping, laundry etc. We therefore devote very little time to our child and he is left up to his own devices. Because day after day he is being put on the back burner, he would feel abandoned, isolated and unloved which in turn would cause him to develop an internal sense of helplessness and the conviction that he can't trust anyone. It would make him very frustrated. He could direct that frustration towards the sick person or other family members, but also towards himself. He could be naughty, malignant, tearful or aggressive (each child is different and acts out differently). He would start avoiding the sick person or become jealous of him. Consequently, the parents would become impatient, scream, and punish him in various ways. Obviously such inappropriate behavior shouldn't be ignored, but it should be understood and the underlying problem solved. Instead of punishing the child we should have a conversation with him. The changes he exhibits are his natural defense mechanisms and his way of dealing with what he does not completely understand. Most likely, we wouldn't have had to deal with that situation if at the beginning of the sickness we had informed the child about the sickness, what it involved, the symptoms and what might happen in the future. We should absolutely make up for that. If we had a sincere, loving conversation with the child he would express what was bothering him. Explain everything to him and answer all his questions to dispel his doubts.

Often children playing during someone's illness is regarded as wrong and inappropriate behavior. This is a misunderstanding that needs to be explained here. A child's world is about play (it helps children to learn) and during sickness this basic need disappears. When a child plays then this doesn't mean that he lacks sensitivity with regards to someone's illness. Don't try to make home a hospital or a funeral home. A child has a right to laugh as before, play with friends or watch television. A change of his behavior should only pertain to contact with the sick person, for instance when the sick person needs silence and peace, but it can't be a general change. Here is an example that best communicates what I am saying.

Three sisters asked me to help their three daughters who each had serious psychosis. Because this problem started right after the death of the children's beloved grandma, their mothers thought it was due to possession by ghosts. It turned out that no ghost was attached to the children. Still the mothers begged my assistant for assistance, they asked for help understanding what caused their children's suffering. In order to help them I had to know their story in great detail. I was getting it in pieces chaotically and I had to put it together myself. There it is:

A single, widowed mother (her husband died in a mining accident) raised four daughters, educated them, and married them off. Each daughter had a good job and an apartment. The two elder daughters lived independently, the middle one lived with her in-laws and the youngest with the widow. They all lived in the same town and were a very loving family. Each daughter had one child and all the grandchildren were more or less of the same age, ranging from six to seven years old. Two of them were attending preschool and the other two regular schools. The grandchildren and grandma were very close to each other. Every free moment the children had was spent with their beloved granny. Her grandchildren became her life. When she was able to dedicate her full time to them she fell sick. The daughters also loved their mom very much and at all costs wanted to save her health and life. Unfortunately her condition grew increasingly worse and when there was no chance for recovery they brought her home from the hospital. At home they made sure that during her last days and hours she didn't miss anything. They were constantly watching over their sick mother. They had to change their family life to do this.

The oldest daughter had a son, Michael and during her time caring for her mom she would leave him in the care of his other grandparents. The second daughter had a daughter, Jamie and she would leave her with a neighbor, while the other grandchild John would stay in his house with his grandparents. This way it was easier for the daughters to manage their additional responsibilities. The daughters suffered greatly because of what happened to their mother and they didn't want their children to witness their grandma's suffering. They would say in agreement: "They still have time to suffer in their life, at least now they can be happy".

Grandma was getting sicker and sicker, but the grandchildren didn't know anything. Her daughters knew nothing about death and they were afraid of this topic. In their homes they didn't talk about her illness or death at all, therefore nothing about this topic was reaching the grandchildren. That is what it was like with the three daughters up to the end of their mother's life.

It was different for the youngest of the woman's daughters. She read a lot about death and thought about it. She was used to it and understood it. With her child she had a different opinion to her other sisters. She recognized that her son, Carol was so close to his beloved grandma, she won't let him go anywhere. He therefore remained at home and was with his grandma until the very end. Carol's mom spoke to him about his grandma's illness from the beginning. Later she told him that most likely his grandma wouldn't recover, that she would get even sicker. This wasn't just one conversation. They talked about it each day, because his grandma's illness was going through different stages almost every day and additional explanations were needed. Besides that she was preparing Carol for his grandma's eventual death. She constantly repeated to him that sickness was not a form of punishment, and that not all people fall sick like his grandma. Carol was concerned that his grandma was sick because of him. She continuously reassured him that that was not the case, and he was not at fault. From the very beginning of the illness Carol wanted to help his grandma. His mom didn't worry that his "help" would disturb more than it will help. She included him in all responsibilities, obviously more so those which a small child could handle.

Carol and his grandma spent entire days together, even when his aunts were taking over their shifts. He played with her when she had good days, and sat quietly with her when she had bad days. As time passed he felt more and more responsible for his grandma and he wouldn't go to another room, because he was afraid he wouldn't hear her voice when she needed something. He also had the time and opportunity to talk to his grandma about all the things that bothered him. This was one of the conversations, and there were many of them, because they spoke almost daily: "Grandma when you die, are you going straight to Heaven? And when I die would I also go to Heaven and would we meet there?" – asked Carol. "Ok, I won't stop anywhere, I would just go straight to Heaven" –his grandma answered. "Grandma, would you recognize me when I die?" – Carol questioned. "Of course I would recognize you" – his grandma said. "But Grandma, I would already be big and I won't look the same as I do now, how would you recognize me" – Carol asked. "I would be looking at you from up there and would see how you are growing" – grandma answered. "That's good, otherwise I would worry that we would never meet again" – Carol answered. It was apparent that they needed these conversations as they strengthened grandma and grandchild spiritually. Grandma spoke freely about death, because her youngest daughter, Carol's mom had prepared her a long time ago for death. Carol's mom was the one to help her mom end all her earthly matters, even though her other sisters were against it. Carol didn't leave his grandma's side until the very end. He was next to her during her death and attended her funeral.

It was different with the other grandchildren – Jamie, John and Michael, whose mothers left them in the care of others and away from grandma. They had only seen grandma when she was completely healthy. Later they were kept away from her and didn't have the opportunity to see her, although they really wanted to see her (as they had in the past). Their mothers didn't agree to that and used all sorts of excuses to protect them at all costs from the suffering. The sisters used the same tactics with their mom, who constantly asked for their grandchildren as she wanted to spend time with them. Meanwhile, grandma's illness was progressing at a fast pace. She didn't suffer much, but she was losing strength. It was less than two months between the time of her diagnosis and the time of her passing. By the end of her life grandma was demanding to see her grandchildren. She wanted to say goodbye, because she was afraid she might not have seen them again.

Only John came to see grandma, and that was right before her death. Unfortunately he didn't recognize her; the illness had changed her so much. Even though she was sleeping he didn't want to get close to her, he was pulling himself back with all his strength. He screamed out, crying – "I want to see grandma, not her". This was not surprising. Not knowing about sickness he couldn't comprehend the situation. He knew a different grandma and wanted to see that one, and not the one who had been changed by illness. From that moment on he changed a lot, he was fussy, didn't sleep or eat and he started getting sick.

They didn't let Michael see grandma either. And while they brought him to her funeral nobody spoke to him about her death or told him anything about her funeral. He stood by her grave with his second grandma and grandpa and constantly asked questions. He forced them to answer his questions because the situation was made him restless. He didn't understand what was happening; he asked about the coffin, the people, and the entire ceremony. He couldn't grasp why people were sad and crying. Probably intuitively, he knew what was happening, but he also needed to recognize and accept it consciously. He was completely unprepared for the funeral, because such matters were never discussed at his home. Even though he participated in it, he knew nothing about it. Finally he asked what the coffin was for and who was in it. Surprised, his grandpa answered – "There lies your grandmother Mary, she fell asleep". Michael didn't know about his beloved grandma's sickness or about her death. He stood there bewildered. His grandparents were glad when he finally calmed down. It was like that until the moment they started lowering the coffin into the grave. He broke free from his grandparents and jumped on the half lowered coffin. He didn't want to let his grandma be buried by sand. He screamed – "How would grandma get out from there when she wakes up?" He experienced real horror. He was defending his grandma and nobody was helping him with it, everyone was against him. From his perspective they should have helped him to get his grandma out of the coffin. Not surprising, he beat everyone, he kicked and he bit them. He was only able to defend his grandma that way. Suddenly he started to lose balance and immediately got a high fever. He was quickly taken home. Every few hours he was given tranquilizers, but he was in shock and the meds didn't provide the expected results. Most of all he was afraid to sleep, because they had buried his beloved grandma when she fell asleep so he was afraid they would do the same to him. He kept waking up at night and hallucinated for many weeks. He constantly needed to save his grandma. In reality he never came out of that state. He was constantly absent-minded, full of fear and withdrawn, you couldn't keep communication going with him for much longer than a moment.

Long after the funeral everyone was still moved by his behavior. At gatherings not only grandma, but also Michael was a main subject of conversation. Most adults agreed that children are greatly affected by funerals and because of that they shouldn't participate in them. Jamie's mom even stated: "During this unfortunate time, I am glad that I spared Jamie any unnecessary suffering". She didn't know yet how greatly mistaken she was.

The news of grandma's death reached Jamie a few days after the funeral. Her school friends told her about it. She didn't want to believe them. She screamed that it wasn't true, that her grandma was alive; she was just out of town (that was what her parents told her). Finally she ran out of the playground and started to look for her grandma. Perhaps in shock she didn't know where she was running to or maybe she simply got lost. Anyway, they couldn't find her anywhere. The police and her neighbors got involved. They looked for her for three days and nights. Finally they found her in a forest, more than ten kilometers from her home. She was in such shock, that despite extreme exhaustion she had kept walking. She was taken to a hospital and given tranquilizers, but she still called out for her grandma.

Almost two years after their grandma's passing John, Michael and Jamie still couldn't function normally. Their school sent them to psychologists and even though they met with a psychologist many times, there were no positive results to report. And how was Carol doing? At the beginning he was very sad, sometimes he cried quietly. He remained psychologically healthy however. He had gradually prepared for his grandma's sickness and her death. He saw how she was when she was sick and he had the opportunity to talk to her, and even said goodbye. He now knew that whatever he did his grandma would be looking at him from above, and when he died she would be waiting for him. In reality he didn't have the great shock that was mixed in with fear and suffering, as transpired with his cousins. For them their beloved grandma to whom they were very close, in one moment had disappeared from their lives, she was buried in the ground without any goodbye. Because of that they felt deceived, hurt and abandoned not only by their parents, but also by their grandma whom they loved so much and implicitly trusted. Added to that was their panic-stricken, subconscious, traumatic fear that a sudden loss was around every corner, at any moment in life. It was not only the loss of loved ones, but also the loss of other things and even their own lives. They couldn't accept that, they couldn't forgive or live with it.

I have had so many clients with identical problems. Even though they were adults, for a long time they still had deep wounds in their hearts for the same reason as the children. "Is there any solution for this?" – I am usually asked. I advise parents to fill that hole marked by suffering, do it slowly and do it with understanding, explain the sickness and the death of a beloved person to children. When a child gets used to this knowledge parents should next take them to visit a cemetery and show them a grave. Only then would they have a chance in their own way to say goodbye to a beloved person.

All three sisters from the case described above reacted identically. They were upset that we offered them "something like this". It turned out that they still had not spoken to their children about illness and their grandma's death. Even the psychologist didn't talk to the children about it, because he didn't know anything about it. Simply put, in these families they acted as though sickness and grandma's death never took place. It's not surprising that the children had such a strong psychosis. When the children asked for grandma, the parents and grandparents didn't say that their grandma had "passed away", but impatiently answered with just about anything else, for example: that grandma had "fallen asleep", "left" or "left for a long trip" misleading them even more. It seemed, completely wrong, to protect their children and grandchildren this way, however they didn't realize that they were really protecting themselves in reality (in other words they had created an illusion that nothing happened). This was done by the mothers, because they still didn't accept the message that their mom had died. In their home a so called silence plan prevailed. They weren't mentioning their deceased mom (grandma), as they had a pretense surrounding her death. Such behavior made it harder for the grandchildren to accept the separation from their grandma which they couldn't understand. Since grandma was traveling or had fallen asleep they were asking non-stop when she would come back or wake up. They were continuously waiting for her. Grandma's sudden departure caused a great wound which constantly festered, because nobody helped the children to understand their grandma's death. As more time passed by the harder it was to reveal the truth. Not because the children didn't want to hear about it, but because they became more and more distrustful.

We proposed to the parents that their youngest sister and her son get involved to help fill the hole in the other children's consciousness. And she did so very willingly. Up to that point she was not allowed to talk with her nephews and nieces about their grandma. The aunts even pushed Carol away from their children so that he would not to blurt out anything about their grandma. Carol's mom started to talk about grandma with her nephews and nieces in a safe and understanding way for their age. She was doing it exactly the same way she had done it in the past with her own son. She told them that their grandma was very sick and that she later died, and now she was lying in a grave. She confirmed to them that not each sickness leads to death and we only die when it's a very serious illness which only happens sometimes. Unfortunately it happened to their grandma, but nobody was to be blamed for it, and they especially weren't to blame for it. Later she began to talk about their grandma's fate, that she was still alive, but she is in different place, called Heaven, and that during her death only her body died and it was put in a coffin and buried in a grave. In order for them to better understand how you could live and simultaneously not be visible she compared grandma's death to a departing boat. She talked about how boats were sailing throughout the seas and endless oceans. She even went with the children to a sea port and showed them how boats drift away and disappear beyond the horizon. Admittedly, they didn't see it anymore, but they certainly knew that the boat was still sailing on the ocean. She told them – "Do you understand now how it is with grandma? Certainly you don't see her, but she is still alive and loves you all very much. You also love her and even though she is not next to you physically she is still in your hearts, memories and thoughts". Carol also got involved in his own childlike way. He said to them that grandma looks at each one of them from above and was waiting for them in Heaven. Only then they started to believe. Since then each of the children has become livelier. In memory of grandma they made farewell cards and collected toys for her. In this way they had a chance to physically say goodbye to grandma. When they were ready they went with their aunt to the cemetery and put all their gifts on their grandma's grave.

As you can see dear reader, the key for these children's recovery was the truth, love, softness and most of all sympathy for their suffering. Their aunt gave each of them the various parts of the reality (grandma's sickness, grandma's death, grandma's funeral) in order for them to put it all together and create a cohesive understanding of all the aspects of grandma's passing. They very much needed that understanding, as without it they couldn't lead normal lives. If the psychologist had known about grandma's death he would have been able to handle this problem. Without all the relevant information however, the psychologist didn't have a chance to heal their hurt.

Were it not for their aunt, who came to their assistance in explaining the facts of grandma's death, the wounds to their subconscious would have remained open until the end of their lives (as occurs with a lot of my clients). This example clearly shows that it's better to provide this information late rather than not at all. As I write these words all three children are now happy and joyful again.

THE DEATH OF PARENTS

Parents are the focal point in a child's life and that is why the death of one of them is always a very traumatic experience for a child. Sometimes it also wounds a child's psyche forever. Along with the death of his parents, a child loses not only a sense of security which is his basic need, but also a role model, after whom he could mold himself. More tragic than a father's death is the death of a mother. She is the one that gave birth to the child and subconsciously the child associates her with a feeling that she protects him from death. When she is not around, the child is confronted with his own mortality and is terrified. Often, the child also holds a grudge against the surviving parent because he/she didn't prevent what happened. The greatest shock is when there is a sudden death.

No less difficult to experience is the death of a sibling. A child then loses not only a sister or brother, but also the parents who are sometimes unable to accept their child's death for a very long time. The parents may have dedicated their time primarily to the care of the sick child and spent all of their free time at the hospital and as a result they didn't have time for their other child or children. If a child is chronically ill then that situation could persist for months or even years. After the death of that child the parents are also gone as they spend entire days at the cemetery and psychologically push their other children away. Children won't understand why that is happening and they would feel left out. Very often they assume blame for the sibling's death because they had taken away a toy, or had hit him, etc. in the past.

I am continuously contacted by clients who, even though they are now adults still cannot free themselves from a feeling of guilt and subconsciously think that their brother or sister died because of them. Often I hear: "Mrs. Pratnicka, my sister died because of me as I didn't want her very much when she was born" or "My parents took non-stop care of my seriously sick brother. I constantly dreamt that if it wasn't for him they would dedicate more time to me. Up to now I cannot forgive myself these thoughts, because they killed my brother" or "My parents know that my brother died because of me, they turned away from me after his death".

Also when one child dies, parents sometimes become over-protective of their other child (fearful of his death) and as a result the surviving child cannot even breathe, figuratively. In such cases the child also suffers because his parents become so concerned with his life they literally don't let him live his life.

CONCEALING DEATH

It is extremely disadvantageous when adults desire to conceal someone's death for as long as they can from their child. The child absolutely feels that something is not right, even though he is being convinced otherwise. This happens in many families, even when someone very close to a child dies. Adults mistakenly think that the child's psyche is unable to accept this knowledge. The early loss of a father or mother is not the natural order of things and will always be a great difficulty to overcome, even for an adult "child", let alone for a young one. However, concealing the truth is a great mistake, because it brings more damage than benefit for the child. Such behavior does great harm to a child (no matter how old he is) because he feels abandoned, almost betrayed by the sudden, and unjustified by adults, departure of the person he was close to. It's much better for a child to see a deceased person, cry and voice his feelings. And that should happen in an affectionate and loving atmosphere, without the child being forced into that situation. It is best to talk with your children in advance about death which would get them used to this tough to avoid reality. Concealing the cause of death only delays the inevitable, but under no circumstances does it reduce a child's sorrow. And, a child should be constantly reminded that he is not to be blamed in the least for a loved one's death. Their sorrow is often accompanied by an agonizing feeling of guilt, even if the children don't show that at all, because they are afraid to admit that.

Unfortunately in many homes silence prevails on this subject. A deceased parent, grandma or grandpa is never mentioned and it is as though a grudge is held against them and there is the pretense that they had just died and left. However, such behavior makes it even harder for a child to accept the separation. There is need for a loving approach to be given to those who we love, even as they are departing from this physical dimension. This wound could fester in a child until the end of his life because he didn't interpret (on the subconscious level) death in the appropriate way. I have been contacted by many people who still suffer because of this even though they are now adults.

Adults see the concept of death as something completely foreign to children so they isolate them from this subject. They are under the impression that behaving this way will protect the children from pain, suffering and fear. They are mistaken. Ultimately children don't live in a bubble. Death surrounds them from all sides. It's in movies, newspapers and computer games. Even quite small children watch television (for instance cartoons) and see animals die and sometimes they contribute to death. Many times they crush a bug, ant, fly or butterfly in order to see death. Or they might have a pet at home and it dies. They are very much affected by the loss of a dog, cat, canary, guinea pig or any other pet. If they don't experience this directly, then indirectly they come into contact with this at the home of friends in the neighborhood, at preschool or at school. Proofs that they are aware of death can be seen in their games. Often they organize all sorts of battles where they themselves or their enemies die. Therefore we can't claim that a child doesn't know death or anything about it. Therefore, when grandma grandpa, an aunt, a brother, a sister, mom or dad dies we shouldn't conceal or mask the truth from a child, because this only worsens an already tough situation. A child should learn the truth; however we should approach him in an incredibly gentle way. This can only be communicated by an adult who is familiar with death, understands it and has accepted it. He would be capable to communicate his own understanding to the child (the same way Carol's mom did it). However a person who doesn't understand the nature of death would be afraid of it and should therefore avoid conversations on this topic, because, among other things he basically wouldn't know what he should say. Unfortunately, at this moment the majority of people are like that. This is also the reason many grown people go through their entire life feeling hurt. They weren't given a chance to get angry and cry in the past.

Even in the case of a child who knows about a loved one's death, mourning could take a long time, even though the adult's emotions cooled down some time ago. Just because a child doesn't cry or express sadness does it mean he isn't mourning. Children in general mourn differently to adults. No matter how long would it lasts; we should help a child going through this. It's most important to bring sadness, frustration or rebellion to the surface and have them express these emotions, however these emotions shouldn't be judged. Sometimes a conversation should be directed so as to answer all the questions bothering a child in a clear and understanding way. And if it is possible, talk about events, feelings and emotions that are being experienced or were experienced by the child as it would help the child overcome his great feeling of loss. Facts should not be hidden, speak the truth, namely that a beloved person still lives that we probably won't fully understand this now, but he is still with us. We can't see the deceased person, but the deceased person can see us. A child would eventually accept life and would be happy, despite suffering because of this great loss. If we don't do that, a child would continuously live in fear of his own or a loved ones' death.

AFTER WE HEAR THE DIAGNOSIS

Upon hearing the diagnosis from a doctor that nothing more could be done, should a terminally ill person simply vegetate and be alone up until the moment of his death days, weeks or months later? Absolutely not! These months or weeks of life could be an incredibly precious and beautiful period for a sick person as well as for his family. This is time that could be used to catch up, meet with family members (and reconnect in some instances), friends and neighbors; think about life; forgive those people who we should or receive forgiveness; reveal secrets that are bothering us or straighten out matters regarding assets. All of that a sick person could achieve with the help of his loved ones. However, a sick person won't be able to achieve that if the people surrounding him avoid him or keep it secret he would soon die.

I would quote here from one of my readers' letters, of which there are many. This is what Mrs. Johnson wrote: "Mrs. Pratnicka, when my mother fell sick and we found out that nothing could be done for her, we took her (similar to what you did with your mom) to our home (before we lived separately) in order for her to end her life here in dignity. Mom was dying and the entire family was there for her. She was dying for over a year, losing and gaining consciousness. All of that was happening in a multi-generational home where my young children's bedroom was next to her bedroom. Downstairs there was a kitchen – always noisy, full of people and smelling of food. In this extremely strange circumstance of life and death I noticed the symbolism of human existence – evanescence, the inevitable end written in our every step, gestures, and feelings. My departing mom in a beautiful way got mixed in with our every-day reality. On their own initiative my children sat down next to their beloved grandma and read her favorite books to her; they were also doing that when she wasn't even aware. When the painkillers worked we would familiarize her with the matters of death. Obviously, we didn't talk just about that. We also brought up other issues, even those unpleasant topics. We were also able to recall the old days and even joke. In that way the children were also learning about interacting with death. We allowed for that, because we didn't want them to think that at some age they would simply dematerialize, they needed to be prepared for the unavoidable – because the end is written for all of us, just as the sorrow, sadness or despair of losing a loved one is also written. Obviously we cried when my mom and their grandma passed away. Even to this day we haven't touched anything in her room. Perhaps this is how it would be until the end of the mourning period. Mrs. Pratnicka, thank you for this wonderful book. If it wasn't for that book, I don't know how we would have survived that tough period. Regards, Mrs. Johnson"

As you can see, dear reader, there are families that are capable of facing up to this difficult task even while they are learning how to behave in the presence of the terminally ill. Other families escape into work and other responsibilities just to be as far away as possible from the sick person.

The approach to life and death as mentioned in the letter above could only be expected in loving and caring families. They were connected through love, wisdom and sympathy. For such families conversations about death were something obvious and natural, because there was nothing to fear. How was that possible, you would ask? Well, when you know enough about death you stop fearing it. If you deeply understand that death involves only the physical body, and the essence of the human never dies, then what would you be afraid of? By thinking and talking about it you familiarize yourself with death and it stops being terrifying to you. Obviously there would still be a period of sadness after the loss of a loved one, but you experience it completely different than you would when you don't have this knowledge. In order to reach such an understanding, death can't be a taboo topic. We can't "protect" even the smallest children from this knowledge or be afraid that it's too dangerous for their psyche. We have to familiarize them with death from early childhood. Obviously, it's completely different between making children aware that suffering and death affects everyone to having them deal with a personal loss. Then our children's pain should be eased, and we should not "protect" them at all costs from the knowledge of death and the experience of mourning.

Proof of this was a young girl. This is what she wrote to me: "Mrs. Pratnicka, it's so good that you familiarize people

with death. For me a very important experience from my childhood which helped me to accept the existence of death was the
passing of a person very precious to me. Even though I later
found out that he didn't belong to our family, at the time I was
very attached to him emotionally. That person was often a
guest at our house and I treated him like an uncle. His funeral
was very detailed and in some ways religious. A few priests
and monks participated. There was also an orchestra. For me,
as a child this was a cheerful way to depart to God. This experience impacted me for the rest of my life and changed my attitude towards my own mortality. It was good that none of the
adults came up with the idea to exclude me, as a child, from
participation in the funeral. When I was grown up I came
across your book *Possessed by Ghosts*, and later also *In the
Wheel of Life*. I understood what death was, and basically that
there wasn't one. This was a very important discovery for me
especially as we didn't bring up such topics in my home. My
dad had feared death very much throughout his life, not only
his death, but also everyone else's. He had lost both of his parents as a child and that had a huge impact on him. They both
caught the flu and died suddenly, and he was left alone with a
group of siblings. There were eight of them, between eight
months and fourteen years of age. They raised themselves, and
they survived the war.

When I was twenty two years old my dad suddenly fell
sick. In a flash he lost control of his life because of this serious
sickness. We found out from the doctors that he wouldn't recover. This was a terrible blow and shocking to all of us. We
didn't know what to do, more so because dad marginalized the
diagnosis from the beginning. He didn't want to accept that
things would change and the rules he had lived by before no
longer applied. Up to that point everything happened according

to his rules. He ran a large company with good results and now had to leave all of that behind. He couldn't accept that. However, what hurt him the most was that everyone, including many of his friends, suddenly disappeared from his life. Yes, people called, approached me on the street and asked about dad, but nobody visited him. When asked about it they claimed that they lacked the courage to visit, they don't know what to do or what to talk about so they chose to run away. They behaved as though they would get infected with his cancer. However dad just wanted someone, from among his friends to drop by from time to time and talk to him. There was a growing anger inside him targeted at himself for falling ill and towards the world for deserting him. He fought with the illness and his own limitations and even with his approaching death. Even though death was close, he absolutely didn't want to know anything about it. I knew how much he feared death and I tried to tell him at least a little about it. However he didn't want to talk about it. I didn't get discouraged, I tried over and over. I did this very carefully as I wasn't dealing with dad, but with the very small, terrified child who had lost his parents at a young age. I told him what I read in your books Mrs. Pratnicka, and at other times I tried to read parts of the book to him. He tried to get rid of me, but I didn't give up. He only got interested when I began to read about what awaits him after death. I remember his relief when he understood that he wouldn't stop existing. When he was strong enough he read your books by himself Mrs. Pratnicka. When he was tired, I read them to him. And even though he didn't usually get out of bed, after he read your books he became active as though he had recovered. Before he would lie in bed depressed and in complete apathy, later however he started to take care of everything that still needed to be taken care of according to him. I am not talking about matters regarding the company and home, because he always considered them as obvious things which he should do before his death. I am talking about those less obvious things. He wasn't discouraged anymore that people avoided him. He faced them himself. He asked each of us to invite family members, neighbors and friends to our home. He wanted to say goodbye to them, thank them, and apologize to them. Our home became crowded once again. People were constantly stopping by. When he felt that the end was close, he asked for a priest to confess his sins. He did this willingly even though I had never seen him pray or go to church before. After a long and very difficult illness he died peacefully. For me his death gained an additional dimension – freeing him from suffering. (…)

Thank you, Margaret." The letter also included some more personal matters which I won't quote fully.

Dear reader, as you can see, often a sick person, for a variety of reasons doesn't want to be aware of his condition. However, with a serious illness it is the time to make him aware of this matter. A person can best familiarize himself with dying when we talk to him about it. However to achieve the expected result, meaning to convince a person, that he doesn't have to fear death, first we ourselves have to understand death and stop being afraid of it. Only then are we capable of talking to a sick person about it and openly and give him support. In this way we not only help him depart, but paradoxically, thanks to death, we find a deeper and true meaning to life.

THE LIMITATIONS OF CIVILIZATIONS

In the examples above, I showed how an appropriate approach to death would look. It should be natural, full of love and sympathy. Unfortunately today's lifestyle, especially in big cities, doesn't make that task any easier. Multi-generational families have disappeared, so we don't see old age, illness and death daily. If someone in a family falls seriously sick, immediately we place him into the care of specialists– doctors, nurses, hospices – and after death funeral home workers. It's not surprising that dying disappeared from our subconscious.

Obviously right after hearing the diagnosis, in the first phase of an illness, loved ones organize themselves around the sick person and his illness. They try to nurture him, care for his needs, and be a so called loving family. They unite around the common goal of care and altruism. During that time any family conflicts are stopped. They don't realize that they avoid them,

not because of the sick person, but because of themselves, because their emotions are dominated by fear. It is the same reason a family would also conceal bad news from those in the
surroundings and similarly isolate themselves from bad news.

Things change when the sickness turns out to be long
term, serious and terminal. Relations in the family change. It
could be said that a carpet is being lifted up under which any
misunderstanding were swept up to that point. It turns out then,
that people seemingly close to each other are unable to honestly and openly speak to each other. Paralyzed by fear they escape into doing certain things, the sick person in is left alone
emotionally. He feels abandoned, pushed onto the back burner.
From the outside it looks like the family and friends are still
very much trying and sacrificing for the sick person, but in reality they don't know the sick person's needs, because they
don't talk to him. They are afraid to sit down next to the sick
person, look into his eyes and hear how much he fears death.
This way, they also push away their own thoughts about illness, suffering and death. They don't understand that experiences are tough and hurtful only when we don't know anything
about them. When we understand them, when we familiarize
ourselves with them, our fears will disappear like the morning
fog.

Unfortunately in our culture there is very little or no
room for death. For most people it seems, life happens beyond
the realm of illness and dying (they choose a life filled with
this illusion). That is why they approach this like something
unacceptable, needless and shameful. They don't want to understand that death is an integral part of life. Most people don't
want to realize that most of us, sooner or later will come into
contact with sickness, old age or death, if not with their own
person, then with their loved ones. This could be completely

unexpected and it doesn't have to be related to old age at all.

Because we approach suffering so lightly we don't take the time to visit our neighbors, friends or even family members, and if we do, we do so very rarely. We explain to ourselves, that it's inappropriate to visit, that the sick person should be left alone with their closest family members during such times. The truth is we don't know how to behave and what to say. We are afraid of seeing suffering, old age and dying, because a long time ago we moved away from the multi-generational family model and we don't have anywhere from which to draw an example of how to deal with these situations. Furthermore it became trendy to isolate children from sickness, suffering and death even when the dying person was someone close to them. It's not surprising, that most children raised this way only expect pleasures from life. If you are a parent raising a child based on such a model, you must consider at some point you will die outside home, lonely and worried. Isn't it about time to change that?

Your, perhaps grown up "child" is not prepared for sickness and death, and doesn't know how to behave in such a situation. They seem terrifying and incomprehensible to him. A different kind of upbringing and a presence at his grandparents' death would have given him a chance to familiarize himself with this area of human life. Otherwise it would remain distant and unreal. And if life were to force a grown up like that to manage this aspect of life, what would he do? He wouldn't know what to do and he would immediately place the sick or dying person into an institution that is located as far as away from him as possible. This is how we raised our children. As adults they have become insensitive, and sometimes even unmoved, but not because they lack a heart. They simply don't know how to act in the face of someone's suffering and death.

They are not capable of suddenly becoming sensitive, even when, the dying person is a close member of the family. This is too great a shock for them. For such a person the sick person reminds them too much of the fragility of their own life and activates fears which they are not ready to face. Basically, we can't prepare in advance for such situations if we lack a model. That is why sickness and death surprises people as so much as it does and causes such a great shock. With all of our strength we escape to an illusion rather than deal with the conscious existence of serious illness and death which affects each one of us at some point.

This explains why people, even in the presence of a seriously ill person act as though nothing is happening. They pretend to be carefree and cheerful because they are afraid to show how much the situation overwhelms them, how badly their fear is paralyzing them. Hence, they view conversations with the sick person about his affliction as inappropriate, even though he expects those type of conversations from them the most. They say among themselves: "Let's not hurt him with these considerations. Let him enjoy life as long as he can". And all of this because they are as deadly terrified as the sick person himself. They are running away from the problem continuously asking the sick person "How are you feeling today?", even though they don't want to hear what he has to say to them at all. Often sick people complain to us, saying: "How can I tell my family about my fear and pain when they only come here to entertain me. If I told them about my feelings they would run away in a hurry and never visit me again".

For the sick person's loved ones it's hard to realize that his life is now flipped upside down, that he has to face up to cruel thoughts about his own death and his trust in his further existence are being shaken. Additionally, any plans and visions

for the future are being substituted by boundless emptiness beyond which is the fear of suffering and death. Healthy people –
as I have already written many times – want to avoid these topics so as not to cause mutual unpleasantness. The truth however, is that they can't and don't want to go into these topics because, they would have to understand the sick person and most
of all address their own fear, according to the rule "what would
happen if I found myself in the sick person's shoes?". They are
shortsighted and become deluded into thinking, that if they
could avoid this topic then sickness and death would avoid
them, which again is the result of a lack of knowledge about
the natural model. There really are only a very few people who
understand these matters.

The sick person seeing and understanding the attitude
of healthy people wouldn't bring up this topic or won't tell his
loved ones the entire truth, not wanting to encumber them with
his own heavy burden. On the outside he pretends that he does
this because he cares about his loved ones. However, the truth
is that deep inside he is afraid to face up to his condition, or
more accurately put, face his fears. In most cases, both sides
are more or less aware of these mutual deceptions, however
they accept them. It is in this way that the circle of lack of understanding and communication is closed. Unfortunately, now-
adays this is the dilemma of most families.

That is also why healthy people are relieved to leave
their sick loved ones and their suffering in hospitals so as to
isolate them from themselves. They don't even want to think
how a loved one feels about being sick among total strangers
and also how it would feel to be sick and die in conditions
where there is constant movement, noise and commotion, and
where there isn't a moment of peace. They don't want to understand that a sick person has no chance to focus on himself

there, when around him he is constantly hearing loud conversations led by patients, staff and visitors, as well as being conducted over the phone. Additionally, there are televisions and radios turned on in almost every room. Do you understand now, dear reader, what great difficulties besides his own sickness he has to overcome?

It's not surprising that in such situations most sick people become lazy or – calling this by another name – escape into ignorance. The sick person prefers to read any kind of book or magazine, just to "kill" time so as not work on himself. And it could be the case that the sick person doesn't have too much time left, and yet he would waste what time he had in a mindless way ... and then what?

Seriously sick people are the ones that suffer the most. They can't, in any way isolate themselves from their environment. They feel that they would die soon and know that they have to focus on themselves, but for that they need silence which they don't have. Hospital conditions and their weakness don't make it easy for them to concentrate on themselves. In order to achieve that, they require inner discipline, and not each person has that. But without concentrating you can't hear your inner conversations regarding the meaning of life and death, you won't be able to reconcile with your own life. In that case, someone from outside could only help. This is why I believe that everyone, without exception, including therapists, doctors, nurses, as well as all other people who work in hospices, retirement homes and hospitals should consider the possibility of the existence of life after death and include this issue in their own advisory programs. All people, who come into contact with death on a daily basis because of their profession, should have open minds and share their knowledge with their patients, and also shouldn't ignore their own experiences. Basically, it's enough for people who take care of sick persons to have knowledge that we never die, after the death of our physical body we continue to live, we don't part from each other and we would always be together. It's about a dying person not being afraid of death and the transition to the other side of death's curtain. If he remains among the living, he would become a part of the mass of stray ghosts. Because of my profession I know, that in this matter it becomes worse and worse.

We shouldn't think that a gap created because of a lack of knowledge about death would be filled by priests and that they would take care of everything for us. Unfortunately, I often saw priests in hospitals, who showed up only to listen to the confession and give the communion or the last anointing which is definitely not enough. In hospices it's a little better. There, the priests come up to the bed in order to stand next to it for a bit, so they could hear out the sick person and... immediately after go over to the next bed. You could say that's good enough. The sick person has a chance to express himself and nobody interrupts him. He however greatly needs a conversation, explanations, assurances and comfort, because he would feel that a lot depends on that moment. I have never seen a priest speak to a dying person, and if so, it would only be about the soul's salvation, not about what the sick person cares to learn about the most.

Dear reader, do you realize that most people currently die in such a tough conditions, because their loved ones isolated themselves from the people suffering by putting them in hospitals and hospices? Moreover, we think this is quite natural, only because, it is comfortable. We say that our current lifestyle, especially in the big cities, doesn't allow us to take care of the seriously ill at home. Such an approach however, isn't natural; even if we try to convince ourselves otherwise.

You don't notice anything unnatural in this until it affects other people, even those closest to you. When this happens to you personally, when you are the one sick or dying, you quickly change your mind, but then you won't be able to do anything about it. Only then would you realize that more and more sick people die outside of their home; lonely, conflicted inside and without any emotional support, even though there are people around them. At that point you would personally become convinced about how tough it is to be sick and die that way.

In such a situation, would you be as happy with the strides made in science as you are right now? Would you still be proud of the developments of modern civilization? When you fall sick, would you prefer for it to be like you don't exist at all, or for it to be as it was in the past. With the latter you would have a chance to die in your own home among loved ones and those close to you. You wouldn't die lonely, and at your death bed you would have not only your close family members, but also relatives, neighbors, friends and acquaintances. You would have the appropriate conditions in which to say goodbye to everyone before your death and make peace with them or share your will with them. You would also have time and the right setting in which to quietly think about your life up to now and to make a decision about what you really desire. A lot is dependent on that moment. Not only, where you would be going after death, but also what desires would bring you back here in your next incarnation, that is, in your next physical life. I described this process broadly in *In the Wheel of Life,* Vol. II.

Ending Your Life with Dignity

In many countries, when the above mentioned problem was noticed greater effort was made to respect a sick person's right to die in peace and with dignity. It is considered each person's right to manage his own life, not only when healthy, but also during serious illness and death (this being normal and natural in loving families).

Each person does not have a loving family next to him that he can count on. Most families don't want to, or don't have the chance to take care of a sick person until the very end. Perhaps family members are too busy, too distant from each other, or live on two different ends of the world. This is also why it's necessary to write down relevant instructions in case of your own serious illness or death. This should be a written will, something like a testament. Each person should write this down as early as possible, even before getting sick. These instructions would be useful later for family members, relatives, friends, and even close neighbors in the case of serious or terminal illness. This would also instruct and inform doctors. It would not only decrease the possibility of, but it would also prevent the use of unwanted, unneeded, invasive or costly therapies. It is a lot easier for family members of a sick person to have ready instructions to share with doctors, and most of all it frees them from having to make important decisions for the sick person. That is how it is in most societies.

Unfortunately in many so called civilized counties, including in our country, a sick person's will isn't respected, more so a dying person. Only the will of a healthy person is respected. Only a healthy person is allowed to decide for himself. In contrast when someone falls sick, in most communities, the doctors, the nurses and family members take over this role. They often make all the decisions for the sick person, and he has no say in these decisions. Not only does the family "protect" the sick person, isolating him from information about the condition of his health, but the doctors and nurses also do this. Maybe not every doctor does this, but most of them do. Most often they do this in good faith; they think that bad news would only worsen their patient's health. In the meantime the sick person lies in bed unaware that he is deluding himself into thinking he would come out of this situation okay, and as a result he doesn't work on himself and his future. He should certainly prepare for death so that he doesn't get surprised by it. It would be a lot better if he did this when he is still fully conscious and has the strength, rather than when he is medicated with painkillers and doesn't know what is happening to him.

In most cases, the condition of the sick person's health is concealed from him and as a result he leaves many unfinished matters, related to: work or possessions. These matters can't be easily discarded, so if the sick person dies unaware, he would want to come back to treat all these matters.

THE LAST WILL

Dear reader, carefully listen to a sick person's last wishes and try to realize all of them. If you don't have the opportunity to fulfill one of these wishes, honestly and openly tell the sick person about it. Otherwise you may experience very unpleasant consequences, which drag on for many years or until the end of your life. Many of my clients experienced this. This subject was extensively described in my book *Possessed by Ghosts*, I would however describe it briefly here also.

We have to be aware that that the sick person's life doesn't end with the death of his physical body and that he still exists and he would demand the fulfillment of promises made to him. Every day I encounter cases in which the ghost of a deceased person doesn't want to leave, because in the past (during his physical life) something was promised to him which has remained unrealized. Often the promise is made just to pacify the dying person t or for peace of mind, however there are serious and sometimes even tragic consequences when it is not addressed. This doesn't only apply to matters within the family or with friends, but also with those related to complete strangers. The following is an example.

A single mother of a large family, let's call her Laura, was suddenly fired from her job. She looked for new one, but without success. Prospective employers didn't want to hire her either because she was older or because she had too many children. Either way, she was unemployed for a long time. Finally, an opportunity presented itself. She was offered a job to take care of an elderly, sick lady who lived in a Western European country. She was devastated. It's difficult without a job, but how could she leave her children without care for so long. To help her make her decision, distant family members and kind neighbors agreed to take care of the children during her absence. She left to take up the job. She was taking care of a wealthy, lonely elderly lady neglected by her family. The elderly lady had children, but they have moved away to different parts of the world. The youngest daughter organized the care for her mom, but she was always traveling. Laura diligently took care of the elderly lady. She fed, bathed, and clothed her like a baby. Even though she didn't need to, she cooked her delicious dinners, and in her free time she cleaned the huge home so that it – as she would say – "wouldn't get buried in dirt". The elderly lady was delighted. She had never had such a good caregiver before. She was constantly talking, she wouldn't be quiet, and Laura kept nodding just for peace and quiet. She knew too little of the language to talk freely with her. One day however she heard very clearly, because the elderly lady spoke very slowly: "You took very good care of me. Promise me, when I die you would take care of my youngest daughter".

"Yes, I would take care of her" – Laura said to comfort her, but in her thoughts she would be with her own children. "But promise" – insisted the elderly lady. "I promise" – Laura answered. These conversations were repeated every day or even a few times a day. This was funny, because her daughter was a healthy, young, independent woman and didn't need any care. However her mother had a different opinion. One evening the elderly lady fell asleep and didn't wake up. Her daughter came immediately and settled up all finances with Laura, giving her a good tip for taking care of her mother to the end. Laura was so happy! She was able to return home faster than she expected and with a lot of money as well.

Sometime after she returned home she started to feel the elderly lady's presence around her. Those weren't innocent memories, but rather intrusive demands for Laura to do what she had undertook to do. Years passed and nothing had changed with regards to this issue.

When Laura asked my office for help she was a wreck. The elderly lady wouldn't let go for even a moment and bothered her day and night. In order to free her from this, we proposed that Laura forgive herself the promise and also ask the elderly lady's ghost not only to forgive her for misleading her, but also to dismiss her from the promise. Laura however didn't want to do this. She was making light of the event saying: "But Mrs. Pratnicka, I only said that to her to comfort her. Why would she have been worried about daughter who was doing just fine…" Laura to this day couldn't, or didn't want to understand that the unfulfilled promise connected her with the elderly lady.

Dear reader, I intentionally gave this example that doesn't relate directly to family or friends. Considering the large number of people who ask me for help, this is not a

unique case at all. Still many idle promises are made in our society. Laura didn't mean to fulfill her promise to the elderly lady. Perhaps she didn't want to upset a dying lady; however the
fact remains that she misled her. If she had honestly told her
that she wasn't capable of fulfilling it, that her daughter would
manage on her own, that God would take care of everything,
today she wouldn't need to suffer.

THE LAST MOMENTS

Death is a part of life and as with life, we should also manage dying. Healthy people often avoid contact with a dying person, even if that person is someone close to his heart. He doesn't understand that during those moments it's enough to just be there. One does not ever need to talk much; silence is also very important. One could offer comfort not only with words but also through action.

Sometimes circumstances don't allow being with a loved one in the last hours of his life. If that happened in your case, don't blame yourself for it. Apparently, this had to happen. If however you could be with the dying person, then move a chair over to the bed, sit down with him, bend over and extend your hand. He doesn't expect anything besides you being next to him. You don't have to hold back tears when they swell up in your eyes. Cry as much as you want if you need to. Tears are a sign that you feel and sympathize; they evidence your care, not weakness. The beloved person also desires to express his own feelings. Perhaps he would find the courage and begin to talk to you. Be ready to listen. Nothing more, just listen to him and be there for him. In that moment it's important to allow him to speak. Therefore, don't interrupt, don't judge and don't ignore his concerns. This would give the dying person an opportunity to express his sadness, and even the entire foundations of his despair resulting from the upcoming end of his life. Talking to him you have to keep remembering that he already has a completely different reality to you. A bedridden person could have a great desire to do some work in his garden, go by the sea, to climb mountains, or something else. All this even though, he may already be unable to turn on his own in bed. Allow him to dream, don't stop him; don't say that his dream is impossible to achieve. In his desires you could read life sorrow. This is felt by almost everyone who is dying no matter their age. Sometimes an elderly person defends himself against death as strongly as a teenager. Everything depends on how he spent his life and whether it was fulfilling. When a dying person feels he has had a fulfilled life he then impatiently awaits its end. He unites with God, and is ready for his departure. He would even rejoice over the thought of meeting his dead loved ones. He feels in that phase more at home among dead people than among the living.

It is different for a person who feels that his life was not fulfilling, that it lacked any purpose. He gets frustrated, vengeful and curses. He blasphemes, because he doesn't want to accept that he is dying and he has no time to do the things that he has neglected. Because of that he is very much afraid of death. He doesn't know what awaits him after the death of his physical body.

Don't be discouraged by his behavior. Know that he is calling for help, even though he is doing so in a very unlovable way. You have an incredible opportunity to help him free himself from this unnecessary paralysis and fear. Tell him about life after death, that he would continue his existence, that he won't be punished, he would just live the life he lived until now. While saying this try to hold his hand and be there until the very end. Be as true a companion during this time of anguish as you were during his happy times. These last moments are an occasion to express feelings which you had rarely expressed before. Even if the dying person is unable to speak, say goodbye to him and reassure him about your love and your hope to meet him again after your death. If you don't have the strength to say anything, don't say anything. Your presence is enough, a soft touch, a smile and warmth will help the dying person.

If you use these last moments well, then later you won't hold any grudges against yourself for not doing something you should have done. Think of the deep feelings which manifested in you, then perhaps in the future this could be a source of strength and comfort in the tough days of mourning.

The people who remain behind should go the extra mile to help the dying person transition to the other side of death's curtain. This is the moment at which literally anything could mislead a soul. It could think that it didn't die at all, that it just seems that way, because what it sees and feels, in reality contradicts its perception about death. Despite our sorrow and pain we should reassert to the soul that it has died. In the dead person's home one should burn a large amount of candles until we know deep down that the time has come when we could stop. That is always an individual decision. When we still feel the dead person's presence, we should talk to him and address him by name. We should say his name in the same way we did when he was alive in order for him to know that it's to him, and not someone else, we are saying: "John, you are not alive anymore. Look: here are your remains. Your body is already dead. Go to God, go to the Light. Don't be afraid, don't stay, you need to go". Almost every one of us in this situation prays for the dead person's soul, but that's not enough. Many souls don't recognize that it's their death, their funeral, their body. This has to be continuously repeated until we succeed. When a lot of time has passed since the moment of death, then a different type of help is needed and here I recommend the book *Possessed by Ghosts*.

If we are dealing with a sudden accident, the help has to be intensified, because the transition to the world of ghosts was shocking and as a result it is very hard for the soul to accept.

Sometimes someone in our circle is unable to accept a loved one's death. Instead of asking the soul to go to the Light, he tries to stop it. Our duty in these cases is to ensure that he doesn't do that even when our heart is also in despair.

You may ask what damage you could cause to the dead person by despairing over his death. Well, a great deal of damage. The moment of death is an instant during which one should stay extremely calm. The dead person has to measure up to his new experience, leave behind everything that was linked to his life and decide what to do next. It's impossible not to feel grief in your heart and cry at that moment. One should cry, but not try to stop the dead person. Otherwise we would hurt not only him, but most of all ourselves. The consequences of a ghost remaining on this side of death's curtain, in other words among the living, are described in the book *Possessed by Ghosts*.

All conscious people have an important role to fulfill, especially those who because of their profession come into contact with death on a daily basis. These are hospice workers, retirement home personnel, hospital staff and obviously priests. Their task is not only to ensure that person dies with dignity, but also to ensure that the dying person is not afraid to transition to the other side of death's curtain and does not join the wandering mass of ghosts.

BEING ALIVE HERE AND THERE

Based on tens of thousands of cases gathered throughout my years of practice I can categorically state that a person is alive just the same after so called death, (when he leaves his physical body), as he was during his lifetime. We may think that we were first alive here, in the physical dimension and later, in the astral world. However the truth is that we are alive there and here simultaneously. This doesn't mean that we are in both places at the same time. We have two states of consciousness and we should be aware of both of them. The problem is that when we are in our physical body we usually aren't aware of the second state. That is why when we leave our physical body we do not realize that we are already in that second state, in our second body that we always have been in it, that nothing has changed for us. This is the main reason so many people miss their own death and mistakenly belief that they are still alive in their physical body, and not the astral. The astral body or the astral state of consciousness is a body and state which we only remember vaguely from our dreams. Every night we leave our physical body (in the same way we would leave it during death) and we move around in our astral body in the astral world. What you call a dream is really a memory of our experiences from that world. The difference between a dream and death is solely that while dreaming you are connected to your body by a silver string (in order to easily come back to it), and death rips away that string forever.

THE MOMENT OF DEATH

At the moment of death the real human with his spiritual body, also called the etheric body, opts out from his physical body and rises above it. However it doesn't yet tear up the final link but remains connected to the body with a silver string. This phenomenon could be observed. We could see a gradually thickening purple haze, taking human form and resembling how a dying person looks. This is the same figure which shows itself to some people, most often to people with whom it was closely connected during its life. Sometimes such a phenomenon takes place long before death. Then the figure is glittery and reminds us in some way of sparklers. By this glittering we would recognize that the silver string is not yet tore up.

People who are in a state of clinical death also remain connected with their physical body with the help of the silver string. Hence, at any moment they could return to their physical life. A person in such a state wanders wherever he wants, but the string doesn't get torn away. We could talk to him the same as we would talk with a living person and it does not matter whether we are next to his hospital bed or on another continent. Not only does he hear everything that we say to him, but he also reads our thoughts and feels our emotions. If we said something in one way, but felt another way, then know, dear reader, that he would immediately recognize that as I described in Ron's story.

I have spoken with many people who were in coma, at death's gate and who decided to return to their own body. In most cases they were rising above their body, observing, how other people were reviving and saving them. I also found myself in such a situation. When I woke up after three weeks of being in a coma, I remembered everything that happened during my surgery and after it. This wasn't a regular day, during which many patients were operated on, but New Year's Eve and twelve o'clock at night. Even though, I was in a critical condition, they passed around champagne and had a toast. All present in the operating room, doctors and nurses alike had some annoyance towards me. They complained that instead of having fun and spending time with their family and friends, they had to be in the hospital and additionally perform a surgery. Some expressed this aloud, while others only thought about it, but I felt all of this with my senses, because I didn't have a physical body which would block the flow of information. After surgery I felt very guilty. When I told the doctor who had operated on me, that I was sorry that I had wasted his New Year's, he almost fainted (there were very few publications back then about life after death and comas). With his legs wobbling he held on to a wall and couldn't move a step. They called for help and took him out of the room. Later he came to visit me every day, sometimes even multiple times. He constantly asked about that evening, apologized and proposed that he perform one more surgery and fix what his friends had "messed up". What he was referring to was a great scar that had remained after surgery. I however didn't agree to it. Somehow inside I knew that it would heal by itself and it did.

Perhaps you wonder, dear reader, whether it's possible at all, for a patient under anesthesia to remain conscious. I would only confirm that he could hear, see and feel. His mind remains conscious of what is happening. Many people after their surgery can't calm down for hours, because they heard something during the surgery that terrified them. Surgeons in many operating rooms have conversations, and even long discussions, not always related to the surgery. They approach a patient routinely, tell jokes, or even have bursts of anger and curse loudly. A lot from that sinks into a patient's subconscious and influences their thoughts and feelings. Such remarks could have a strong, positive or negative, influence on a patient during his recovery time and later. Sometimes a patient gives up and dies on the operating table because he heard a negative prognosis about the state of his health. I am writing this, so doctors could be more careful about what they say, think and feel, because patients know that, although not all of them recall it later. This obviously doesn't change the fact, that this information remains in the subconscious and from there acts upon a person in a positive or a negative way, sometimes until the end of life.

Almost every person that shared their experience of clinical death with me saw a light or lightsome "spiritual" being, standing sometimes at the end of the tunnel. At that time, no one felt pain, despite having suffered significant body damage. When they were made aware that their task on Earth wasn't yet completed, they immediately returned to their bodies and started to feel pain and physicality. They had the opportunity to return because they were connected to their physical body through the silver string as previously mentioned.

I performed regression sessions with various people, meaning sessions to return them to their previous incarnations. When they were transitioning from one life to another, they often reported how the process of leaving their physical body occurred. These were some of their statements: "I left my body", "I saw a wonderful light", "I was drawn in to a wonderful being, a source of energy, a light", "Wonderful people came up to me. I was not afraid. They came to help me", "I felt very light", "I felt very much at peace", "I was resting after the troubles of life. I left all my bodily afflictions behind", "I was at peace and happy", "This was an amazing feeling… wonderful, as though the sun would always shine here", "This light was so bright", "The light was a source of strength. Everything comes from the light", "This energy comes from the light", "I was drawn in by a magnetic force and my soul went there right away", "I was among friends. I saw many people. Some of them were my loved ones, others were not. Everyone was waiting for something". Many people said that, but everyone had more or less the same thing on their mind. Those who had feared death up to that point weren't troubled by it, but rather puzzled, and even grateful.

DEATH AND WHAT'S NEXT?

Dear reader, you already had some knowledge – even though until now just theoretical –that there is no death, and what you thought about death until now, was simply getting rid of the physical body. This resembles taking off your clothes, and you as a real human gain an opportunity to move forward along the path of your growth. However, that entire issue is not just based on putting away that uncomfortable and bothersome covering, but also on completely freeing yourself from it. It would allow you to finally feel free and liberated. This resembles the process of a caterpillar feeing itself from its cocoon and being transformed into a butterfly. The caterpillar doesn't stop existing during this process. Analogically the soul freed from its physical body continues living in its own spiritual body. It's free and like the butterfly can literally go anywhere.

This, which we routinely call "death", is therefore not the end of life in this world and the *beginning in the other*. We are dealing with a continuation. In order for the dying person to feel free after leaving his own body and fly like a butterfly, he must have knowledge about this subject while he is alive, and at the moment of leaving his own body remember to use that knowledge.. A butterfly that leaves its cocoon also has to have it before it frees itself from cocoon, otherwise it would get the idea to stay in it permanently right? Nature, equipped the butterfly with the instinct of self-preservation: this is the source of its knowledge. People in contrast have intuition; however most often they are blind and deaf to what it suggests to them. They prefer to live unaware, in delusion. That is also why, after the death of their physical body, instead of going high into the sky like the aforementioned butterfly, they want to remain in (or by) their physical body at all costs. For this reason the number of souls who remain suspended between "heaven" and "earth" that don't make the decision to go to God is constantly growing. There could be many reasons for this. I will describe them one after the other.

The most important of these is the fact that after death souls don't know or don't believe that they have died. Nothing changes for them. They overlook their own death and think that they are still alive. They don't realize that they could go to the light. They think that they are still alive and belong on Earth. Even if they suffered for a long time due to a serious illness, they think, that they are now healthy. If they were old or disabled people they suddenly feel rejuvenated or at least that they have gained strength and energy (this only happens at the moment they leave their body). They still, as though through a fog, see the physical world and think that they can function in it (this is caused by being wrapped in their etheric body, which I will describe in a moment). They don't see other souls who are in the same situation as them. There is a great amount of such souls next to each other, but more often than not, they don't see or hear each other for a long time (obviously they could see and hear each other, but first they would have to accept that they are no longer alive). With every passing moment they continue to believe that they are still alive, in their physical body and that nothing has changed. There are battalions of lost souls still overwhelmed by this illusion and as a result leading a life of delusion. Very often those are our loved ones: fathers, mothers, brothers, sisters, beloved grandmas, grandpas, friends, neighbors and persons from school or work.

When I ask wandering souls: "Do you know that you are not alive?" Usually I am met with great bewilderment: "I didn't know. I am not live?" They often experience momentary shock. They were not told before that life after death was so real. I have heard that thousands of times before and I still hear it almost every day. Unfortunately, great ignorance prevails in this area.

One of the reasons I decided to write this book was a desire to share knowledge which would allow everyone to understand this important issue. It's about readers being able to prepare themselves and their loved ones for happiness in their future life behind death's curtain, that is, in "heaven". Everyone, sooner or later would have to face this problem. In Eastern cultures conversations about death, what happens to us after it is a completely normal, everyday thing. Even young children know about it. Because of their attitude they are not surprised by death. Their knowledge in this area protects both the dead and the living. It's worth it to transfer this custom to western culture. Helplessly, wandering ghosts would not be as lonely and unaware of what to do with themselves, with nowhere to turn for help in a seemingly incomprehensible situation.

If we don't engage in these conversations on a daily basis, then the most appropriate time to bring up this subject would be when someone reaches old age or is seriously ill. It's very important to gently convince the person who reaches that point to discuss what he plans to do if he dies. Naturally, this may not be easy. We don't want to scare him, we also think the conversation might be inappropriate. Perhaps, we are concerned about what he would leave behind and for this reason want to stay in his good graces so we are considered a great friend. We could also be afraid that he would think that we desire his death.

However when would he settle his matters, if not when he is sick or old? I am not speaking about illnesses such as a running noise or cold, but rather illnesses that he may not survive. Conversations around this subject don't mean that the sick person would die right away. It's about "What would happen if I died?" On the deepest level of his consciousness a sick person knows if he is going to die, even when his loved ones and doctors tell him otherwise.

Conversations about death are very important for both the dying person and people that remain behind. The main reason soul's overlook their own death is because they lack knowledge about their existence changing very little after the death of their physical bodies. If they knew, it would be much easier for them to understand that and they would be able to confront their new state without being surprised. It is even more difficult when people don't believe in the afterlife before their death. Even when they recognize that they have died they don't know what to do with themselves. People who were sick for a long time or died at an old age also find it difficult to believe they are ghosts.

What happens then to souls where sudden death surprises

them? On this this side of death's curtain, among the living, a great number of ghosts wander, who were surprised by death at the best moment of their life. Until then they never thought about death. They were young, healthy and suddenly they were no longer alive. They were surprised by the sudden accident, no signs of death approaching and with time for reflection. I am talking about car, plane or mine accidents. Such souls don't want to hear that they are no longer alive. In the blink of an eye their physical life was gone and in that instant they were dead. They did not notice when it happened. If they had known about life after death, they would possibly have realized they were no longer alive. They don't want to believe in the situation they found themselves in, no matter who and what tells them about it. For many of them death is an end of everything, not a path to further life.

Some souls are even stunned long before their death. When they go through it, they are unable to recognize their true state. These include terminally ill patients who received strong pain relievers also drug addicts and alcoholics. The mind of a sick person who received anesthetics could be compared to that of a drug addict's mind. Long after death he is unable to bounce back. When he recovers consciousness, he would still lack knowledge of the afterlife. The consequences of such ignorance I described in the chapter "Dangers During Death of the Physical Body" in my book *In the Wheel of Life*, Vol. II.

The next reason some souls don't go to light is that they are afraid of being punished for their deeds. These don't have to be great sins, as I described earlier in John and Carolina's case. They were able to heal that aspect of their lives. If however they don't, then most likely they would feel like sinners unworthy of traveling further to "heaven". They would stay like many others in the world of ghosts, leading the life of wandering souls. Most of the ghosts that remain on this side of death's curtain have quite small "sins" in their consciousness and only infrequently bigger ones, however while alive they believed in a horrible, vengeful and punishing God. That is why they now feel unworthy of receiving forgiveness. Even though, awaiting them in the moment of death is wonderful assistance consisting of spiritual guides, the loving Light and loved ones who died before them. They turn away and refuse to go further. They don't believe that God would forgive them their sins. That is because they could not forgive themselves their own sins in their physical life.

The next big group that remains in the world of ghosts is souls who while alive didn't believe in God, and therefore they didn't have anyone to go to after death. They thought that life ended in the grave, and after that there was just an abyss, nothingness. And yet other souls believed greatly in God, but thought that they would have to lay in their grave until the "Judgment Day" and it was only after resurrection that their body would go to "heaven". Therefore they became victims of what they believed in, specifically, in what religion ordered them to believe in. Now they feel deceived not knowing what to do with themselves. Wait for judgment, punishment? But where should they wait? Wait in their grave? They are still alive; therefore they can't wait in a suspended state. They realized that only after death, when it was already a bit too late. You may ask: "Too late for what? Too late to go to the Light. In the moment of physical death they were supposed to decide where to go.

This group also includes people who took every precaution while they were alive and planned their afterlife in detail thinking they would lie in their grave until Judgment Day. Those are people who while alive, built tombs for themselves and their loved ones, opulent monuments; they also planned what they would wear in their coffin, in order to look their best in the coffin. They wondered how many people would attend their funeral and what would be said in the eulogy.

The all need energy in order to exist just as people need air. They hover around cemeteries and steal that energy from people who come there. This may seem like a joke, but it's not a joke at all. There are many jokes about the deceased getting up from their graves. Members of this group strongly identify with their body, but we as human beings are not really our bodies.

This is how many ghosts get stuck on the road of their transition in the afterlife. When, after death they realize what has really had happened to them, it is a great shock to them. They don't know what to do with themselves however, because the time for their transition to the other side of death's curtain passed long time before. They don't have any other choice but to draw energy from people or penetrate the body of someone permanently.

In the world of ghosts perhaps the largest group of ghosts that stay after death are those, who while alive were very attached to earthy matters. They are now unable to free themselves from those earthly matters. Those could be attachments to material or non-material things. They could be stopped by their own home, car or other possessions. Everyone has certainly heard of haunted houses and the frightening ghosts in them. Others loved food, alcohol, drugs, sex, or gambling too much while alive. Yet others liked deciding their loved one's matters so much, interfering in everything, that now it's hard for them to stop wielding that power.

Another reason ghosts remain is their willingness to fix mistakes they made while alive. They think that by staying on this side they could possibly fix what they did wrong.

There are also ghosts who cannot leave in peace because someone cursed them, attacked them or used black magic against them, and what's more they believed in it. It's not a curse or black magic that holds them, but their faith, thinking that this is as it should be. The next sizable group is made up of those who committed suicide.

For some souls it's very hard to leave Earth, because they left someone, who they felt, need to be taken care of, for example: a parent leaving a young child behind, caring children leaving their elderly, lonely parents behind, etc.

The abovementioned souls stay on Earth because they made the decision to stay. There is however a great number of souls who would very much like to transition to the other side, to "heaven", but their loved ones' despair don't allow them to do that. These souls are divided between their well-being and the well-being of those who they left behind. They could even be aware that for everyone's well-being it's better for them to leave, but their loved ones won't allow them to do that. Therefore, one has to remember that while mourning, despite the sorrow, it is important to think about those, who have a right to leave. We should do that, so as not to hurt them or ourselves. I know, how hard this is, because I went through it myself. My mom however was able to demand I not stop her. How many souls do that? Very few do that.

Isn't this a surprising fact, that after death someone finds his reality to be the world he believed in while alive? If he believed in "heaven", then he goes to "heaven". If he doesn't feel worthy enough to enter "heaven", or was afraid of punishment for his violations a hellish reality is in store for his loved ones and for him.

THE TRAIN GOING TO HEAVEN

The moment following death can be compared to a train going to heaven, and only those persons who have a ticket can get on the train. Everyone who thinks he is worthy to enter heaven gets a free ticket. And, after the train leaves the station, a crowd of ghosts remain, who don't know what to do with themselves.

Until then they had help from everywhere, enough energy and a goal. They had a place to go. From the moment the soul closes itself to the benefits of transitioning behind death's curtain to so called "heaven", it has to manage by itself. It then starts to wonder what to do next. Most often, it returns to its loved ones, family or to the people with whom it was directly involved. There it feels the safest. It may also come back to its own home, the hospital where it was; it may also return to work, to friends, to the cemetery, to its grave, to church if it liked being there, to properties it owned, to the bar where it could drink as much vodka as it wanted to, or to the place it got high.

Most souls, who die in an accident, remain at the scene of the accident continuously replaying it. This replaying of the accident serves to awaken the soul and make it aware that it's not alive anymore.

You may certainly wonder why some souls don't leave on that proverbial train to "heaven". Why they resign themselves, even though they are invited to enter? Well, they are all very afraid of punishment. A violation, that they accuse themselves of, and which doesn't allow them to leave (because in their opinion it requires punishment) could literally be anything: backtracking on a promise, not repaying a loan, consuming meat on a Friday, not attending mass on Sunday, various kinds of fraud, abuse, through to the most heinous sins such as banditry, felonies, rapes and murders. They are afraid of punishment and they want to avoid it. As many ghosts as there are, there are as many types of fears of punishment. They could have easily forgiven themselves these violations, but they didn't know that they were dying, because, for example their loved ones concealed that from them.

Therefore, at the train station between "heaven" and "earth" there are ghosts who have small violations on their consciousness as well as great sins. They don't believe that it's enough to forgive themselves their own sins. "Why does this happens?" – You may ask. Well, God gave us all free will. If we want to feel guilty and punish ourselves non-stop for our own deeds, then we could do that. God doesn't do anything against our will. If however, we free ourselves from feeling guilty for sins we committed, we would have a chance in that instance to go to the Light. Ghosts without this knowledge are resigned to their circumstance as they think that it's too late for them. They expect severe punishment in the form of purgatory or hell. They want at all costs to avoid it, that is why they fight fiercely with death and remain on this side of death's curtain among the living. They don't realize that they brought the fate they greatly feared upon themselves because they stayed in the astral world, among the living, creating a reality which happens to be worse than what we call purgatory or hell, but more about this in a moment.

Why can some souls, including those who even have serious sins on their conscious, forgive themselves and transition to the light, while others don't? It all depends on whether the specific soul loved itself, others and God while it was alive. If that person had despair, sadness and a lack of hope in his heart then he lacked room for love. Love is the substance which brightens the darkness in a person's heart. It gives him great power. A person, who loves himself, won't hurt himself or anyone else. He would be loved by his environment. He believed that God loved him and as a good Father-Mother will forgive his child. Such a person could forgive himself and others.

Someone who doesn't love himself is unable to love anyone else. He hates everything and everyone, including himself. He also hates God. He feels like an evil person, he only sees evil around him and does evil things. He thinks that because he is evil then his Father is also evil. And as such his Father wouldn't forgive him. He doesn't want to and is unable to believe that it could be different, that God is love, and could forgive everything. How could he believe in love when he doesn't know what it is? Love is God. Meanwhile he doesn't believe in God. A world without love and without God not only seems, but is also cruel. Living a cruel reality, people become cruel to themselves and to others. They don't forgive, doesn't sympathize, they use rules such as "an eye for an eye, and a tooth for a tooth" around

which a vicious cycle revolves. Love in such a world is associated with weakness. What a paradox. That, what in the world of
kindness is the greatest power, is associated with weakness
there.

At some point this cycle needs to be broken, and the time
leading up to death is the perfect occasion for that. There is time
then to forgive oneself, others and even God. The people who
are alive after the death also have an opportunity to forgive us.
God also forgives us. Even when someone is no longer among
us, we could forgive him. It's never too late. In this process, we
are helping not only the dying person, but most of all ourselves.

THE HUMAN BODIES

Dear reader, in order for you to understand the essence of death, you should fully realize that you have more bodies than just your physical body. You use a different kind of transport for traveling over the sea or air, and yet another to move from one place to another on the Earth's surface. In the very same way your soul and spirit use various bodies in order to have certain experiences. I am using a metaphor in order to show that each subtle body serves the soul and spirit so that it can experience different things. Even though, we use these bodies every day, most people are not aware that they have all of these bodies. This knowledge may seem unnecessary to you during your physical life (which is a mistake, because with the help of it you could significantly improve the quality of your life), however it becomes absolutely essential in the afterlife with the death of your physical body.

To the basic human bodies belongs: the physical body combined with the etheric, the astral body, the mental body and the spiritual body. All of them are true copies of the physical body. Each of these subtle bodies is – on a greater or smaller scale – an oval field of energy, resembling an egg, which is surrounded by another egg and then another, to an increasingly higher levels of vibrations. This resembles the Russian babushkas – one doll fits into the other, and the next one fits into another and so on. These bodies are simultaneously penetrating each other. The vibrations of the subtle bodies are significantly higher than the vibrations of the physical body; that is why most people don't see them, while others don't have any problems recognizing them. In order for you to better understand this, imagine dear reader that you are looking at a plane's propellers. When they are still or spin slowly, you see them without a problem. It is the same with a human's physical body: it vibrates quite slowly and that is why you see it. The other bodies vibrate much faster than the physical body, which is why you don't see them. It is the same with a plane's propeller. When it spins faster and faster, you are unable to see them, as though they don't exist. Do the propellers disappear? No. You simply stop seeing them, because your eye is unable to observe them because of how fast they are moving.

The etheric body's vibrations are similar to the physical body, because it's a subtle replica of the physical body, meaning a physical look-alike. It's a copy, not only in terms of the shape of the physical body, but also in terms of each organ, the knuckles, the veins, the cells and the tissues. The etheric equivalent of a given organ can't leave the etheric body even when its physical equivalent is surgically removed. The etheric body only stops to exist when the physical body dies. Only then (after a short or long time) does the etheric body disappear from the physical plane. It's located between the physical body and the astral body, meaning the emotional. The etheric body is basically a physical body, but just more subtle than physical body (it vibrates a bit faster than it) and that is why it is invisible to the average person, who doesn't know anything about it. Dear reader, the etheric body gives you life. Do you realize that the physical body doesn't have any life at all? That is why I keep repeating that it's only clothing. Any energy needed for action comes from the etheric body, meaning the spiritual body, not from the physical body. You must fully understand this, because it is an important, if not the most important thing you need to know concerning death. The etheric body is always young, always beautiful and always healthy. Even if they cut out one of your organs during surgery you still have the prototype in your etheric body from which you could rebuild it. You still have the astral body, which you occupy during sleep and your mental body which you use for contemplation. If you want to learn more about this topic please read my book *In the Wheel of Life*, Vol. II and III.

Now I would like to show you the difference between dying with full awareness and dying without awareness. Many people die unaware, because they greatly fear death and punishment for their sins. This causes them to choose unawareness, because they don't want to know the consequences of their actions. They race through physical life applying the rule: "Whatever happens, it happens. I don't want to know anything about it". As a result of living that kind of life they experience that kind of death.

Dying with Full Awareness

The people who are fully aware of the nature of death are those who also think about it a lot. Yet during their physical life they know that their life doesn't end with their physical death. And since they are not dying, they are also realizing that they are never being born. Therefore they understand that their mom only gave birth to their physical body, not to them themselves. They know that during so called "death" only their physical body dies, and they as the real human continue to live. When this moment comes, they don't hold on to life with determination, but welcome death without fear. They are aware that during so called "death" they don't perish and become nothing, but rather transition from a physical state to a spiritual state, in the same way a student goes from one classroom to another. This comes from a deep understanding of the entirety of Life, thus they look at it from a broader perspective. They know that they live eternally, and physical death doesn't deprive them of life. This certainty or trustfulness in eternal life is reflected in their physical life. It's of the highest level. They are not afraid of death so they soar as high as they desire during their physical life. They are not afraid of death, therefore they know that even if they fall, they won't die, but instead in the future they would soar again. They said "yes" to their entire life. There is no fear in them, and even if some appeared, they quickly manage it, because it's not too great. They are not afraid of life and are not afraid of death, whendeath comes. They face it with trustfulness and peace, the same way they would face a friend who they haven't seen in a long time.

This is possible, because they were psychologically and physically prepared for it. This positive attitude ensures that they remain fully aware of themselves and of each moment they find themselves in. Remaining aware they are masters not only of their own life, but also of their death. This protects them from very unpleasant experiences. I write about them when I discuss the consequences of dying in unawareness.

What I write about here has nothing to do with religion. One could be a so called atheist and still realize that death is a natural part of the greater life and be religious and not understand that.

As you can see dear reader, someone who is aware of further existence after the death of his physical body lives in physicality completely different to someone who is unaware. The former is always trusting and calm deep down while the latter is full of worry and anxiety. When a person realizes that in reality he never dies, his every thought, word and desire takes on a different meaning. He looks at life from a different perspective. He knows that time or space would not erase anything. He would understand cause and effect much better. On the other hand a person who is unaware of the nature of death treats everything as impermanent and insignificant. He believes that everything depends on fate, good or bad, that he doesn't have any influence over what happens to him. When he begins understanding death, everything starts to take on a much deeper meaning. He notices conditions and other matters not only as fleeting phenomenon but also significant events that have their inspiration in some specific reason. He doesn't expect with a sense of dread the end of his earthly journey. He treats death as a return Home and an opportunity for rebirth. This awareness means every moment takes on incredible importance for him.

A person who is aware and still in physicality understands life on a deeper levels, and not superficially like most people (even the very religious). He understands life as a constant process of development; hence he transitions from one phase of life to another with trustfulness and calmness. He knows that in order to become a child he has to leave his infancy state. And next: he wouldn't have become a teenager if he didn't first leave his childhood stage, nor fully grow up if he didn't leave his puberty stage. Do you remember with what happiness and optimism you welcomed these stages of life? Then you knew the benefits of transitioning from one stage to another. Going through life we continually grow until we reach the end of our journey on this side of curtain. Leaving the physical state we transition to the spiritual state. And during our so called "death" we don't enter nothingness, we simply lay down our physical body and go forward as the real human, in order to continually grow and develop.

Natural life is a process of continuous progress and growth. You can't understand life – life in a greater, general sense – in a different way, through that "death". That "death", the "death" of the physical body, makes you realize how life transforms. In reality you are immortal and wise. Every day you are becoming wiser and wiser.

Someone who understands that death is a natural transition from one state to the other accepts death and surrenders to it without fear. He leaves his physical body without sadness, because while being alive he already had knowledge that the physical body (which most people considers as their being) doesn't have any life on its own. He understands and accepts the fact that he is alive thanks to the energy coming from his etheric body and allows for, or also agrees for that part of his being to peacefully withdrawn from his physical body. In such a state, death is gentle and painless. For the real human, withdrawing from the physical body is not difficult because the subtle, spiritual, higher bodies are his real world. He knows perfectly well that one of them, his etheric body; c is used when he powers himself with energy to act, and his second body, meaning his astral body he uses during sleep each night, and his third body, his mental body, he uses when he thinks. Perhaps you are not aware of your spiritual bodies; however accept as a fact, that you have them. You would fully realize them after the death of your physical body. However, to be fully confident that you have reached this phase of existence (only this phase is characterized by a lack of fear of your non-existence), during your physical existence you need to know more about this subject. If you don't feel your subtle bodies, you should read about them, so that while contemplating and meditating on this, the knowledge could reach you that you have them (I described these matters broadly in *In the Wheel of Life* Vol. I and II)

For someone who is aware, death is the removal of one of his bodies for the purpose of living in other bodies. For his soul this is like taking off clothing. The soul doesn't understand death to be the final end. I repeat this every so often for this to

stay in your subconscious. This is the same as applies to memorizing a poem. When you read it only once, you will remember
very little from it, but repeating it would facilitate you remembering it permanently. If you die, you won't make a mistake, because you would have a map of consciousness, which would
lead you further. When you encounter some worrying phenomenon, you won't be scared of it, because you would recall the
cause of its formation. Understanding of its essence would make
it disappear like a bad dream in front of you.

      Dear reader, I am trying to present the subject of death to
you from various perspectives, so that you have a chance to recognize, that life and your seeming death (during which only the
physical body is taken off) makes up a whole. The soul is eternal, and its desire for knowledge and enlightenment continues in
the material world as well as in the spiritual world. The process
that allows for the soul to circulate between these two areas we
call reincarnation. It makes this search easier, allowing the soul
to continue learning as it strives toward perfection. If you are an
opponent of reincarnation, know that in the past everyone was
conscious of it. It was only during the time of Emperor Constantine, when the texts of the New Testament were chosen, and all
passages mentioning reincarnation thrown out. I will explain
further in this book how that happened. Faith in only one life
creates many problems. One of the most important of these is
responsibility, basically a lack of it. People who are convinced
of this concept don't feel the need to care for others and about
the world in which they live. They try to get out of life as best as
they could and at all costs, by neglecting for instance our beautiful planet. In an irresponsible way they abuse our natural resources and contaminate the Earth. Through human nearsight-
edness and the belief that we are only here for the period called
life, they act in ways that lead to imbalance in the ecological

system. This is only a short list of problems caused by thinking that we only live once.

DYING UNAWARE

It won't be easy for you, if you will consider yourself as only a physical body. You would live in continuous fear that despite the fact that unconsciously you also use other bodies. You would be constantly afraid of death, despite not knowing about it. You are not alone. Most people eject this knowledge from their consciousness because of the fear of looking a little bit beyond their own body – into an unknown area. This doesn't have great negative consequences during their physical life, however after death everything changes in their perception of reality. Then they have a feeling that everything they had up to that point has been taken away. This is a normal consequence of their mistaken thinking that they don't want to, or need to know anything about physical death while they were alive. Such a person is terrified in the moment of death. He doesn't know what will happen to him. He therefore drags his feet to stay in his physical life as long as possible. Nobody can dissuade him from this choice, because he has free will and could always – even in the moment of death, as well as after it – take advantage of it. However, he develops the mistaken belief that a persistent fight to hold on to his physical body is his only option. He doesn't want to understand that this is against nature. At the end, death wins, it also happens to be incredibly painful. It's not because this is death's nature, but because it's forced to break him out of his physical life. The more someone resists death, the more he fights with it, then the more suffering he experiences. When a dying person gives in to the natural process of life, and swims gently with its current, life carries him on its shoulders. However when someone resists Life, he behaves as though he would swim against its current. He holds on to whatever he can, but the current is ultimately too strong however.

Certainly, many people would approach death differently if during their physical life they knew that their life wouldn't end with their physical death. What great comfort they would experience during their physical life with this knowledge. They would not be full of fear as previously mentioned and even if they were fearful it wouldn't be so great. Perhaps they would realize that since they don't die they basically were never born and in the past only their physical body was born. They would also come to the conclusion that they had lived an infinite number of times before and they wouldn't defend against physical death so bitterly. I understand that not all people are able to grasp this because they are paralyzed with fear which prevents them from understanding.

In the meantime the Guardian Angels and other helpful souls which they really do exist help people after death when they are already in their spiritual state, to join their loved ones who transitioned to the other side before them.

When the etheric body is withdrawing from the physical

body, the physical body becomes deprived of life. I repeat: the physical body on its own never had life. Its liveliness comes from the etheric body which in part is also physical, even though for many human eyes it remains invisible not because, it can't be seen, but because people don't want to be aware of its existence (because of their feelings of fear). When a person dies, he dramatically changes his point of view. Nevertheless, many people hold on to their etheric body, mistakenly thinking it is their physical body. One more time I repeat: the physical body on its own doesn't have life. Knowing about this, it doesn't make any difference for us if we are in our etheric body, or in our astral body, once we have rejected our physical body. Otherwise, a person dying would hang on to his etheric body mistaking it for his physical body, as a result most people drag along their etheric body or part of it after the death of their physical body. By the time he frees himself from it, he is in, even if for just a moment, in an unconscious state. This is a very important moment, because that unconscious state carries with it great unpleasant consequences (more about them, when I will describe imprisonment in a cocoon). The etheric body gives energy only to the physical body, but on its own is not a tool or machine like the physical, astral or mental bodies. This is also why a person holding onto his etheric body is incapable of any action in the astral world, in other words, where he should transition after the death of his physical body. However people dying in a conscious state, who during their physical life recognized the essence of death, in one moment free themselves from their etheric wrapping. However, it is different for unconscious people. Best case, the etheric body imprisons them for a few hours, and worst case because of a complete lack of knowledge this could last many days, or even weeks or months. The less a person is conscious of the essence of death, the more he is afraid of it and the longer this lasts. For people who are spiritually advanced this lasts shorter or doesn't happen at all, because there is no fear of death inside of them. The next step in this process is the transition of the real human to his astral body.

To summarize, a person who is too attached to the physical world and to his body, doesn't allow for the etheric body to go away, wanting to hold on to it. He doesn't understand that he could do this for some time, however at the cost of pain and much unpleasantness and by that hanging onto the etheric body he cuts himself off from both worlds at once – the physical and the astral. He thinks that he still lives the physical life, but he doesn't realize that he is surrounded by a thick, grey fog, through which sees the physical world unclearly. Everything is shadowy and barely visible to him. This is because of his unwillingness to recognize that his physicality drifted away from the field of his experiences. If he accepted his own death and wasn't afraid to see, he would notice that his physical body lies completely lifeless. This results from fear of nothingness and non-existence.

Even though, such a soul lives in horrible conditions, it doesn't want to abandon its etheric body and fights to retain it. It feels this is the link that connects it with the only world that it has ever known. It wanders like that lonely and unhappy until extreme tiredness forces it to finally leave the etheric body. Then it transitions to astral life, which it could have entered immediately after getting rid of its physical body, without feeling pain and unpleasantness.

However, before this happens, the soul despairs because of the necessity to leave its own etheric body (which, as we remember, it considers its physical body) and often tries to blindly take over the physical body of another person. It's very determined and in many cases it succeeds. This is how possessions happen from the etheric level. I dedicated an entire book, *Possessed by Ghosts* to this, and in it I described possessions and its effects. I recommend this book to people who are interested in this topic.

HOW DO POSSESSIONS OCCUR?

Because souls who refused to transition to the other side are commonly called ghosts I also use this term. Sometime after death of the physical body a ghost slowly notices that he is running out of energy and doesn't know where to get renewed energy from. If he were in contact with others ghosts, then he would certainly realize, how to manage, but at the beginning he wouldn't notice his companions and is therefore left on his own. He is blinded by the fear of death because he doesn't know that he died a long time ago. He becomes weaker and weaker, more and more apathetic and has great difficulty thinking. Instinctively self-preservation kicks in. On Earth, there are many places ghosts can draw energy from. Those are water veins and faults. Some ghosts find these places. They don't realize that on the other side of death's curtain they could lead a wonderful, care-free life full of love. When there was an occasion for that, they didn't have enough courage to believe in a forgiving God. They weren't capable of forgiving themselves and they were afraid of punishment so they didn't transition to the other side. Now they don't know how to do this, and therefore, according to them their fate has already been preordained. Sometimes they are being sought by loved ones, by souls who died earlier and are already on the other side of the curtain. Sometimes they very much love a missing ghost and decide to resign from living in "heaven". So they lower their vibrations and transition through the curtain to rescue him. Sometimes the search lasts a very long time and is completely ineffectual. This happens because this is an unnatural process. Sometimes an intercession prayer by people on Earth helps ghosts, and then one of the spiritual guides comes to rescue him and transition him to the other side. When this doesn't help, one needs to ask an exorcist for help. I met many ghosts who spent hundreds of years suspended between "heaven" and "earth" and some of them were from previous millenniums. Such ghosts usually can only be helped accidentally when leading other ghosts away.

Many ghosts don't know from what source to take energy and often decide to steal it. Some of them don't see anything wrong with it while others feel bad, thinking that they are doing something punishable. The latter ones most often don't attach themselves to a specific person, but draw energy from various people little by little. Most often they dwell in places where there are large groups of people. All ghosts who don't transition to the other side of the curtain must find a source of energy in order to function. They could ask for it from God, but they don't want to or they don't have courage. They rather steal it from an animal, human or plant.

In order to better understand what this looks like, I would try to illustrate this by comparing it with diving under water. At the very beginning of diving we feel perfect, we look at the beauty of nature and make a decision to stay under water forever. We don't consider that this is an unnatural environment for us. We see only what we want to see. We think: "It is so wonderful here, and only unpleasantness awaits us up there, perhaps even punishment. There is nothing to think about. We are staying". We are alone, finally free and happy. But what is this? Slowly we notice that we start to run out of air. We didn't anticipate that. We wanted to outsmart nature, but nature is a lot more intelligent than it seemed. We notice the boat which we arrived in is long gone. Where do we get air from? We are afraid that we would die soon. We notice a fish swimming by and we wonder whether it would be possible to steal a little bit of oxygen from it. Miraculously, we did it, somehow. We feel relief, we can breathe again. As we continue to draw air from it, unknowingly we enter its interior. We know we didn't become a fish, but through the fish we could at least for some time function, admire the views, and most of all avoid the unpleasantness and punishment.

A ghost who decided not to transition to the other side of death's curtain often returns to the family it recently left. In his home there is grief. Everyone is heartbroken, glum, and discouraged. Mourners would very often give anything to turn back time so that the soul of their beloved could be with them in the world of the living. By behaving like this they prevent the spirit from leaving. The entire time they are crying and begging: "Stay, don't go. How are we going to live without you?" This is a very egoistic approach to life and it's a sign that we don't understand the essence of death. You could say that you did this because the loss hurt you so much, because the despair overcame you. You could say that you were losing your mind, you weren't yourself, and you weren't able to think about anything else. I understand you perfectly well. After the death of my mother, for half a year I was also unable to live. If it wasn't for her attitude and her request that I not hold her back in this world I certainly wouldn't have let her leave for the other side of the curtain. Assuredly, you remember how I described her clinical death. She returned from it and cautioned me, that she couldn't die, because I didn't want to let her go. I resigned myself to her death because I loved her so much. I gave her freedom, but still suffered greatly. I mourned so deeply, that were it not for my newborn daughter and my six year old son the world would have stopped having meaning for me. Only my little ones mattered to me at that point, and also how to take care of them. Besides that I wasn't capable of anything else and I didn't even remember what was happening with me and around me.

I am not trying to convince you not to mourn. Mourning needs to be experienced with as much intensity as is possible. This is very important for our psychological health. We were left alone, unhappy, often lost and with lots of problems which perhaps, we had never dealt with before. Let's give ourselves as much time as we need. This is a time during which we should only think about ourselves and those who are in the same situation as us. I strongly appeal to you however, to let a deceased person leave even when we feel that this is not good for us and when everything insides us rebels against doing so.

When a ghost who didn't go to the other side of death's curtain returns to its family and the family desired it return, it doesn't have even the smallest problem finding a source of energy. It simply attaches itself to family members and draws energy from them. Mourners usually are so heartbroken because of the misfortune, that at the beginning they don't notice that ghost penetrated one of them. When they do notice, often it's already too late for a reaction. Fortunately, this only applies to adults.

Most children come to this world with special protection. Unfortunately, ghosts sometimes also steal energy, and sometimes the body as well, from young children. I described quite a number of such cases in the book *Possessed by Ghosts*, in chapters on homosexuality, mental illnesses and autism.

In a normal psychological state, someone wouldn't allow anyone to take away his energy or allow himself to be penetrated. Ghosts feel this and look for people who would allow themselves to be compromised in this way, so that they could attach to them permanently, like leeches. They steal energy from people who are weak, sick, old, under the influence of alcohol or drugs, tired, sleepy, upset and depressed and frightened; in order words from people who are already short of energy. They can't feel the ghost's activity and react appropriately. Quite often a person in this situation doesn't suspect that he has a companion who comes for daily food for the energy which God gave him. He loses health and strength without knowing why. Ghosts who do this can cause exhaustion in someone's body, which could then cause serious illnesses, and sometimes even death. They often remain outside of the person, but sometimes they can accidently enter the person. This is like a ghost walking past a hidden entrance and accidently leaning against a door which opened, and it fell inside. This is exactly what occurs when a person is possessed by a ghost that didn't plan it or meant for it to happen.

There are ghosts, who consciously stay in this world and need a body. It's not enough for them to be attached to someone in order to steal energy. They demand a body so that they could function in our world. Therefore, they look for a victim from whom they could steal it. From the moment they possess a person, besides his own spirit there is also a spirit of someone else inside him. It's not rare that one person is possessed by a few or even a dozen or more ghosts. Often these ghosts don't know anything about each other. Most likely, the person doesn't know about them either that they possessed him because he lost consciousness. His loved ones notice it quicker, but when they tell him, he simply doesn't believe them. It is conceivable that at any point in time h there could be more than a hundred such uninvited guests in a living person. The Holy Bible uses the word "legion" to describe such a large of ghosts.

When one ghost attaches itself to a healthy and strong person it could initially go unnoticed. Admittedly, he would feel a loss of energy, but most likely he would blame it on the weather or tiredness due to work or school. When a few attach, things start to change. The person becomes apathetic, sleepy, and doesn't want to do anything, and is also very sensitive. Sometimes he becomes sick. But at the beginning he doesn't notice that something is not right with him.

Ghosts prefer to draw energy from healthy, strong people or function in such a body. How is it possible, some people might ask, that a ghost could penetrate a person's body? It often occurs when we lose awareness for some reason, for example, when we have surgery and go under anesthesia. Another opportunity for a ghost is those moments when we lose consciousness, even for few seconds when we are hit in the head or during when we experience accident related shock. All events filled with alcohol are also the perfect opportunity for a ghost. Teenagers more and more reach for drugs and open themselves up to penetration by ghosts. Even moments of small change in consciousness, such as during smoking a cigarette enables possession by a ghost. Sometimes when we are sick, discouraged, we unconsciously allow ghosts to appear in our body. During mourning we are practically helpless when we immerse in despair for the dead person and open ourselves to that side. Then a large number of ghosts could possess us. Not only the ghost of the deceased person could possess us, but also those ghosts which are nearby. When we play with séances, especially when we don't know anything about it, it is possible that ghosts could permanently enter the bodies and minds of the participants. You need to be able to lead away ghosts that are summoned, but people who organize these séances don't know that. Moreover, most people, who call themselves distinguished experts in this area, are possessed by ghosts (people who truly understand this world wouldn't touch it just as someone doesn't put their fingers inside an electrical outlet). It's easy to be possessed when we play with tarot cards, not knowing much about it, or when we meditate in an inappropriate way. Ghosts often attach themselves to people or penetrate them, when they lose control over their emotions and have a tendency to identify with negative energies such as anger, hatred etc. Never however be afraid that ghosts would attack or possess you because that acts like a magnet. If you will live consciously, nothing bad would happen to you. And even if in some way you attract ghosts to yourself, once you stay attentive, you would recognize it and won't be interested in its thoughts and emotions, and it would quickly get bored and leave. A conscious life is the best, constant protection from ghosts. It is like an alarm's sensor detecting the presence of strangers non-stop.

Ghosts usually attach themselves to an unaware person. It does this because it seems to him that it is the only way to access energy. It is similar to when it penetrates a human's body. It may know that it is doing a wrong thing, but it seems to him that he won't be able to exist and all the more to act, as he would like to. This is more of self-preservation or survival instincts, than the ghost's maliciousness, a many people think.

At the beginning, after penetrating a person, a ghost is as

intimidated as anyone who has found himself in a new situation. He doesn't as yet know how to behave, how much he can allow himself to do. He simply investigates the area. A lot depends of which ghost penetrates which person. A ghost is looking for a person who functions on similar vibrations. If he was aggressive while he was alive then he would look for a person with similar tendencies. This works on the basis of attracting similarities. In this way, a greedy person after penetration of by ghost would be even greedier, a jealous person even more jealous. Each specific characteristic would be amplified. That is why at the beginning it's hard to figure out that something isn't right. When, for example, a person gets unusually upset about his friend's behavior at work, he would think that the surroundings caused his excessive reaction, in this case a friend at work, but not a ghost. When a person gets penetrated by a ghost acting on different vibrations, it could be different. None of his faults would be strengthen, instead different ones would appear, which until then he didn't have at all. A common characteristic for people possessed by ghosts is increased sensitivity on one hand, evidenced by contentiousness, sometimes outbursts of rage at the least expected moments, and on the other hand sleepiness, lack of enthusiasm and crying. The person would begin to have mood swings: from great excitement to great depression. A person, who until then was psychologically and physically strong, wouldn't really know what to do now. This would be equally burdensome for him as it is for his loved ones.

When a ghost is unsuccessful in possessing a living person its life gradually starts changing. With time it realizes that something in its life has changed, but it doesn't know exactly what yet. It realizes this when it could see its friends in the physical world but cannot communicate with them in any way. It notices that when it talks to them they don't respond, and when it touches them, they don't sense anything. But it also tells itself that it is all a dream or it offended them in some way. That is because the ghost, at all costs wants to believe that it didn't die, that it still lives in the physical world (since it is still conscious of itself. And why would it think differently?).

THE EFFECTS OF FEARING DEATH

If you agreed with the death of your physical body, while leaving the material plane you would be sufficiently awake for nothing bad to threaten you. If that applies to you, in the future would not need to be concerned about the consequences I write about below.

Things are different when you are frightened by the thought of dying as you approach death, you would escape into unawareness (which happens automatically to most people.). Besides being wrapped in an etheric body, which I described above, you would be at risk of different, yet more serious consequences. The cause of all of them is the fear of death. If you are afraid of death in your lifetime, then know that while dying this fear would intensify in you and you would find yourself in a state similar to panic. You already know that when you have fear you would resist death want to preserve your life, wrapping yourself in your etheric body, mistakenly considering it your physical body. Such defense reaction would cause you to stop being aware of yourself and what is happening around you. When someone doesn't want to be conscious of himself and escapes into unawareness due to panic, the situation would be used by his astral consciousness. The astral consciousness is a consciousness of your astral body, which moves around in the astral world (it is comparable to the way the physical body moves around in the physical world). The emotional body and astral world are built on emotions.

In physical life, sometimes you burst out with uncontrollable emotions. If you don't want to have control over them, they start to have control over you. In essence they take control of you. It's the same when you don't have a physical body. If you express a desire to be unconscious (because of your fear) then your astral body starts to act for you. It's goal is survival, hence it would try to form its own particles so as to not only withstand the attack of death, but also any other attack to which it could be exposed in the future. An astral matter is a lot thinner that physical matter and this characteristic allow it to maneuver the particles of a human's astral body. Therefore when formed the stronger ones, created from the thickest matter, lay on the outside, creating a barrier or hard shell – obviously for astral condition, resembling a coconut. The identical process occurs during your physical life when you decide not to take control of yourself in challenging situations and have outburst of negative emotions. However we don't deal with regroupings of matter permanently, because when you calm down this state ends. The rest of cells, the weaker ones, or in other words, the more delicate and more subtle ones form on the inside in a shape resembling the structure of a coconut. When you desire unconsciousness (due to your fear of death,) after getting rid of your physical body and transitioning to your astral body, the consciousness of the astral body forms cells in concentrated layers along the same lines. Subtle particles are placed closer to the center because they are too delicate and therefore useless for defense. Therefore, there are particles of panic, fear, anger, hatred, rage and malediction on the outside of this structure. Then there are more subtle emotions, such as sympathy, and hidden on the inside is love, affection, and sympathy. Its composition in this way resembles a coconut. Its structure could be compared to a coconut because of its very hard outer shell and the delicate contents on the inside (like coconut milk). From a different perspective it could also be said to resemble an onion somewhat, with it characteristic concentric layers.

The astral consciousness creates this cocoon as a durable barrier from death, in case of friction, so that it could stay as long as possible. I ask you to recall what I wrote about the caterpillar in a cocoon. In order for it to get out of the cocoon and transform into a butterfly, it has to have a consciousness of itself. Otherwise she won't fly up to the sun, but rather remain forever in a cocoon. It is similar with a human but not exactly the same. He also needs to remain conscious of himself, however unlike the butterfly not so as to get out of the cocoon, but rather so as not to get enclosed in such a cocoon. People allow their astral consciousness (focused on survival) such maneuvers, because they mistakenly belief that it acts in a mutually beneficial way. Just like the astral matter, they don't want to die and fight against death fiercely. In the astral matter's limited understanding it is helping, but does it really do so to the advantage of the real human?

In a moment you would get a chance to see, that a person enclosed in such a cocoon loses greatly as a result. Why does someone allow one to be created therefore? Because he doesn't want to be conscious of himself and more often than not acts automatically. When a tough situation presents itself, he chooses unconsciousness, thinking: "Whatever happens, it happens. I don't want to know anything about it". On the one hand he does this because of fear, and on the other hand because of habit. Ultimately, it is identical to how he has behaved most of his lifetime. When a situation came that was emotionally challenging, he chose unconsciousness by drinking alcohol, smoking a cigarette, taking drugs, being a workaholic, being a sex addict, or losing himself in other addictions in order to at least, for a moment not be conscious. People who escape into unconsciousness don't realize that they have no control over something that they escape into, but obviously they think the opposite. The same type of behavior is activated inside of them upon death. They don't realize that even a short period of unconsciousness can result in various, very serious personal consequences. During physical life, drunkenness or drug addiction could very easily lead to an accident; after death it could come to the regrouping of the astral body from which a cocoon is created.

Dear reader, the astral body doesn't have to regroup at all. When astral matter moves around freely in the entire astral body the person would be free. He was already free during his lifetime and now he would also be free after the death of his physical body. When he is not afraid of death, there is no need to escape into unconsciousness, hence in his case the maneuvers of the astral essence doesn't take place. In order to have a control over it, we must be fully aware (only then do we have a chance to control our emotions) and conscious of ourselves as a whole, not just of the physical aspect of our existence. We could then decide whether our astral body should regroup and, if we belief that it is inappropriate for us, we could oppose it. However, we can't impact the physical or the astral worlds unless we are conscious of them and know the rules that guide their operation.

Unfortunately, with regret I must say that people's knowledge in this area is anchored too deep in the physical world. They are constantly reaffirming to themselves the mistaken belief that everything they have is tied to their physical body which they want to preserve at all costs for as long as they can. They are very much afraid of death and because of that they escape into unconsciousness during their lifetime. And what happens to them after death? Unwittingly, they allow for the regrouping of their own astral body in order to preserve it for as long as they can as well. They don't know or don't want to know or realize that they are aimlessly and in vain fighting death for their body (first the physical and later the astral body). After all, it's their own soul that chose to abandon the body, because it didn't need a body anymore. However they don't want to know that and as a consequence there is this bitter fight.

Dear reader, as you can see, everything depends on the state of consciousness. When we are conscious of Life as a whole, not only of the physical aspect of it, then we are also prepared for the respective stages of it. When we don't know anything about the topic, most often we mistakenly think that we don't have influence over anything and what's worse that everything happens on its own that someone, some savior would take care of everything for us. It's not advisable to travel far away unprepared and death in some sense is such a trip. Leaving everything up to fate could bring great unpleasantness, and in fact possibly also tragic consequences in the future. If we don't familiarize ourselves with the topic of death, at the moment we leave our physical body a fight occurs within us which is not won by the strongest, but by the most conscious. If someone doesn't take care to consciously ensure his own future happiness, the cells of his astral body, also known as his astral essence, would do this at the expense of his suffering. When a person remains fully conscious, both sides benefit from it: his real human body and his astral body.

In the book, *In the Wheel of Life*, you can learn a lot more on this topic. Now, I would just say that the regrouped astral body in a cocoon could as well be called a suffering body. For the average person, let's say a kind person for instance, this could entail many unpleasant consequences. In the case of a person who during his lifetime was very selfish, this body is downright insufferable. Furthermore, in the latter case it is extremely strong. It is very hard to break it and any outside help is quite often impossible.

AN OVERVIEW OF LIFE

At the moment of death, even an unexpected death, the person who dies reviews his entire life after adequate rest. Everything he experienced in his past incarnation moves in front of him down to the smallest details. He sees every second of his existence, even those periods where he was not active were recorded and saved. He would review everything like a member of the audience in a movie theater, but he is simultaneously the viewer and the principal actor. He recognizes the causes and the effects of his actions. Only now, in the light of truth, he would recognize what kind of person he truly was without embellishment and without lying to himself. He would see all his good and bad moments, all his highs and lows, what he loved and what he despised, what he achieved, what he could have achieved or do better at, what made him happy and what made him cry. He would recognize what he should have learned, but he didn't despite having so many opportunities to learn which he missed out on.

He would look at each of his relationships separately. He would recall all his conversations. He would analyze reasons for his actions. He would also feel what other people felt in a given moment. He would feel their fear, pain, confusion, intimidation, rejection, etc.; everything that he had earlier caused. He would look at the good and bad moments which had some meaning to him. Even the most hidden and shameful ones, when he was upset, when he felt sorry for himself, and he would also look at those moments where he was proud and happy. He would now know that everything, literally everything, each attitude and opinion were a source of positive or negative energy that he was fully responsible for.

Do you better understand now, why among other things, we should not disturb a deceased person? Why the living should remain calm and peaceful? Our laments and cries bother our loved one at this very important moment.

Following are a few descriptions of the life overview after death: Andrew understood that his life was full of greed, violence, falsehood, hatred and prejudices towards others. This ultimately led him to experience great violence. He understood why his house was burnt and his wife killed accidently while she was inside the house. After his wife's death, he realized that love was comforting at each painful moment and his role was not to punish or judge people, even those who had burnt his house and were indirectly responsible for his wife's death (karma and Divine laws take care of that). His task was to understand and forgive this. Unfortunately he wasn't able to do that and he died embittered.

Matthew, the manager of a large company, understood that he shouldn't judge people too quickly. Everyone had to be honest in their dealings with others. It was only after death that he noticed how many lives he had ruined due to rushed decisions and judgments he had made.

Melanie, a beautiful woman and model, came to this world with the task of believing in herself, but unfortunately she was unable to accomplish this. She was supposed to believe in her own feelings and instincts and not allow herself to be constantly influenced by others, especially men. While dying, she noticed that they had supremacy over her, because she did not believe in herself. She had given them too much power, simultaneously taking it away from herself. She had felt this throughout her life, but could not put an end to it because she did not love and accept herself.

Christina, a homemaker and mother of three kids, immediately noticed that she learned great anger and assumed an air of self-importance towards people instead of learning the opposite. This resulted in her not having control over her life. She desired to boss people around, but couldn't. She understood the deeper cause of this state of affairs: from the very beginning she felt condemned. She did not have a cheerful outlook about life, she did not have faith and she constantly had doubts. She came to the world to learn to believe; but she chose doubt instead of faith. She also inculcated this in her children.

Richard, an entrepreneur, was lost all his life. He was also here to learn about having faith, but he had difficulties learning this. He was supposed to belief people who were trustworthy, but he couldn't distinguish them from those people who were not. Therefore, he spent his entire life thinking b that everyone wanted to hurt him. He did not want to believe anyone, so he disbelieved everyone, even his loved ones and people he knew well. He kept a great distance between himself and people and situations he could have benefited from, and got entangled with people he should not had kept in contact with.

As you can see, dear reader, during our life on Earth each one of us has to take care of ourselves, and what directly affects us and compromises us as a whole. Certainly, each one of us has to learn many lessons, but we always learn them one at a time. When we pass one, we can deal with next one, never sooner. When we have already learned all of our lessons we would understand what our fellow human beings need and what they lack. We would become a harmonious unity.

In almost all cases, leaving the physical body is completely painless. Even after a long and serious illness, you would see peace, comfort and a smile on a dead person's face. The consciousness of the real human leaves the physical body and for a short time stops in his etheric double. This is the exact moment mentioned earlier that constitutes whether we are dying consciously. It's not essential, if we are dealing with a sudden death or if the death is preceded by illness or old age. What is critical however, is the extent to which we familiarize ourselves with the topic of death during our physical lifetime.

THE TRANSFORMATION KNOWN AS DEATH

Many people lack the consciousness that they have an astral body in which they spend quite a lot of time at nights during their lifetime. Hence, after the death of their physical body they don't recognize that they are already in it (this is the result of their mistaken beliefs). Some people are deluded into thinking that after the death of our physical body some noticeable changes would occur, however nothing would change at all. They are not aware when they enter the astral world just as they were not aware of their astral body during their lifetime.

When we are conscious of ourselves and know enough about death, there is no need to be afraid of life after death. There is no prize awaiting us in the form of a so called "heaven" or a punishment by a harsh God in the form of a "hell" or "purgatory". We would only find the results of what we believed in, thought, felt, did and spoke about during life in our physical body. Nobody forces us to do anything, or awards us, or even punishes us there. If you died at this moment you would live the same as you did until now.

After the death of your physical body, you awaken to the consciousness of the astral body and see exactly what you got used to in the physical world. Up to this point you would not have realized that the astral world is an accurate copy of the physical world, therefore you wouldn't quite understand exactly what was happening to you. Since you still have the consciousness of yourself, it would seem to you that that is proof that you did not die at all, that you are still alive in your physical body.

In order to have a comprehensive understanding of this, imagine that at this very moment, in a fraction of a second for some reason the physical world ceased to exist. You would still do the same thing that you are doing at this exact moment, with one difference; you wouldn't already be in a physical reality. Most likely you wouldn't realize that at all. You would still see the walls of your home, outside the same trees, streets and the same people, in other words everything that you were used to observing. Consequentially, for many people it is difficult to recognize the fact of their own death. They could still hear, see, think, and feel while in their imagination death means that they should become a stiff corpse with no feeling and movement. For this reason most people in that situation desire to return to their physical live (because of their fear of the unknown, among other things), and only a few decide to go further. For those who remain on this side of the curtain and decide not to do the right thing, in order words to depart to higher worlds, I dedicated an entire book *Possessed by Ghosts.*

They remain stuck between "heaven" and "earth" because religions do not teach their followers what to do in the netherworld, meaning in the astral world. One references the "Last Judgment", but not what to do until then: just lie there and wait for it, or wander around? Therefore, priests of these religions don't have the correct knowledge on this topic themselves. In my practice I have met with tens of priests, nuns and monks of all religions who were already on the other side as ghosts but were having serious problem with their further existence. Hence, my confidence in the importance of familiarizing yourself (during your lifetime) with what awaits you after your physical death. It would preempt many unneeded fears, tensions and suffering.

If every person learned more about life after death during his physical life, he would have a guideline, sort of a roadmap which would help him to move around the new territory that is the astral world. Instead, most people have many misguided concepts which create a flawed roadmap that every now and then fails them. Throughout their entire life they were told to believe in something, what in a face of real existence in astral body is senseless. False perceptions instead of leading to the astral life of peace and blissfulness as God intended from the beginning, for most people starts a real "hell", created as a consequence of accepting those perceptions. Therefore, instead of living in truth they continue the deluded existence which they created with their perceptions during their physical lifetime.

RETURNING HOME

When a soul decides to leave and the physical body dies, the person's consciousness, with astonishment sees that he is still alive. He is in energetic body, even though his physical body is wept for and buried in the ground. For the consciousness this fact could remain unnoticed. It sees itself as such during its physical lifetime – still sees, hears, feels warmth, coldness, hunger, thirst.

After leaving its physical body, the soul notices other loving souls around him, souls that died earlier who were now waiting to greet him and guide him in the further journey. The Guardian Angels and Spiritual Guides who loves also wait for him. We easily recognize them. In this important moment, no soul is left without help or left alone. There is a wonderful, ceremonial atmosphere, full of cheerful expectation before the great journey. The soul is free of earthly matters then, and with the assistance of loving beings moves slowly towards the Light that radiates with love and happiness. It feels safe because it knows that it is loved and expected. Souls who were exhausted by sickness, unconscious or semi-conscious before death, because for example, they were given strong painkillers, now receive special help. This could be compared to the medical help they received here on Earth. Strength is brought back to these spirits in order to allow them to go on with their further journey.

I already described how the transition behind death's curtain towards "heaven" looks. Unfortunately, few people decide to go that way. Only those persons who were trustful and are conscious of themselves, of their own life, of death during their life on Earth transition this way. They were honest with themselves, with their loved ones and with God. They were all mature souls internally; they were harmonized during their lifetime and at peace with themselves and with the world. These souls were warm and heartfelt people during their existence on Earth. While living they already knew what would happen with them when they died. They did not have to be anybody special. Many of them led the life of an average person on Earth. They experienced emotions like everyone, had various things on their consciousness, they experienced highs and lows and successes and failures. Sometimes like all of us they did something which would not have pleased God or did not do something, which according to them, God expected of them. This could have been one, or many constantly repeated faults. These are so-called sins that the Church talks about. Many souls who transitioned to the Light had many faults and displayed many negative emotions. They could have been jealous, greedy or lazy at times. They could have cheated, stolen something, betrayed someone, manipulated others in order to gain something, gossiped, criticized, mocked, or eaten meat on a Friday, didn't go to church on Sundays or didn't have control over themselves and started fights, etc. Obviously, not all sins listed here were committed simultaneously or by one person.

However, it is human to make mistakes or to have sins on our consciousness. What we call a sin is basically a lesson which we have to learn here on Earth. A person has to learn that each act carries specific consequences. In Eastern culture they call this karma; Jesus said about it "As you sow, so shall you reap." I would describe this in the following way. When we do, speak and think good, we receive goodness. When we do, think and speak bad, we receive evil. Each soul was here on Earth many times and what it has learned hundred percent, consist of its consciousness. Consciousness is nothing but the memory of what we have already learned. For example, we remember not to steal, because in another life we stole something and we were publicly flogged or had a finger or hand cut off, or perhaps even lost our life. Now, when we have an occasion to steal something our consciousness speak to us saying it is better not to do that because it could end poorly for us. The person who listens to his own consciousness is calm, because he knows he is doing right. The person who proceeds against his own consciousness exposes himself to various consequences due to his actions. Either way, your consciousness speaks again and again in the form of guilt. We would say: "I have pangs of conscious". However it only speaks when we have already passed a given lesson.

Things are different when it comes to a lesson which a person didn't yet pass – then our consciousness would not suggest anything to us. Let's say that a soul in any incarnation didn't work on the subject of betrayal yet. Opportunities to betray would show up in her life one after the other. She must ex-

perience what it means to betray and suffer all the consequences; or be betrayed and feel the pain associated with it.

At that moment, it is good to rely on intuition, turn to a
wise family member or the environment in which one lives.
However, there is no guarantee that we would listen and do the
right thing. Whatever we do, it would be good for us even if we
react incorrectly. This would become the topic of one of the lessons we came to Earth to learn. We would gain a chance to
make a mistake and learn from our discomfort how to act correctly.

So, the only souls that go to "heaven" are those which at
the moment of death are reconciled with their own life and have
a clear consciousness. Certainly, they committed sins in their
lifetime, but they were able to forgive themselves and others.
Deep inside they knew that sins, even the biggest ones, were just
lessons to be passed. And, before death, these souls finished
their matters on Earth. They said goodbye to their loved ones,
family, possessions, and work without sorrow. Detachment from
earthly matters let them go forward, not looking back, not re-
gretting anything that they left behind. They believed in a loving
and forgiving God. In their lifetime they decided what they
would do when they died, not leaving anything up to chance.

Consciousness of the So-Called "Heaven"

When a soul frees itself from its physical and etheric bodies, it leads further life in its astral body. That is nothing new for a soul. It enters the same body it was in each night during sleep, in which it freely moved around wherever it desired. During our physical life we live in the physical sphere as well as in the spiritual. We are simultaneously alive on both these planes. Most people are not fully conscious of this state that is why when they die, they don't recognize it as there is not much change between both worlds; they don't recognize that they don't have their physical body anymore.

This is also why, dear reader, quite often a person enters "Heaven", but is not aware that he has done so. It's too similar to the physical world. The only difference is that we have to wait for what think about to materialize in the physical world, however in the astral world everything materializes immediately. That is because astral matter reacts on the person's thoughts and desires with a greater ease and speed than in the physical world. And as a result everything materializes around the person immediately, without any delay. That includes not only his wishes, but unfortunately also his worries, fears and concerns. Imagine his fascination, when he desires something and it immediately appears in front of him. Now imagine a person who is frightened by something. This would immediately materialize in front of him as well. What that person desired, feared and was concerned about in his physical world would later dictate his further life in the astral world: how it would proceed and whether it would be a happy existence or not.

Let's say that he thought "Oh, how would I manage here?" suddenly, in the same breathe, he would face challenges that he couldn't manage no matter what. If he thought "I hope nobody assaults me (robs or kills me)?" he would immediately be assaulted (robbed or killed). And, if he thought "How beautiful it is here…" right away it would be a wonderful world in front of him or if he thought "How beautiful and free it is to live here" immediately he would be living like that. In the physical world all our thoughts also come true, however in the physical world we have to wait for the results.

After leaving their physical body many people are unable to understand the laws that apply in the astral world. As a result they don't take advantage of its specifics as they still have a body as they did in their physical life – because the astral body is an exact copy of the physical body – they are unable to understand and accept that one of the great advantages of living in the astral world is a lack of tiredness and complete freedom from many things essential to the physical world, such as eating and drinking.

Therefore, although people are freed from eating, sleeping and going to work etc., they still cook, and eat food and work. Those needs in turn force many others burdensome activities upon them, such as shopping, preparation of meals and cleaning. They garden, build homes and many others things which they customarily did. When for example, they build a home, they still laboriously carry bricks and plaster, even though they could think "build a home" and it would appear in front of them in a second. In order to achieve this, they would have to see a ready to move in home with all its comforts, instead, they just see individual stages of the construction of a house. During work they could make the plaster or bricks light in weight, they could remove the need to climb to different floors and use doors to go from one room to the other. Instead of walking they could comfortably float in the air. However they are used to slogging around so it is hard for them to accept that it could be different. When they do notice that it is possible to do things through thoughts that were impossible to achieve in the physical world, they would think that it only seems that way or that it is only a dream.

As a person stays longer in the astral world he would gradually start noticing the differences between the astral and physical worlds. He would better understand the astral world. Ultimately, he would recognize that he stopped being tired, feeling pain and that he is younger, more skilled and freer. Then the moment would arrive where he fully realizes that he is not living his physical life anymore and he doesn't have a material body. Only then does he have an opportunity for real life in "Heaven".

THE TRUE LIFE BEHIND DEATH'S CURTAIN

Some people call this place "Heaven", others "Paradise", and yet others "Eden". And even though there are many names defining it, they all reference the same place. This is not yet the true "heaven", but it is a small part of it. It seems to be "Heaven" because self-conscious people can create everything they desire there (we are talking here about the higher astral world). Space does not play any role and as a result each conscious person can have his own universe, not only homes, gardens, parks, theaters, museums, schools and villages or cities.

Hence, each conscious resident of the astral world creates the conditions he wishes to live in and the scenery. He chooses what he considers to be beautiful and desirable, whatever seems essential to his new life.

In the astral world each person imagines his reality differently, therefore great diversification prevails there. This is obviously not needed to live there. Many people, however, to feel safe, imagine their own surroundings and create it to their liking. Rules we should live by do not exist there. That is why it is only then that we discover who we really are and what desires we have. Everything is realized immediately there, after our thoughts and feelings appear. Obviously, everyone can, at any moment, change their desires whenever and to whatever they want. I would repeat however that these types of actions are reserved only for those people who are self-aware and with the understanding that they have accepted their death. Many don't do this at all, because they are not aware that something like this is even possible. Most residents of the astral world create unconsciously at the beginning, but with time even they begin to understand that matter is an illusion and only thought is actually real. From that moment on they start creating consciously.

If we were able to see this with our physical eye we would see beautiful lakes, magnificent mountains and wonderful gardens which exceed in their beauty anything that exists in the physical world. We would also see things so wonderful that for many of us living in the physical world would seem to be too fantastic, almost unbelievable. However for residents of the astral world their reality is as real and as tangible as houses, churches or schools built from brick and stone are to us. A great number of people live happily in a fantastic, quite fairy-tale-like environment for many years, continually creating anew their environment with the help of their thoughts.

Everyone creates for himself. When people want to be together they collectively "paint" or imagine things so that together they could create a collective reality. If they want to be together, they have to create collectively, otherwise their individual creativity would separate them from each other, and as a result they would be on their own, in the world they created.

People who are together have to be connected by common goals and passion. This would be due to vibrations based on the principle like attracts like. Even though anyone could live with anyone in the astral world, just as they do in the physical world, people group based on various commonalities: religion, nationality and interests. Those people feel a mutual attraction and create groups, the same as they did in the physical world. Therefore, in the astral world nobody lacks companions.

Members of different groups could obviously visit each other, nobody forbids this, but more often than not they prefer to spend time in a group of their own friends. Our lesson on this and the other world is to get closer, not only to those people who have the same vibrations as us, but also with those whose vibrations are different from ours.

As you can see, dear reader, in the astral world which is commonly called "heaven," a person is really free, could do whatever he wants, whenever he wants and pass his time as he pleases. However not all people take advantage of the wonderful possibilities provided to them by the astral world, in other words by "heaven". Why? It is because they are constantly looking for "heaven".

IN SEARCH OF HEAVEN AND GOD

Dear reader, did you realize that a large number of souls in the astral world still search for God and heaven, even though it is already there for a long time? They do not see God, or heaven, or the promised prize. How is that possible? Well, most people had a mistaken concept of heaven and God during their lifetime. Many souls search for God in so-called "heaven", however no matter how great their efforts are, they are unable to find Him. Sometimes this lasts entire centuries and is ineffective, not only because God is not there, but also because of their mistaken assumptions.

It is not about a single follower, who made a mistake because he incorrectly understood his religious teachings, but about the majority of souls, even those dedicated followers who the Church deceived with its mistaken teachings, including obviously, priests, monks and nuns as well.

Dear reader, perhaps you don't realize how great a problem this is. In today's world around 150 thousand people die every day. In their lifetime they lived in various places on the globe and followed different religions. Each religion, and there are countless, points to the existence of a different God and therefore to different "heavens". Imagine the prevailing chaos when, after the death of the physical body each of them tries to find a path to their own "heaven". The problem is not the amount of religions, or their geographic location, but the mistaken belief system they were taught by their religion and to which they remain faithful after death.

Each of the deceased people believed in his own religion and at times was too extremely loyal to his religion yet he did not feel God in his physical lifetime. Over the millenniums nothing changed in this matter. To prevent followers from rebelling and leaving, most religions found a solution.

Knowing that it is not able to arrange a meeting between followers and God in this life, they postponed this for after death. Followers were convinced that they do not need to see God because they are sinners and unworthy of Him, however if they will die with devotion, God would take them in. They would not only see Him then, but they would also receive a prize for being loyal to their religion.

This explains why even the most devoted follower, priest, monk or nun, waste their current life in search of God somewhere outside of himself, even though this doesn't make any sense. Many of them even when they feel Him deep inside their heart do not trust themselves and do not believe that this is possible, because their religion claims otherwise. This isn't a characteristic of only one religion. Many religions want their followers to search for God the outside of themselves and in most cases they successfully convince these followers.

Lost souls, who stubbornly search for God after the death of their physical body, would have believed in their Church unreservedly at one time. In their innocence they sacrificed their life for faith, in order to receive a generous prize for their sacrifice after their physical death. This explains why in one religion people fast and hurt themselves, and in another people are willingly to sacrifice their life as a suicide bomber and yet in another they waste their life in the mistaken belief that the Savior has already atoned for all of their sins. In their understanding, it is enough to just go to church and give a financial offering and expect God to take care of the rest.

It is easy to live so unaware on the physical plane. The difficulties only start after the death of the physical body. At that point person after person experiences great disappointment. They recognize then that nothing their religion told them is true. They go through life accepting that and after their physical death they find themselves trapped. They believed in their religion during their physical life and now after the death of their physical body they experience real horror. They search for God, but they can't Him. In their lifetime they were misled with the promise of a wonderful prize, and after death they got a different reality.

Perhaps you understand better now, why your loved one changed so much after becoming a ghost and also why ghosts that haunt churches are so vicious, lost and terrified. There are souls that instead of living according to God's intention, continuously wander around, because they are convinced beyond a doubt that God and the "Heaven" in which they believed really does exists and they have just lost the path to them. That is how they search, sometimes for a very long time, in vain.

I know about this, because on a daily basis I deal with ghosts disappointed in this way. I met thousands of them in my life. As I have already mentioned this group also includes priests, nuns and monks from all religions. Almost each one of them met all of the requirements of their respective religions, and now they wander around in the netherworld and do not know what to do about themselves. I am not only talking about those, who remained on this side of death's curtain and as ghosts cause problems for living people, but also those who trustfully transitioned beyond it. In their lifetime they bragged about belonging to a Church, they fasted, gave financial offerings and met all other religious requirements. They believed as deeply as possible in their church's dogmas. In the netherworld this deep faith instead of being their guide, misleads them. Basically, it could be said that it only seemed to them that they believed in God. They really believed in religion, but not in the true God. They believed in deceiving promises, and not Truth. And even if they gain a chance to understand this in the netherworld, they don't want to understand it. They search for God in the figure of a person and "Heaven" in the form of place, however nothing like that exists. But, they already have God in their heart; however they do not even try searching there.

Dear readers, these are not nonbelievers or people who go to church sporadically. Quite the opposite and that is why their faith is dogmas and happens to be so deep. Otherwise, considering alternatives would be a lot easier for such souls.

What they experience in the netherworld is a consequence of a deep belief in something, which isn't true. Since these people throughout their entire physical life relied on the teachings of their religion and turning to a God who was on the outside (sitting somewhere on a cloud), after physical death it's hard for them to look for Him elsewhere; on the inside, deep in their heart. They don't realize that in their lifetime, as well as after death they act like someone who is looking non-stop for his eyeglasses while there are right on top of his own nose.

However those persons who were not strongly connected to religious dogma or were not connected to it at all, have a lot easier life in that regard. They more easily accept the fact that they are already in "Heaven" and they enjoy being there. It was easier for them to find "Heaven", because they did not a have a prior misconception about it.

Perhaps you think a lack of faith is better because it prevents mistaken beliefs. However, a lack of faith causes souls to fail. Without God there is no life. A person who does not believe could squander not only his present incarnation, but also the next ones. This would last until his soul awakens.

Believers are more awakened and even though they are looking incorrectly, they do however believe that God exists and they are open to Him. Nonbelievers however do not want to awaken at all, because it seems to them that they don't have anything to awaken to. They think that after death there is only nothingness. Even when they awaken they do not know what to do with themselves. They do not have a goal. They wander around indefinitely until their consciousness changes. They leave things entirely up to chance. They do not realize how painful the results of such actions could be to them.

That is exactly why this book is written, so that you dear reader, could take a look at what lies beyond death's curtain and understand that it does not end our existence, and our further life will be determined by what we believe in. Only people who familiarize themselves with this knowledge fully and recognize it on the deeper level of their consciousness, will gain the chance to live the way they desire in the future. The time after death it is not the time to acquire this knowledge. That is the time to reap the rewards of many years' preparations. Someone who ignores death and does not want to know anything about it is not discharged from the effects of his "carelessness". After death there is no time for sorrow and excuses. You would have nobody to complain to. Besides, complain about what? That nobody told you what you didn't want to hear or think about, that God or some other higher power would take care of everything for you? Did lack of knowledge save anyone from the execution of the law? Could you protect yourself from an electric shock if you didn't know that electricity is flowing through the cable you are holding? It is identical with life and with the transition we popularly call "death". Therefore, knowledge of the visible and the invisible powers is an absolute necessity for us.

Most people do not realize that "Heaven" is a state of consciousness, not a specific place. It is an awareness of God and Truth that you can only reach during your lifetime.

Many people may ask why almost none of the major religions pass this basis knowledge on to their followers. One cause for this is the lack of awareness in priests, even in those priests who hold high positions in the religious hierarchy. Otherwise priests, monks, and nuns would not wander around after their death like most other souls. Members of church organizations simply do not know the truth. How this came about, you will find out shortly. Priests teach what they believe in. I am sure that they are not aware of the consequences of their teachings –souls wandering around in the other world.

This is also why, dear reader, you must rely on yourself, because only you can discover the reality in which you exist. Nobody could do it for you, because it is located inside of you, deep inside your heart. The person who takes steps towards that way would discover a true gift. Remember, that no matter what happens around you in this or the other world always listen to yourself, to what is inside you.

Dear reader, perhaps you are very devoted and loyal to your religion and my words cause you some discomfort, fear, disbelief and confusion. Remember, that these matters need to be understood while you still have a physical body. After death it is already too late. The basic problem is not a lack of faith in dogma created by human minds, but a lack of faith in the truth. Sickness or poverty is not a virtue or truth, even though many religions impose that as a belief.

MESSAGES

I would like to repeat that I do not condemn religions as such, and I do not claim that they are unnecessary or bad. I just want to say that the founders of most of them did not understand the intention of Jesus, Buddha, Mohammed or other Great Persons from whose inspiration they created various religions. Most of these religions were created by people who had nothing in common with These Great Enlightened Beings, for example because, they were born many years, sometimes hundreds of years later, therefore long ago after Their departure. These people only knew Their teachings from messages which circulated by word of mouth. The messages were not written down, because writing was not yet widespread.

A message can be interpreted differently by people based on the understanding of the receiving party. This is well demonstrated in the game Chinese whispers. Even when we provide a simple, longer text, along the way while it is being communicated by word of mouth, its content changes so much that at the end you don't know what the original message was about.

It is the same with gossip. There is a different intention at the beginning from what is seen at the end. Even if we give a message to only one person, it may be misunderstood and distorted.

I have experienced this many times myself. I gave interviews during which I said what I wanted to be written. Later I read the article with astonishment and thought that from what I said very little was understood and put to paper. If I did not demand prior authorization (that the editor send the text for verification prior to publication), nothing could be done about it, because the article would already be published. Even if the editor had good intentions, the fact remains however that readers of the article would be misled, despite my sincerest intent and the editor's goodwill.

It's the same with the Bible and New Testament. However, the biggest problem here is not that the interpreter incorrectly translated these works. Each interpreter translated the text the way he understood it. In order to understand a spiritualized text well, one has to be on a very high development level or have lived in the times during which the given text was created. Otherwise many mistakes could arise from the translator/ interpreter not understanding letters and symbols unknown to him. Already these types of mistakes bring us readers many problems with understanding a translated text.

The real problem with a large part of the New Testament's texts is that they were purposely distorted. During the early period of Christianity, while Cesar Constantine was ruling around 350 AD, many mystifications were consciously inserted with his cooperation, to purposely undermine the true message of the Gospel. While the New Testament was being written countless fabrications were made about real events, substituting them for the original stories. Quite a big part of the historical data was distorted and erased. Constantine, ruler and founder of the Catholic Church did this on purpose. He wanted to be in control of the growing Christian movement. Therefore he decided to put an intermediary between God and followers– a priest, who he would have control over. From that time on they started to persuade people to search for God outside of them, where they did not have a chance to find Him – instead of in their own heart. Either way, we currently use and rely on the false texts of the Bible.

In today's world because of habit and/ or ignorance some religions and their theologians teach about God as a Creator. He certainly created a perfect world, but in His masterpiece he made a great mistake. He created imperfect people who were capable of committing sins. Do you see the logic in this? I don't. How could a Perfect God who with such precision created each thing, the largest as well as the smallest, make a mistake and create anything imperfect, in this case a human being? Additionally, so that He can punish him eternally?

A long time ago religion, with premeditation included in the Bible parts about God's anger and vengeance and now religion watches over you to don't find out the Truth. If you find it, and more importantly apply it, you would no longer need religion.

However even this distorted version of the Bible could be a very precious signpost showing how to go along the path of life from the beginning as a human until enlightenment. However by relying on the Bible one needs to realize that it doesn't include the entire Truth. You could still work with it, because it's an invaluable treasure. Simultaneously you should avoid its falsehood. How do you do this? Open yourself to intuition and it would lead you and suggest what Truth is and what is not. Throughout centuries much blood was unnecessarily spilled, because the Bible was too literally interpreted.

Things would look differently, if the people who fought were aware that during Jesus' time many words had a completely different meaning to what they currently have. Jesus spoke and taught in Aramaic. That dialect was not completely understood by Jews, just as the Swiss German is incomprehensible to Germans. Even though this was just a dialect, it completely subjugated the official Hebrew language which Jews in Palestine used at the time.

Besides that, one needs to be aware that Jesus' words were communicated by word of mouth. They were spread along the lines of storytelling or gossip. Only seventy years later, when Jesus was already gone, were they written down in Greek. I am sure that by then many words appeared that had a completely different meaning to what Jesus was communicating, not to mention that those were two different languages with two completely different cultures.

After many centuries the New Testament was translated from Greek to English, and yet later to Polish. During that period hundreds of years passed during which each language developed and changed. Therefore, is there any point to focusing on individual statements or passages when words taken out of context wouldn't reflect the original meaning? Only when read in its entirety, do we have a chance to get a sense of what Jesus wanted to communicate to us as presented in the Bible.

A large amount of falsehoods were included when the New Testament was written. Most likely it was thought that this would remain so forever. Constantine didn't realize that in each civilization there existed a Bible just like ours. This means that many Bibles remained after the New Testament was written. It isn't important if it were written down on porcelain boards, clay boards or on papyrus. Thankfully this biblical knowledge was communicated to all civilization according to the same model or system, therefore falsehoods and changes were easily discovered. They were found by archeologists looking for lost civilizations. They continuously find new, undiscovered gospels. Therefore, many researchers have at their disposal the true and full text of the Bible, which unmasks Constantine's deception. Researchers are stunned, and at the same time frightened by their discovery of this fraud.

This is quite easy to figure out, because all civilizations use the identical chronological system which throughout centuries didn't undergo any changes. Even though the texts were written many centuries before our Bible, they describe the same events what our Bible does. As you can see, dear reader, the Gospel is timeless and it has been like that from the beginning of history.

Even though the deception was already discovered long time ago, the present Church still convinces people of untruths and demands from them to they believe in it. As you know, one of the largest religions says that it acts in the name of Jesus, meanwhile it relies on His false imagine. This false image was purposely dissected and imposed by medieval priests, during times when the Church accepted religious wars, slavery and persecution.

The church's description of history is not based on the four gospels in order to show Jesus Christ the way he really was, but quotes Isaac's poetry which portrays a false image. That is why only a few know Jesus as a very educated person, perfectly dressed, prosperous, with impressive looks, great magnetic strength and full of authority and power.

Instead of this true ideal, the present Churches demand we accept as a model a person who was lonely, poor, treated contemptuously because he was born of low social class and had a low social status and further was ignored by those who were of higher social standing. Our ideal person became someone who didn't have friends, saved fishermen, sinners and outcasts. He was often naked and hungry, took politely insults and persecution and in an act of mercy raised his hands in the air when the world was condemning him.

Times has changed, meanwhile Catholicism sits tight. Instead of showing Jesus Christ full of Wisdom, Love and Power, it focuses on His supposed docility, humility and submissiveness, meaning characteristics thanks to which He supposedly abided evil and injustice (doesn't the church wish for his followers to be a faithful personification of these characteristics?).

Religion made out of Him, however, only to take away God from humanity, for whom He lived. He overcame death, humanity's greatest enemy and rose from the dead; meanwhile religion continuously only celebrates His death and suffering. After He rose from the dead He lived among physically living people for fifty years, however religion is silent about this. Why?

Isn't it to feed followers with false ideals, which say: "Be humble, bend down before your tormentor, give yourself into the hands of he who wants to hurt you, when they beat you, turn to them the other cheek"? Isn't it easier to have a control over a person who accepts such imagines?

You don't believe that it was different back then, than how your religion claims it to be? I propose you read history. From Talmud you would find out that during Jesus' time each

Jewish rabbi, meaning teacher, had to practice a craft. This was a law back then. Saint Paul was sowing tents, Rabbi Johanna was a blacksmith, and Rabbi Isaac was a shoemaker. The fact that Joseph was a carpenter wasn't an insult, but an honor. In addition to practicing his craft, each one of them was greatly educated and personally respected by everyone.

Jesus stood the highest of them all. He was a man with greatly impressive, majestic and powerful looks. In the Gospel we can also find confirmation that: "He taught them as someone who had authority, His words were full of Power". Hence, constantly repeating that Jesus was poor and disdained is total ignorance.

One shouldn't blame priests for that. Few of them want to find out for themselves what really happened. Most of them rely on what they learned in school. In this way they gained the "knowledge" they pass on further to followers. They teach the supposed truth, however they themselves fall into their trap as victims of their own learning. They teach about God, but they don't have the consciousness that in reality they don't actually believe in God. If they believed in Him, would they still be stuck in an illusion? This explains why scholarly priests, enlightened by the Truth, after discovering it and coming to a higher understanding immediately leave the priesthood. By knowing the Truth they are not able to serve the Church further in its present structure, because these are two mutually exclusive realities.

After Jesus Christ rose from the dead his apostles wanted to create the Kingdom of God on Earth in which there wouldn't be hunger or suffering caused by evil. This idea was that the effort put in by each person would contribute to the growth of each individual person. The Kingdom of God is sort of a perfect community in which everyone has equal access to God and His wonderful goods. Did the Church ever achieve this task? As a whole, meaning as an institution, it honors more temples, religious practices, rituals and holidays than humans.

God puts in front of each person bigger task to accomplish than considering some days and places holy. Ultimately, the entire Earth is a holy place as well as all human days, because they were both sanctified with God's love which realizes the Divine purpose and shows to each person his greater destiny. Thanks to this vision, the apostles' teachings were as powerful as Jesus Christ's teachings.

In building early Christianity, Constantine, the founder wanted to take over the spiritual power of the apostles, but he didn't want to take over the vision which was to become its base. If the early Church had gone for that vision so would have the spiritual power. He didn't understand that the Power was contained in the vision itself, and not in the institution, the Church. When he resigned from this vision, he immediately lost spiritual Power. This could also be explained differently. The church never had that spiritual Power, because from the beginning it didn't have a vision to build the Kingdom of God. That is why God was placed somewhere far in Heaven and followers were ordered to pray to Him, at the same time establishing an intermediary between humans and God – the church and its priests. The church could have acquired Power and be born anew, if its goal was to build the Kingdom of God on Earth and certainly if people were found who knew how to achieve this. Then it would transform or ascend followers instead of giving them the illusion it does currently.

THE NATURE OF GOD

I will try to explain to you, dear reader, why people search for God in vain after death? This happens because they don't understand His True Nature. They look for God in the form of a person, because that's what religion taught them, meanwhile He fills Himself all Heaven and Earth. It's hard for a small, absorbed with limitations, human mind to grasp this if you don't know anything about Him and if you don't contemplate and mediate about Him. He is the highest knowing power, penetrating each form in the whole universe. He is the Life, Wisdom and Energy of any and all creations. God, in other words, the Presence "I Am" is the source of everything that is. This means that we live in God, move in Him and we have our existence in Him.

You heard something different in church? However don't all holy books and inspired scriptures claim exactly that? Each one of them point out the existence of an Omnipresent, Omniscient, Almighty Source or Energy which in different languages people call differently. Most often we call it God.

God Almighty holds in his hands all Life. Our human outer senses deceive us; as a result we fall into illusion. It mistakenly seems to us that we are independent, separate beings, however the truth is different – we live in the Omnipresent, All-pervading Ocean of Spirit.

You cannot live without God, the same as you cannot live without air and fish without water. Moreover, the Life-giving Spirit is a lot more essential to life than air, food and water. You can survive even a few months without eating, a few days without water, a few minutes without air, but you won't survive even a fracture of a second without Ether or Prana (this is almost one and the same), which is a basic component of Life. People who are capable of living without food they nourish themselves with Ether or Prana.

I don't have in mind only the issue of getting to know God, because each person knows Him. It's about getting this knowledge and making the inner you conscious of it. This knowledge is inside you, but was effaced from your memory. Getting to know God is not based on discovering something new, which until now was unknown, quite the opposite, it is based on the constant disinterring and recovery of Him in own memory. Dear reader, you knew God since time immemorial because you were created by Him. For uncountable centuries you were with Him on a daily basis, very close to Him and you had full, conscious memory of His Presence.

You would reach this knowledge quicker if you found the courage to get rid of the fear once imposed on you, not only the fear of knowing about God, but most of all the fear of God Himself. A long time ago you came to believe (I described this in details in *In the Wheel of Life*, Vol. III) that your greatest sin was that you stood against God Himself. You mistakenly thought that you got separated from Him, what religions call the original sin. This fear, not only exists in you, but also in every person, religion stokes it keeping you in this mistaken belief. Because of this mistaken belief in separation you are on a subconscious level sure that God would punish you. That is also why constantly anew on a subconscious level (perhaps on a daily basis you don't even realize it) appears a great fear that you did something wrong.

This mistaken belief about a punishing God has nothing in common with the real God. God is Love. It's only your subconscious' fear of Him, controlled and stoked by your ego, which changes God of Love to God full of hatred, punishment and revenge. Through this mistaken belief God, who is your beloved Father-Mother and true friend again and again becomes now your enemy.

God didn't come up with that, but people did in the past. It's hard to discover this dishonesty because it was done with incredible scheming. The main goal of creating this mistaken belief was to create in people the biggest possible fear in order to more easily manipulate and control them. That is why you need to try to recognize, whether you are a believer or atheist, that inside you exists – often completely unconsciously – the feeling that you did something incredibly wrong. Reach for this fear. It's about time you recognize it inside yourself and face up to it. You have carried this unpleasant feeling with you for thousands of years so it's about time you got rid of it. That is not an easy process. I went through it in the past myself and I felt it in a painful way. Just the thought of God, when I started to think about Him differently to what my religion taught me, resulted in me getting a strong cough attack. This lasted few months until I finally processed this topic. Later I was coughing less and less until the cough stopped completely. Today I can write, speak and talk about God without any problems. Not everyone has to go through this process as painfully as I did. It all depends on how deep your faith in mistaken teachings is, mine was tremendous.

This is not an easy road; especially at the beginning when there would still be a lot of doubts inside you and who knows maybe everything in your world is falling apart. You need to find the courage and determination to take the first step forward, later with each further step it would get a lot easier. One day you would suddenly discover that everything that is bad, by itself falls off of you. Certainly, it would still remain somewhere behind, but it won't have any influence over you anymore. I wish this for you from the bottom of my heart.

It is the same with sin. People are constantly being frightened by sin, but sin doesn't come from action. Whatever "bad" you did, it's never a sin, but only an experience which helps you to learn. You cannot be punished for something that you are learning. You have to be experiencing because without experiencing your soul wouldn't have an opportunity to grow, to improve.

Therefore, what you commonly call sin, is not actually sin itself, it is your reaction and interpretation of your own action that you recognize as unclean and unethical. Sin is a consequence of your own mistaken, thoughts and feelings, which as a result brings to your heart concern and remorse. You commit inappropriate action because instead of aiming to perfect what is inside you, you fulfill the egoistical caprice of your own ego, meaning your external, little "I". When you cool down from the first excitement which your ego suggests to you, your own intellect will accuse your mind of inappropriate behavior, judging it as faulty, immoral, and unintelligent.

As you could see, sin is nothing else, but your own judgment, this is your negative thoughts that flout your dignity, intrude on the peace of your heart, filling you with fear and remorse. This only happens for you to again aim to own interior and to perfection.

God is an All-Wise and Understanding Spirit. He is Omnipresent and Infinite. There is no place He wouldn't be. This means that one cannot resist Him in any way or ignore Him, because He penetrates everything. His intelligence is infinite. God who is One, rules the entire universe as well as your body. You sense Him as the deepest sphere of motives for your actions. As a rule, you don't have clear and constant consciousness of that sphere of yourself. You sense it intuitively as a hazy and closer undescribed desire, as a secret, inconceivable strength pushing you through life in directions often not understood by you. You don't understand it consciously, because a long time ago you forgot about the purpose of your desire, which is why you came to Earth. This is exactly the part of your life that you realize as a mission, sometimes it would seem to be against common sense and your own interests. Often you are not conscious of that fact, because your Divine "I" is covered with a too exuberant ego and/or a thick layer of anger, hatred, fear or other low emotions.

There aren't people on Earth that wouldn't be worthy of God and His mercy. There are only those who contradict His existence, turned away from Him and fell into illusion.

Dear reader, carrying the correct picture of God in own heart is the most important thing in the world. You could then approach Him in a direct way as to you Father-Mother. Only then would God answer you, giving you all the good things you ask for. God penetrates all conditions. If you allow God to be expressed from your interior (as you did in the distant past), you

would feel with your entire being, that you are connected to
Him. Only then would you honor God for real and glorify God
of the entire human family, and not just God of one religion.

Most religions are deprived of the true image of God. It
is proclaimed that faithful people search for Him on the outside
of themselves where you can't find Him. This is nothing but
giving honor to divine idols, idol worship. Then you won't hon-
or the true image of God, but the human perception of Him.
Meanwhile the commandment says: "You shall have no other
gods before me".

A person looking for God outside of him doesn't grasp
the sense of his own life, as it really is in reality. I am talking
about Life in general, not only about physical life or further existence in the netherworlds. Such a person is continually lost,
full of fear, frustrated and doesn't recognize what is the cause of
it.

God is not some external entity who you have to bow in
front of, but an integral interior aspect of your own being. Your
life should be focused on these truths. When you come to understand this, you would stop being afraid of God and it would be
easier for you to imagine His brilliance, power and the possibilities which He has provided. Then you would start to regain control over your life. Talking about the Great Principle of God that
is inside each of us, He penetrates your physical body as well as
all your subtle bodies, meaning your etheric, astral, mental and
higher bodies. Everything, the entire universe, including all your
bodies is built from God's substance.

God couldn't be just on the inside of you, or just on the
outside of you, because He is Omnipresent and All-Pervading.
This is the Highest Intelligence, Thinking Substance, from
which all things came into existence, it is everything, through
everything, and which constantly looks for fuller expression and

life. God is the source of all Energy and Power allowing the flow of Life and invigorating all things. He also invigorates you in each moment of your life.

Perhaps, you don't feel Him at this moment. Know however, that when you try to come to know Him, first there appears in you a very small, barely noticeable feeling. As you continue, with time this sensation intensifies until you finally begin to feel a powerful current or a stream of life inside your body, brain and heart with your entire being.

If you still look for Him on the outside of your body, you would never find Him. Your outward senses would probably suggest that He doesn't exist at all and you would fall into illusion's trap. Hence, some people who don't know that they should look for God on the inside agree to the theory that God is far away from them, somewhere in a distant "Heaven" and they don't have a chance to see, hear or feel Him. They do this so as not to feel total emptiness and hopelessness.

If you don't have a true image of God, visualize that He is a lovely Entity of Light and try to feel Him in your heart as your Father-Mother. You are a child of this wonderful, loving Entity who cares very much for you. God is All-Love and this unconditional love He sends to everything that He created, and not only to those who deserved His love.

Because most people have already forgotten about, *Who They Are in Essence*, why they are on Earth and where they are going, they can't open their minds and hearts to God and His plan. And since God is Omnipresent, then according to definition He has to be in each person. One cannot separate something that is Unity; therefore one cannot separate God from a human.

You turn away from Him when you stop loving, but this doesn't mean that you have separated from Him. Even though God is in your heart, he never imposes Himself on you. In order to find Him there, you have to come to believe and try to come out to meet Him.

If you still have doubts that God exists, know that this is not unnatural. People throughout many incarnations who went through various experiences throughout many lives were influenced by the Church's teachings. You are not the only with regards to this matter. Many great people, even those regarded as saints during their lifetime said that throughout much of their life they didn't feel closeness to God. However later in their life something changed and they experienced an epiphany. Therefore, experiencing the illusion of separation, the nonexistence of God or having doubts about His existence is something completely normal on the path to achieving true faith. They are a part of your maturing, sometimes painful, but necessary journey.

Always, at any moment you can return to Him and be with Him as you have been so close to Him for a very long time ago, since the very beginning of your existence. Do you remember the parable of the prodigal son? It talks about you. In order for you to return, you need to love God with all your heart and soul. However, you won't achieve this if you won't love yourself first. This is not about you loving your small, personal "I", but yourself as a whole. This includes your physical body as well as your great Divine "I", meaning the Presence of God inside you. Empty prayers and fasting are good for nothing. These are proof that you don't love God and yourself.

God desires for you to fully live your life which you received from Him, to enjoy it and don't resign to it. When you are cheerful, satisfied, fulfilled, God knows that you are happy and that you are experiencing your life correctly. By denying love to yourself, you are denying God; you don't allow Him to settle in you. Love is God. God is Love.

Love is an omnipresent energy; however it is up to you if

you open up to it. Here is one requirement. In order to love and accept God, you have to first love and accept yourself entirely. Then your love is transferred to God and then on to other people. By loving God in yourself, you also love Him in another person. It is never the other way around.

If you want to love others only for them to love you, you would fail. Why? Even if others love you very much, you won't sense their love if you lack love in your own heart. God loves you, but if there is no love in your heart, you won't feel His Love, which is everywhere, it is Omnipresent. It depends on you only, whether you reject His love as most people do presently. You have free will and you have the right to use it however you want. Is it worth it to use it in a way that would harm you?

You should pay special attention to compassion, not only in regards to other people, but most of all in regards to yourself. When with compassion you will look at you lessons, you would also understand the lessons of other people. If there is no compassion in you, you start to take pity or feel sorry for yourself and for others. You would burden them or yourself with this low negative emotion which could pull down you and the person that you pity all the way to the bottom. This would be a great mistake. When you take pity and feel sorry, then you send to yourself or to others signals: "You are in a situation without a solution, and the world is a bad place". This behavior is similar to closing the only exit with a huge rock. You plunge yourself or someone else into even greater hopelessness than currently exists instead of encouraging yourself or someone else to look for a way to get out of a tough situation.

The situation changes dramatically when you feel compassion. Then you send a signal to your own personality or to another person's personality which says: "I know that you are in a tough situation, but you picked this tough lesson for yourself.

When you come to understand how you attracted it to yourself, you would pass it and free yourself even from the toughest situation".

This gives you the strength to go beyond yourself, to learn your lessons instead of just receiving them. When you follow this, at some point you would suddenly understand that God created a perfect world and a perfect human. It cannot be different, because He created you in His own image and resemblance. However to notice this perfection, you first have to notice it in yourself and accept it: "I am perfect as my Heavenly Father is perfect".

RELIGIONS

Religion should be at the forefront of awakening people's consciousness about what I wrote above. Since the early days of the world, all religions in their original, true form had the task of serving as the basis of life and freeing people from the limitations and captivity created by our own misconceptions. Surely, religions wouldn't have been needed or created if humans had full consciousness that they live in God and move and exists in Him (As it was in the past. I wrote about this in the book *In the Wheel of Life*, Vol. III). If we have full consciousness, we would listen to God and comply with his counsel.

The question arises, do religions as they currently exist, fulfill their role and are they even needed? The answer is: yes and no. Yes, because even though in a mistaken way, they do point out to people that God exists. If it wasn't for religion, a person in today's world wouldn't even know that God exists.

It's thanks to religions that we have the possibility to find out about Him.

However, most people don't manage this knowledge because instead of with God, they enter into a very rigid relationship with religion. They don't know that a mistaken faith in God could be as bad as a complete lack of it. Mistaken faith takes people nowhere. And they only find out about it after the death of their physical body. Most religions, irrespective of their great diversity, are stuck in the same place. They desire you look for God through them, because this is the only way religion could be absolutely certain that you would remain their follower, and not God's. Meanwhile they put God far away from you that you have no chance to get to know Him. If you, in some way miraculously discover the Truth, they would quickly try to get you to doubt in It, telling you, that what you discovered isn't possible. If you hold firmly to your new opinion, you would discover to your surprise, that you always had this great knowledge inside of you. Therefore, most religions instead bringing a person closer to God basically move him away from God. Almost every religion wants to mediate your contact with God, which is unnecessary from one side and quite impossible from the other side.

Dear reader, no human, including priests, rabbis, or any other type of religious leader is capable of transferring any rights in this area from him to you. Besides, why would they do this, each person is equally equipped for all possibilities. Perhaps, dear reader, at this moment you don't see this as clearly, but this will become completely clear to you and completely discernable when you develop and raise your consciousness.

Notice that a priest who tries to transfer his rights to contact God to you is erratic. All that the priest can do, is show you the path (that is the purpose of religion) through which you can expand the pursuit in your heart to fill yourself with the goodness that is God. Therefore, at some stage of life and development each person rises above religion, because none of them are capable of fulfilling your inside desire, which is a need to constantly strive higher to God, to the Light.

While contemplating deeper on it, we quickly come to the conclusion that average priest basically cannot know God. In theological school he studied various areas; however he was mainly taught how to get to know God with his mind. After graduating from school, he still concentrated on theological problems contemplating dogmas; sometimes he studied to compare other religions. Therefore, most priests spent time contemplating dogmas and teachings.

I know this topic very well, because I receive many letters from priests as well as from students at theological schools. I read, for example: "I went to theological school to find God, but they don't talk about God there. I passed my first, second, third and fourth years and still nothing. Here, only the year of study changes, but the content usually remains the same" Or: "Mrs. Pratnicka, how do you know all of this? In my church, there is no God at all, God is just discussed". Many devoted people were greatly disappointed by their religion and they walk away from it in massive numbers.

Well, the Creator cannot be analyzed in detail and with the help of the mind you will discover that God is a heart that radiates with love. Defining God rationally and experiencing the love which He is in essence, are two very different things.

Most religions for centuries were stuck in one place, while Life is a constant forward movement. Nobody comes to a halt, because they would be going backwards developmentally. That is why many religious people "grew out" of their religion. Somewhere deep inside they know, that each soul has to go on that last piece of path to God alone. Courage is needed for this, and not each person can find this courage. Many people prefer to turn back or be stuck in the same place with their religion rather than to find the courage and move forward. Hence, those less brave, and here we are talking about the majority of people, are lost and feel trapped. They don't find the fulfillment of their needs in religion, because what they are looking for just isn't there. They feel a strong inner desire, almost an urge, but they cannot fulfill it, because they can't determine for themselves, what it is. Something is breaking away from them, but they don't know what. Not understanding their deeper nature they start to fear themselves. They are afraid to leave their religion and simultaneously they don't have the strength to be a part of it. With time they start to fear everything, and most of all God. That is why, while getting into the heart of the Great Principle of Life, which is God, one should find the courage to go beyond what is known and beyond religion. Only then would we reach the True Great Wisdom of God.

It wouldn't be necessary to walk away from religion if religion would revise its teachings and start to teach the truth. However we would then regain our former power and most likely we wouldn't need religion anymore. The church cannot allow for this. Without you and people like you, the church would cease to exist. This is why the biggest religion of the world persuades its followers that God, for example: seen through Jesus lives in Heaven and in the moment of death would come out to meet you and take you with him. For this reason dead people very stubbornly look for their own God and their own "Heaven". They don't have access to Him, because they too eagerly believed in the Church's teachings and thought independently too little. Such dedicated, dead persons feel greatly disappointed, bitter and often want to take revenge. When such persons as a ghost possess a living person, it causes the Church many problems, for example: it curses, blasphemes. That is the type of ghost that the church calls a devil or Satan. The more a person is dedicated to the church during his lifetime, the more trouble he would cause his family and the Church after his death. I have lots of proof of that. It comes from the thousands of families who have had to deal with possessions by so-called "devout" ghosts.

Here is a very important notation. I am not writing this to separate you from religion or convince you of new theories which are contradictory to yours. I write this to awaken inside you an obliterated memory. It's inside you and awaits your discovery. This Truth is an integral part of you. You would come to understand then, that the mistaken understanding of the Being of God shown by some religions is the same as you not believing in Him at all. Therefore unfaithfulness is not the lack of faith in the teachings of some religion, but lack of faith in the Truth. You should know that memorizing parts of the Bible is not enough. Praying with just the movement of your lips without active actions is worth nothing. It is so easy to read or speak about love, compassion or faith. However to truly love, truly show compassion, and believe in God with all your heart requires a change of consciousness, obviously not temporarily brought about by drugs, alcohol, or the flow of momentary emotions. A permanent change of consciousness could only be achieved through knowledge and understanding. Only specificity and practice could sustain it. This is the assimilation of something almost mystical; putting it into practice must become an everyday habit.

You are here to love and learn. Do you really think deep inside that you soul lives only one time and afterwards for eternity sings psalms and plays on harp for God? Would your soul be happy with that? And when you are limited by the physicality of your body, would this momentary, one-time existence make any sense? I would repeat here: I don't want you to start believing in what I do, or blindly accept anything that I write. I would like you to find this knowledge deep inside you and only then when would you accept it as the truth, believe it wholeheartedly.

Find the courage to break this outer shell of your mistaken perceptions which is stopping you from accessing your own interior. Only then would you find God and countless layers of wisdom, love and power.

Dear reader, I am assuming that you are not aware that you have already lived many, many times. If you remind yourself of this then your life in your physical body and after death won't disappoint you anymore. All wisdom is in you. You were collecting this wisdom throughout all your incarnations. You just have to break this precious piggy bank, and you would get its abundant contents that are deeply rooted inside you.

You would certainly recognize that God is always with you, forever, and He can't be separated from you or from any of His creations, because He is Almighty, Omnipresent and All-Wise. He is Everything in Everything, and therefore He is also in you. He is absolute Truth. He is the only reason for all things.

THE RESULTS OF MISTAKEN BELIEFS

I would like to return to the description of the fate of a person who found himself in the place known as "heaven" where all thoughts materialize immediately. People who were very religious during their lifetime experience great discomfort in "heaven". Initially it appears to be unease which grows more and more over time to be transformed into panic and fear. This is caused by various kinds of thought forms, which are omnipresent in all religions in the present world. Thought forms pertain to various matters – hell, fire, the devil, the beast, various afflictions, agonies in purgatory, meaning everything a believer has occasion to be confronted in their church. There are countless amounts of such thought forms because once such a thought form is created it could exist for many centuries, in other words for many incarnations. How does this happen? Well, it's a form of energy and it has the properties to assimilate with the thought forms of other, similarly inclined people. The effect is that it doesn't die, as it is constantly stoked anew with energy, meaning with similar thoughts of other people; so that it actually grows in strength.

When a person in the astral world encounters thought forms that he believed in up to that point he falls into a state of great terror and suffering. Even though they are false and an illusion, they act with great strength on his terrified senses. The state of panic in such a person could last for a very long time; until he finally realizes that he is the cause of his problems and that is why he can't free himself from the fatal effects of his mistaken perceptions. Most often it's thoughts of Satan, the angry and cruel god or deity, eternal condemnation, hell, and purgatory. How does a person create such problems that it impacts them so strongly after the death of their physical body? He does this through his own thoughts and perceptions, as well as through those he took over from other people, including his own religion. He could have created them himself, because during his lifetime he didn't pay enough attention to control his thoughts so that he could see them as fleeting and meaningless where necessary. He could have also contemplated such topics, because he liked feeling fear. Perhaps, he didn't understand back then that each thought is extremely important, that it exists in the subtle world. Either way, he created his own thought form (or took it over) and his own suffering. After the death of his physical body he should come to understand that his circumstances are a direct result of his own, mistaken thoughts and they are neither true, nor were given to him as punishment.

Therefore, until he realizes that his own thoughts created or his own thoughts attracted various thought forms, he would have no chance to change his fate. He would stay in that state until he understands that he is the creator of own life. It is only then that he would automatically stop harboring feelings of fear. Therefore, it isn't thoughts forms that are threat to him, but his own judgment or perceptions. Proof of this would be the person who in his lifetime didn't believe in such things. Even if he comes into contact with the same thought forms which caused panic in someone else, it wouldn't raise any fear in him, but would disappear like a morning fog. You already understand yourself that it's faith and fear or lack of them that decide whether given thought forms cause us great suffering in the astral world or we choose to be indifferent to them and suffer no consequences.

The type of our life behind death's curtain depends on how we imagined life after death when we were still in physical life. Unfortunately, it can't be said that we are doing well in this area. Most people create a version of the astral world in the physical dimension based on apocalyptic visions, most often based on what is postulated by their religion.

If you want to take a closer look at how various images that are realized after the death of your physical body look in the astral world I propose to you, dear reader, you watch a great movie "What Dreams May Come". It's very realistic and contains many truly well-presented details. Then you would come to understand that people who are aware of themselves, and are therefore creating their own goodness, are in the astral world for a shorter period than those people who allow themselves to be programed during their lifetime to believe that horrible conditions await them after death. An additional positive aspect of this movie is its great plot.

Dear reader, isn't it worth to revise your images about the netherworlds at this moment? When you honestly work on yourself, you would discover soon enough, to your surprise, that you are at that moment the gardener of your soul, the guide of your own life. Learn about the laws that rule your thoughts and realize that the power of thoughts and the factors of the mind influence the formation of your character, circumstances and fate. If each one of us realized how much influence our daily life had on our future life in this and in the other world, wouldn't we wonder about every step and every thought?

Unfortunately, it is only when we pass to the netherworld that we start noticing thoughts as specific things. They are as solid to us as if they were made from wood, cement or iron. Therefore, it's an illusion that a thought is fleeting. A thought has its own energy and is subject to the same rights and rules as everything else is on our planet.

SPHERES OF THE ASTRAL WORLD

The astral world as an extension of the physical world is to a great extent similar to it. In the astral world there exist seven different levels, spheres or octaves (I broadly described them in *In the Wheel of Life* Vol. II). Each one of them corresponds to certain kind of vibrations which are created by emotions, feelings and thoughts: they can be "heavy" such as fear or "light" such as compassion. For souls that are in the astral world, the essential thing is the level of vibrations they are operating on at the given moment, because that determines the quality of their existence (it's understandable that someone lives differently in the constant vibration of "fear" to how they would live in the vibration of "compassion").

Nobody, who feels guilty or unworthy after the death of their physical body immediately find themselves in a happy world, meaning in spheres of higher vibrations. This can't happen, because he would be automatically pulled to his level. A person who is fulfilled and happy is very different to a person who is lost, meaning unhappy. These two states are mutually incompatible, and therefore like a magnet they repel each other.

This mechanism resembles the physical world. Ultimately, no middle school student would get into college right away; similarly a person with low social status won't be accepted to an exclusive club. Social status or education level can't be raised in a day. It's the same with the vibrations of the astral world. There is however the possibility that a soul with high vibrations (high social status) lowered them, which would obviously cost that soul great discomfort or even suffering.

Why do so many people vibrate on the level of heavy, meaning low feelings? Most of them love to fear. You don't believe that? Look around you and you would notice that in most cases people take delight in abominable things and as a result they create those thought forms for themselves. This functions in the physical world as well as in astral world. Creators of heavy thought forms could even be happy about them and experience a kind of satisfaction, for example, people who are passionate when they watch horror movies. They could take delight in even the most terrifying scenes while other person would look on in with disgust, because it creates fear in them, distaste and other negative emotions. Therefore, one person would avoid such scenes, and the other would miss them, depending how he steers his own imagination. In the astral world there is great diversity. Next to levels of goodness, peace and beauty exists various levels of beasts, devils and hells. Such thought forms to a great extent were created by the imagination of followers of different religions. In a great part they consider themselves as hardened, unworthy sinners, and in advance they are prepared for punishment, condemnation and being burnt in hell.

More devout people in the meantime imagine their life in heaven and create thought forms of various deities, depending of what religion they belong to. Yet others go to an imagined purgatory where they experience various forms of torture (in the psychological sense obviously, because here we only deal with imagination).

However, the fact that someone believes in fear because he likes it, doesn't mean that you also have to give in to such visions and experience them. That is their decision to create such abominable things, not yours. Perhaps, you look at them with pity, because you are an atheist. However, people who in their lifetime didn't believe in anything and thought that after death there is only nothingness are not doing any better. These very people are the most lost because they are not even able to believe that they are still alive, not to mention other options which they could have benefited from if they had allowed themselves such thoughts. When at some point they leave the astral world and transition to worlds of higher vibrations, it would turn out surprisingly for them as they were completely mistaken with regards to their perceptions. The description of further life after death exceeds the scope of this book. If you are interested in this topic I recommend the book *In the Wheel of Life,* Vol. II.

STUCK IN A THOUGHT FORM

Dear reader, you have had already multiple occasions to become convinced that what is experienced in the netherworld depends on our experiences up to that point, in other words, it depends on how we look at certain things. It depends of us whether we would see things the way they really are, or we would give in to the suggestions of other people, who may not know anything or very little. Hence, it's absolutely necessary – in this world as well as in the other – to review and filter what is being said, written, shown by others and reject what doesn't harmonize with the suggestions of our intuition (meaning, indicators of our Divine "I"). Your own messy knowledge could also mislead you. This is why you should doubt everything, including your perceptions, until you reach the Truth. Never rely on a ghost's opinions because they could mislead you the most. And everything is relative. A few people looking at the same thing would describe that same thing completely different. Everything depends on the level of your consciousness. Your level of consciousness would also determine your visions. Even if they seem terrifying, in reality they were not so at all. It's your judgment that makes them terrifying, and you always have full control over your judgment. Each of us decides what we want to see. Sometimes people get stuck in their own thought form and they are unable to get out of it. Their own fear and mistaken beliefs that things have to be a certain way, enchains them to a thought form.

I became convinced about this many times while helping to resolve this type of situation. That usually happens when the living person in some way becomes involved in a relationship with a ghost imprisoned in the astral world. It persists until I manage to awaken the ghost, then a change happens immediately. This is not an easy task, because the ghost would be in a state similar to what we know as shock in the physical world. In the physical world, you could shake a person, hit him on the cheek, and pinch him. These things can't be done to a ghost. A ghost is entirely convinced that it imaginations are the absolute truth that it deserved them and nothing is capable of changing that. The ghost falls into this state because it wants to, not because it has to. And that is a huge difference.

Protestants are in an especially tough situation. It's a little bit easier for Catholics, because they believe in purgatory and know that no matter how long they handle agonies (I repeat: agonies that come from their own perceptions), at some point it would pass. I don't have to emphasize that this suffering is completely unnecessary. Certainly, we are dealing here with an illusion, but it's very real and painful for the soul involved. That was also the case in the example below.

One day Lucy reached out to me. She was an educated,

married mother of three children who suddenly started to experience horrible anxiety without any apparent cause. She wasn't able to function. She visited all the well-known therapists, but no therapy had helped her. She felt great fear, but didn't know what it pertained to. She even assumed that it came from traumatic experiences in previous reincarnations. Therefore, she went through sessions of hypnosis and past life regressions, which I firmly advised her not to do, but they didn't bring any success either.

When she reached out to me I discovered a panic-stricken ghost attached to her. It turned out that it was her beloved grandpa who in his lifetime was a warm, good and kind person. He also had these characteristics after death. I couldn't find out why he experienced such great fear, because I wasn't able to make contact with him. He was not getting any messages from me. He was in great shock caused by fear. Therefore, it wasn't Lucy who feared, but she felt her grandpa's fear and thought it was her own. It was hard to reach Lucy as well. She feared almost everything. I had to break through her wall of fear and make her realize what caused her problem. I was doing my part, and I suggested to Lucy (this should be done in each case like this) that she needed to forgive herself and grandpa and also to ask grandpa to do the same. Such action would make them both busy, loosens them up and also free them from the chains connecting them and corrects any mistakes. I was constantly explaining to her that it wasn't her own fear paralyzing her, but grandpa's fear. However, she wasn't managing this knowledge or her fear. We taught her how to differentiate between her own fears and fears that originated from outside of her. For quite some time she couldn't do that. I found out more when I started to ask about her relationship with her grandpa. She explained how much they loved each other and how grandpa's death affected her very much. She still missed him. "If you didn't fear him when he was alive, why do you fear him now?" – I asked. "Ultimately, this is the same soul, with the same character as during his lifetime. Your mutual longing for each other isn't allowing grandpa to peacefully leave. That has connected both of you as though with a great chain". Only after these words she woke up. She understood that she was the cause of her problems and she started to distance herself a little bit from the fear that was coming from her grandpa. Up to that point grandpa and granddaughter were strongly connected through mutual longing and fear and I couldn't help either one of them. When Lucy let go a little bit I was able to take care of grandpa. Finally I was able to make a weak contact with him. It turned out that he got stuck in a thought form about hell and was greatly afraid of it, because he was convinced that there was no way out of it. "How come you are in hell? Hell doesn't exist..." – I mentioned. Grandpa was trying to convince me however that since he was in hell he must know what he was talking about. Indeed, grandpa was stuck in his own thought form which presented itself as hell. For the first time I then attempted to take a person out of his own "hell". I thought that this would last weeks, but it literally only took a second. "Do you understand now that what you saw was a delusion?" – I asked grandpa. "This was a trick of your imagination". Immediately, the devils and hell disappeared. Lucy's grandpa finally noticed the beautiful light. It was there the entire time, but it was covered by his illusion. For some reason he was expecting punishment and this expectation created it. He wasn't interested anymore in anything else, but in his happiness and left Lucy immediately. Dear reader, as you can see from this example, even good people could find themselves in "hell", if they don't believe and can't forgive something. I hope that this would make you realize how important forgiveness to others and yourself is during your physical life. Soon after that Lucy called us. She told us how great she felt and that the fear literally left in a moment. She asked for it to remain like that forever. And it did. When grandpa was in the other, better world, he didn't have any reason to tightly hold on to Lucy because he stopped feeling fear. Hell as a place of eternal condemnation obviously doesn't exist. Despite that religions still frighten their members with it. This situation was changed after the official message from Pope John Paul II in 1999. During one of his trips he spoke on this matter. He said that hell is not a punishment from God, no matter what other people had claimed. He said that hell was just a not too wise choice which people decide to make. To be more specific, hell was the state in which people that separated themselves from God experience "suffering, frustration, and emptiness without God". Artists, who tried to follow holy books presented hell as a world of fire which is controlled by devils with pitchforks. The Pope perceived each of these images as a metaphor only. (source "The National Post", author Robert Fulford, 21.12.1999).

IMPRISONED IN A COCOON

Behind the death curtain there are also souls that are imprisoned in a cocoon. This is not the same as imprisonment in a thought form. A cocoon is created by emotions and a thought form is created by thoughts. I already described how cocoons are created. If you need to refresh your memory go back to the chapter "The Effects of Fearing Death". Here I would just repeat that a cocoon is created beyond the person's consciousness when he doesn't want to control his own fate. A more careful person that is enclosed in a cocoon would notice with time that the various afflictions start affecting him, but by then it would already be too late for any reaction. When the cocoon is created, the real human sits in it as if in prison, or in other words, as if in an astral cage. At the same time he would begin to have the impression that everything around is changing for the worse. He would feel that way because the exterior layer of the cocoon would be aligned to his coarsest emotional qualities, because these are the heaviest and thickest, meaning the most durable against friction.

In the astral world there is a law based on the mutual attraction of similar characteristics. The astral body having on its exterior surface only the coarsest particles would only attract similar elements in the astral world. From the outside it would only reach him therefore only as sensations corresponding perfectly to these particles. If the lowest characteristic of a given person was hatred, jealousy, and fear, which would now define all of his experiences. At one time during his lifetime he loved, hated, was brave, was paralyzed by fear and was jealous, but there were also longer or shorter moments of being free of these negative emotions. Now nothing else would reach him besides those which were stronger than during his lifetime (because he doesn't have the protection in the astral world which his physical body provided) hatred, jealousy, and terrifying fear. Therefore such a person wouldn't be able to perceive the entire astral world, but only the small part of it that corresponds to his coarsest vibrations. It's similar to someone enclosed in a well from childhood looking at the world through a tiny aperture and based on that assuming that the entire world looks that way. That is a subjective view, but real for that person his reality based on his consciousness That is because at that point he constantly hates, is jealous, is full of fear and it would seem to him that he is among haters and jealous people who are residents of the astral world who fear everything. He could be surrounded by living people or people without their physical body whose astral bodies are normal, meaning not regrouped, but he would not be capable of feeling or noticing higher characteristics above and beyond those through which he looks at in the world surrounding him. Because of that all the people surrounding him would seem very evil and criminal to him; people without any positive qualities.

Also, former friends and family won't seem the same to him anymore, because he won't notice their good sides, instead all he would see is their faults. It's not surprising that in such conditions the astral world is viewed as hell. However, the reason for his predicament would not be the astral world, but the person himself. Firstly, he gathered internally a lot of low type matter which he absolutely should have gotten rid of during his lifetime. Secondly, he programmed himself for unawareness (among other things through various addictions) and he allowed for his astral consciousness to control him and regroup his astral matter in this specific, unfortunate for him way; in other words, in a cocoon.

Every day people reach out to me for help for themselves and their loved ones. Everything is alright, until they find out that the cause of their extreme suffering is a ghost that is someone very close to their heart, for example, their mother, father, husband, wife, child, beloved grandma, grandpa, friend, etc. They couldn't believe that this person who was kind to them during their lifetime suddenly became such a monster. "What happened to his love for me" – they ask. I hope that they understand now. If not, I recommend they carefully read the chapter dedicated to the cocoon. I also think that the following examples would help you understand.

Margaret, the mother of two grown, married daughters and a single son, suddenly fell sick and despite the best medical care (one of her daughters was a great doctor in a local clinic) died after a few months. During her lifetime Margaret and her children comprised a wonderful, loving, peaceable, cheerful and caring family. There were no fights between them, betrayals, alcohol or anything else that would point to negative characteristics. When Margaret fell sick, however she gradually started getting madder at the "injustice" of fate. When she was finally able to enjoy life, as she said, "the children had left a nest", she was dying. They hardest thing to accept was the fact that after her death her husband would meet another woman in the future and make love to her. She couldn't stop thinking about that. She became obsessed with that. During her lifetime she couldn't talk anyone about it, she couldn't even confess it to her husband. He worried so much about her illness, that she thought it would devastate him even more. She never talked about such personal topics with her daughters. Besides, everyone was assuring her that she would soon recover and that everything would be as it was in the past. They all refused to accept her death. According to them, it was a waste of time and energy to contemplate something that would never happen. However, despite their best efforts she died unaware, intoxicated and poisoned by the pain relief medicine.

When her loved ones reached out to me a real horror prevailed in their homes. None of the family members were possessed by ghosts, but all of them were disturbed by them; so much so that for a long time nobody slept through even one night. They were haunted physically and mentally. When I discovered that the ghost was their mom and wife, nobody wanted to believe it. "What you mean its mom?" – They asked "But she was like a saint. She wouldn't even hurt a fly, and this ghost disturbs us with great premeditation and on daily basis. And even if in her lifetime she was a beast, she died three years ago and the horror has existed for half a year at the most. Mrs. Pratnicka must have made a mistake." Since they didn't show too much trust, my assistant recommended they use the services of someone else, perhaps contact a priest. They agreed. After a few months they reached out to me again. "We have already gone to all the priests and lay exorcists" – they screamed to my assistant over the phone – "but nothing worked. Instead of things calming down, something now attacks us with even greater fury. None of the people who we reached out to for help told us anything about mom. When we mentioned her, they laughed. "Then what did they say?" – My assistant asked. "Some said that it's Satan, others that it was black magic, yet others that it was a curse" – they answered amicably. They always organized a conference call and were all present on the phone. "Now what do you propose? Do you agree to cooperate with me on my terms" – I asked. "We don't have a choice. You are our last hope. Otherwise we would go insane". "I would do my part" – I said "But you all have to firmly do your part, meaning, what I tell you now. Firstly, you have to forgive your mom, also yourself, everything that comes to mind. Secondly, you have to ask your mom for forgiveness. You have to do this as long as is necessary." They agreed to it. "Besides that, you have to constantly tell your mom, at least a few times every day that she has already died (how and when), because she is not completely aware of that and thinks that she is still alive." – I said. "How could someone be unaware of their death?" – they asked with doubts. Then I recommended them to my previous book *Possessed by Ghosts*. They were supposed to read it many times until they fully understood my words.

My intuition was not wrong. Dying unaware and intoxicated by medications, Margaret allowed herself to be enclosed in a cocoon. Her jealousy and anger stoked by sorrow over her lonely death, were on the exterior layer of her astral body and created a solid shell. Besides that, like many other ghosts, she wasn't aware that she was not alive anymore. She thought that in some miraculous way she had recovered and the promises given by everyone around her were fulfilled. In her view, she had simply returned home healthy, without any signs of pain.

She just couldn't understand why her loved ones didn't want to talk to her and why they changed for the worse, towards her. Inside she felt love and kindness, but on the outside she only looked and felt only through the prism of feelings she had on the top of the cocoon. She was however convinced that it was her husband and children who had changed dramatically. She was talking to them and they were ignoring her, she was asking them questions and they weren't answering. What was worse, they started to do everything at home in their own way, arranging and changing things as they wanted. She couldn't allow for that. They didn't even ask her for permission. The same was happening in her children's homes. Before, they would always come and ask her for advice, and now they treated her like air. "How did I raise them? They don't even have the smallest amount of respect for me. I would show them! Since they want a war, then they would have one" – she said with an eagerness for revenge.

She obviously didn't know that it was her who underwent a change and not her loved ones. Even when I was explaining this to her, she couldn't believe it. I had to remind her about this for a long time before she began to understand everything and at the same time change for the better. Her loved ones were helping me with this. When she doubted my words, she heard them from her loved ones (for instance, that she is not alive anymore). Obviously they didn't hear her, but she thought that they were answering her questions.

I told Margaret to forgive everything what she holds against herself. She was also supposed to forgive others. They were also forgiving her and were asking her for her forgiveness. This looked to her like a dialog with them. The hardest part was to forgive her husband because a woman appeared in his life. This provoked a great amount of anger and hatred. When both sides forgave each other and asked for forgiveness, the cocoon's shell started to slowly dissolve and finally Margaret freed her-self from it.

Everything that we did with such difficulty during the exorcisms, the family could have done during Margaret's life-time. It would have been enough if they had spoken to her dur-ing her illness and not leave her by herself with the pain associ-ated with illness and her growing fear. Furthermore, if they had understood then, what death is, they wouldn't have fought so much for her life and would have allowed her soul to leave when her soul was ready, when it was the time. Negative emo-tions wouldn't have emerged in her, and dying in full awareness, she wouldn't have gotten enclosed in a cocoon. And even, if one had appeared it would have been delicate, created from positive characteristics, from love and kindness which had prevailed in her entire life.

Now, let's consider another example: Rob was an aver-age person during his lifetime, and there are many in the world, neither very kind nor bad. Sometimes during his lifetime he would drink with his friends for Dutch courage. He wouldn't be called an alcoholic. At his home there would be bottles of alco-hol standing for months and he wouldn't touch them, but he couldn't refused his friends when they offered him a few beers. Then it seemed as though something had entered him, because he would become a completely different person. When he drank, and even sometimes when he didn't drink, he would blame eve-ryone for everything and insult them, and during his outbursts of anger, he became so angry he was capable of violence. After some time that would pass. He wasn't really sure about the cause for these outbursts; hence he didn't strive for change. Af-ter the sudden death of his physical body (his heart didn't with-stand one of his outbursts of anger) he allowed his astral body to regroup. Before that all his bodies were mutually penetrating and their particles circulated freely. Now they got enclosed in concentric spheres. On the very top of the cocoon was hatred, anger and fear as the strongest and most resistant friction particles. During his lifetime Rob was kind and warm. He remained the same inside, but he begun to perceive the world through the prism of his exterior layer's cocoon vibrations. He not only saw the world full of hatred, but also heard and felt it. He could have been in the most beautiful place in the world among his most dedicated friends; however he wasn't conscious of their existence. Through the exterior sphere of the cocoon's filter nothing else was reaching him, and the subtle particles of his astral body were closed on the inside (he could have reached these if he wasn't in the cocoon). He only felt other people when they were in a state of hatred, anger or malediction. He wasn't aware of his limitations. People seemed like monsters to him. In self-defense he often attacked them.

When Rob was dying, his neighbor Joanne was outside the country. She had lived in England for years prior to his passing. There she had started a family and had a good job. Her family lived in Poland and had reached out to me to help her. For some time Joanne started to beat herself all over her body. When she was having an attack, her body was covered with bruises so large it was as if the punches had been thrown by strong man, and not by her tiny hands. "At the beginning we suspected her husband" – her sister said "but later we were convinced that he was protecting her from herself. During such fits of anger she cursed aggressively, however with a heavy, masculine tone of voice".

My assistant asked how long this has been going on. It turned out to be a few months. At first, tiny bruises and scratches appeared, but later with each passing day this started to intensify. Her family was afraid that Joanne would seriously harm herself. I found a very strong ghost next to her. In order to identify him I asked for a list of deceased people her family knew, but the ghost wasn't on that list. I asked them to broaden the list, by including distant family, friends, and neighbors and then I found Rob's ghost. I made contact with him. Initially he complained that he was possessed by the ghost of some woman he couldn't free himself from. Rob thought that Joanne had possessed him and that she was the cause of his misfortune. By beating her, he was trying to free himself from her.

When this became clear, I started a long and strenuous exorcism process. The ghost couldn't be led away as in other cases, because the cocoon in which Rob was enclosed didn't allow for that. We had to wait until the shell dissolved and freed him from it. Meanwhile, Joanne's task was to recognize with what thoughts or emotions she was attracting Rob's ghost to her. It turned out that what was attracting them to each other was their mutual vibration of great rage; in Joanne's case it was feelings towards changes that occurred at her work. The next step was to heal her psyche, in other words, change the thoughts and emotions that attracted the ghost. Joanne was forgiving him and herself, she was constantly telling him that he was not alive and that he was a ghost, not her. Finally, it worked. Joanne stopped beating herself and stumbling, and Robert had left her. He didn't quite free himself from the cocoon, but Joanne was free from him.

I hope, dear reader, that you now understand on what are based laws of the astral world and as of right now you would start working on yourself. That way in the future after leaving your physical body you won't allow elementary desires (your astral substance) to regroup in your astral body. Most of all, I trust that you won't be scared by your death and remain in constant awareness (that is essential). Furthermore, you would ensure that you don't get overpowered by any addictions (during your physical life). When we allow our addiction to control us, we are in its clutches and then the addiction would dictate our fate in the present and in the future. Then freeing ourselves from the addiction would be basically impossible. In the present with the correct understanding and determination we have absolute power over it. Addictions and the cocoon have the same cause and if you have a problem with this, dear reader, I advise you to read the chapters about addictions that are in the books *In the Wheel of Life* and *Possessed by Ghosts.* It's necessary for you to fully understand the essence of addictions and get rid of them while you still have time. Otherwise, after leaving your physical body you would suffer very much because you wouldn't be able to quench them. Quite a number of people have problems with addictions, but they don't admit it to themselves or they think that they have it under control. Reaching out to a person with a common sense from your own environment and asking him whether in our case you may deal with the addiction requires courage, but it could turn out to be truly priceless. In general, it could be said that everything that we use regularly to improve our mood, points to the existence of a strong addiction.

When it doesn't come to creation of a cocoon, particles of the astral body have the possibility to freely move around it, the same as takes place in physical life. As a result of that, people don't get closed into one zone (level)of the world and their own astral body, and retain the freedom to move on all levels, depending of what kind of particles they have in their astral body. In other words, they could move around throughout all spheres of vibrations which their own astral body offers to them. If their feelings and emotions vibrated in their lifetime on a high subtle level, then despite being in the astral world, they won't be attracted to its lower regions and would be under the impression that they were living in heaven. From an analogical point of view, if their feelings and emotions were coarse, it would seem to them that they were in hell. All these levels located between the proverbial "heaven" and "hell" correspond to Christianity's purgatory. I am reminding you again, that we are not talking here about objective places that actually exist, but about subjective states of mind.

One more note for the future. Elemental desires encompassing the semi-conscious fear of its own fate would always strive and at all costs, seek to project unto the people who are defending themselves from the regrouping of their astral body, its own fear. This is possible only in the case of people who fear death. However, people who understand death and are not afraid of it, will immediately recognize that this is not their own fear and further it comes from the outside. As a result they won't give in to pressure to regroup their astral bodies, as this would lead to the creation of cocoons.

People who fear death would think that this is their fear. As a result their fear would strengthen. I emphasize again: it's only about a delusion, to which you must not give in. That fear is only suggested, whispered. When you reject it, it bursts like a soap bubble or disappears like a fog. Because of that it's worth knowing, during your lifetime, the laws surrounding the transformation commonly call death, and get used to these laws so as to remember them well in the future.

ADDICTIONS

A person's happiness or misery after his death depends on how he accepts the loss of his physical body. If he feels he lacks it, then most likely he would suffer. It would be even more so if he had additions or desires. Addictions and desires would without exception manifest in the astral body as vibrations and a field force or in other words a magnetic force. When we are still in physical body, the largest part of this field force is occupied with setting heavy physical particles in motion. When we don't have our physical body anymore, the entire force of these vibrations sets our astral body in motion and then every desire (and obviously addictions and urges) manifests in our astral life with a greater force than in our physical life. In other words, we feel them with increased intensity.

If a person doesn't learn how to control their desires and addictions in their physical body, after death they would suffer greatly and for a very long time as they would not have the chance to quench them. If you want to see what you would have to go through, try immediately to refrain, from this very moment, from your addiction for a very long time. Then you would receive a small portion of desire which would hit you. I am saying "small portion", because you still have your physical body and the force of the desire wouldn't reach the intensity that you would feel when you only have your astral body. And now imagine that the time would come when you are completely incapable of quenching your addiction. Shouldn't you immediately start working on it?

It doesn't matter whether it is alcohol, compulsive smoking, drugs, sex, work addiction or anything else, without quenching it you are unable to live. If you are in an even worse situation and you are an addict whose desires are stronger than your reason, your common sense, sense of decency and family feelings, then think what would happen to you later. While entering the astral world you would feel the particular desire a hundred times stronger and you won't be able to fulfill it in any way. That situation would turn into a true hell. Many people are in such situations. On no account, should we claim that that situation is punishment for bad deeds. Simply, such people are harvesting their own deeds, thoughts and emotions. They planted certain habits which grew into strong addictions. We are dealing here only with the consequences of our prior behavior. Dear reader, I am certain that you would agree with me on this matter.

And even one day of great suffering could sometimes seem to last centuries; however with time, very slowly the given desire when not fed with new energy would become weaker and weaker until it disappears completely. How long does it lasts? Time in the astral world doesn't exist. Everything is measured by the strength of our feelings. "Very long" would therefore apply with a very strong force of unfulfilled addiction. For the soul it could seem that this lasts centuries. This is how we come to understand the false idea of hell and eternal condemnation aroused in great measure by the image of a person going through his own tortures and unfulfilled desires.

It would seem that the described suffering arises only in extreme cases of addictions. Nothing could be further from the truth. For many people, their unfulfilled desires are the result of various attachments to the physical world which become a great torture. To this category we could add: dedicating yourself to business, dedicating time to aimless social activities, habitual television watching, habitual shopping, playing, practicing sports, playing video games, surfing the internet, in other words everything that serves the purpose of killing time. For such a person the astral world would be a place of inexpressible emptiness and boredom, a place where he wouldn't know what to do with himself. There is neither time nor things there nor activities to "kill", in other words all those things which the physical person strives for and desires so much. There is no gossip, judgment or idle chatter on which much social contacts are based in physical world.

THE STAGES OF RETURNING HOME

The Path Home has many stages and stops. Each one happens on a different world, on a different plane. I described this topic broadly in the book *In the Wheel of Life.*

Here I would just say that the astral world is not the final stage of our journey. It's also not a true "Heaven". Perhaps, you would ask how long a soul stays in the astral world. It varies greatly. It's different for each person. A soul is in the astral world as long as it takes to deplete all the energy which originated from the soul's feelings, emotions and passions accumulated in its physical, earthly life. Therefore the contents of the astral life are all the emotions and feelings, but only those which contain a personal element.

If the physical person's thoughts and feelings were mostly selfish then they create for the astral person quite a tough life, or even a very difficult one, because he generated many disadvantageous thought forms which would later turn against him. If a person was good and kind, then such thoughts would ensure for him a relatively nice astral life. However to some degree, a lot depends on how a person takes his death; mainly, whether he is aware of it and whether he accepts it.

If a person's feelings and passions were strong during his physical life then his astral body would have a great lifespan and his stay in the astral world would last long (several dozen or even several hundred earthly years). If his past life was mostly characterized by intellectual work and was based on integrity, and not on passions, then his stay in the astral world would be relatively short (around fifty years). Writing "short" I have in mind the average length of life in that world. While comparing lifespan in the astral world to lifespan on Earth, it should be emphasized, that often the lifespan in the astral world is multiple times longer. Therefore, isn't it worth to think about it today while you still have direct influence over it? Characteristics of the astral body are being created during your physical life through your passions, desires, emotions and indirectly through your thoughts and physical habits, such as nutrition, intake of liquids, purity, abstinence etc. This doesn't mean at all that the purpose of life is mortification of the flesh or refraining from the pleasures of physical life. It's about understanding the relationship between cause and effect and avoiding matters which would cause suffering in the astral world. You are in the developmental process and you shouldn't get too attached to earthly matters. It's worth it to apply the knowledge presented here for your well-being here and there. Ultimately, the soul's purpose after its long journey is to return Home, to God.

Dear reader, as you can see, our future life depends exclusively on our physical life on Earth. It has a decisive influence over our fate, present as well as in the future. This was emphasized for the longest time by sages, prophets and Masters. Even the astral life, which is often longer than our physical life, is only an intermediate stage in life and death's cycle and it prepares the soul for further existence.

Once again, I would like to repeat that death in the earthly sense doesn't exist. Those are only the next levels of the same life, following one after another world. The quality of life on upcoming, specific planes depends only on the human, in other words of his thoughts and feelings. Death of the physical body doesn't change anything in this respect. Life in higher worlds is only a continuation and the result of a person's current emotional-mental situation. If we want to translate this according to religious beliefs, the astral world would be the equivalent of purgatory, and the mental would be the equivalent of heaven. Those are however subjective states of consciousness, and not objective specific places. Also, hell is a state of consciousness and not a specific place. A person believing in the existence of hell and purgatory creates for himself extreme sometimes unpleasant experiences, for instance as demonstrated by the fate of Lucy's grandpa. Staying in this type of proverbial, self-created purgatory or hell could cause you great suffering. But even this mistaken perception of reality at some point comes to an end.

Dear reader, the state of your consciousness creates your reality. This is nothing else, but a deep knowledge on some topics reflected in a feeling of certainty. This knowledge is created in your physical life, and not afterwards. Everything is in your hands. Isn't that good enough proof to adequately prepare for it? Where to start? Most of all, we need to recognize and change thoughts disadvantageous to us which are followed by our emotions. They should be changed from negative, fear filled to those more perfect and full of love and beauty. This is extremely important. When our physical body dies, we wander to where our thoughts lead us. If we were full of fear, in despair, full of hatred or anger, then after death we would find ourselves where it is appropriate for the vibrations of those thoughts and emotions. Therefore, this would be the equivalent of hell or purgatory, if we have to describe this in the religious terms of many believers. If our thoughts were noble, full of peace, appreciation, love and forgiveness we would find ourselves in the equivalent of heaven. This is already a lot, even though this won't be a true heaven with capital letter "H" yet.

THE FUNERAL

Let's return to the living people. When a soul departs, the living people are obligated to organize for the body, in other words the exterior covering, a funeral. In reality, the funeral serves a purpose for the living people, and not for the real human. I repeat: we organize a funeral for his body, his clothes which has very little in common with the real human. Most people don't understand this. It's hard for them to understand that since a soul decided to leave the physical world the funeral ceremony, embalming, cremation or other rituals have no significance to the soul. They are important for the living people, but not for the departing soul. The soul took off a body, similar to taking off old, used, unneeded clothing and as a real human gone further. The soul doesn't need any preparations. The soul's transition resembles crossing through an open door or curtain. I am writing about this, because living people often ask me to ask a given soul whether its body should be buried in a coffin, cremated or dressed in a certain way. For such decisions there is enough time before death. After death, the soul departing beyond death's curtain is completely disinterested in this.

As already mentioned, it also doesn't interest that large, unaware group of people who don't want to die and who want to hold on tightly to life. They want to live, not die hence matters regarding a funeral don't interest them, but rather it sickening them because it is terrifying. The people mourning have to decide this for themselves. However, they have to remember that they are dealing with an abandoned body, not with a real human. In the grave only his physical part would rest and that belongs entirely to Earth, and his soul is already not there. The soul left to go to God, to the Light and even if it didn't leave, it's not in the grave anyway. Perhaps a soul wanders around between "heaven" and "earth", or has already possessed someone. Many people every day visit graves and for hours talk to a deceased's body mistakenly thinking that they talk with his soul. Meanwhile the soul left a long time ago. You can talk to a deceased person anywhere on Earth, even through your own heart. The deceased person would certainly hear you, because you never disappeared from his eyesight. Therefore, you don't have to hang out at a cemetery. In a grave rests just his body abandoned like old, used unneeded clothing. Meanwhile many people consider the body as the person who deceased person was during his physical life or even something more, because he is already close to God. In reality the deceased person is as close to God as he was earlier, and not a bit closer. If you don't understand this correctly, you would suffer unnecessarily and expose yourself to possession by ghosts which want to take advantage of your mistaken thoughts on this topic and the situation you found yourself in.

In the moment of the soul's definitive, final departure from the body, the silver string is torn once and for all. This is the moment at which the etheric body leaves the physical body. Then the physical body's cells begin to lack prana, in other words a life force, because the physical body by itself never had life's energy. Therefore, the body lacks the bonding force which kept its cells unified. The dead body, deprived of energy becomes a concentration of independent cells which results in the body's decay. However the physical body's cells don't die. Each one of those cells begins to live their life having previously served in the body's wholeness. This is why hair and nails still grow. However, even after they recognized that the body was dead, in many cases three days are needed before the soul would leave it.

THE PARTICIPATION OF CHILDREN IN FUNERALS

Whether people should take children to funerals is a very tough and quite controversial topic. I believe it depends on whose funeral it is. If a person close to a child dies, with whom the child was emotionally connected, then obviously you should take the child to the funeral. Without that, the child wouldn't be able to say goodbye to the person, and the funeral serves that purpose. If the child loved, for example: grandpa, and during his funeral the child was sent to be somewhere else, then the child would feel a gap later in life. The best approach is to ask the child whether he wants to participate in the ceremony and act according to his will. At the same time, the child has a right to refuse. If a child participates in a funeral you should prepare him for it, tell him what the ceremony involves to avoid any sort of surprise.

Things are different when it comes to the funeral of distant or foreign people. Then the child shouldn't participate in the funeral.

Besides that, it's very important for a child to know about the sickness and death of people close to him. Perhaps this fact was diligently hidden from a child. A child shouldn't be sent away to an aunt during the time of sickness and death and later shown the body of his deceased grandpa and be expected to participate in the funeral. Firstly, this leads to a shock. Secondly, the child won't recognize his grandpa who would have been changed by sickness and death, and as a result he would be scared of grandpa. If a child actively participated in caring, for example, for his beloved grandpa, knew about his illness and was made aware of his death, then the child shouldn't be forbidden from participation and saying goodbye to him. If the child doesn't want to come up to a coffin then he cannot be forced. It's the same with regards to convincing him to kiss his grandpa or aunt goodbye. I have many clients for whom such childhood experiences turned out to be very traumatic and they still can't manage them even though they are now adults.

If a child participates in the ceremony then we should be watchful with regards to what could happen during the ceremony, even if the child has participated in funerals in the past. I would use as an example my son when he was little. He was almost six years old when his beloved grandma passed away. When he attended prior funerals he was very calm. It was probably because we adults didn't show any special emotions. It was different with grandma. He was involved with her sickness the entire year and was extremely connected to her emotionally. He was greatly affected by her death and his despair climaxed at the funeral. When the coffin was being lowered to the ground, he jumped on the funeral home worker and started to hit him with his small fists. I had to explain again that this gentleman was doing his grandma a favor, because we have to bury her body and grandma herself was already in heaven and not in the coffin. Later, when I was talking with him about this occurrence and asking him why he did that, he said that he didn't know, and that it happened by itself. After giving some thought he later said: "Perhaps I wanted to stop that man from putting grandma in a grave". Later, we talked about it many times. He always assured me it was correct to take him to the funeral, otherwise he wouldn't know how to explain to himself the sudden disappearance of grandma. He said that he would have worried about her even more, and now at least he knows that grandma is with God.

Dear reader, as you can see, keeping illness or the death of his loved one a secret from a child is definitely a negative solution. In the child's consciousness an emptiness that is impossible to fill would arise. He would wonder why his beloved grandpa (grandma, mom, dad, sister or brother) with whom he was so close suddenly disappeared. And why he left him? This creates constant, unbearable suffering which is a lot worse than participation in a funeral and letting out the entire bitterness all at once. A child despite his pain still feels at that time loved even though his beloved person passed away and not betrayed or abandoned, because his beloved person disappeared suddenly.

Things are different when the child knows about someone's death, but doesn't want to participate in the funeral. One must, if possible fill in this gap and tell the child about the funeral later. Over time, when a child is ready, we should take him to the cemetery, in order for him to connect your conversation about the funeral with the physical reality. Usually, children in such situations write a card or take with them a toy to leave there. Adults shouldn't discourage them from doing that, because for children this is a way of symbolically saying goodbye.

On the other hand, children who participate in the funeral may desire to put something in the coffin – letter or favorite toy – and adults should allow them to do that.

Adults often don't want to take children to funerals, because they are afraid of their misbehavior, that everyone would be sad or that the child would be running around church or step over flowers on graves. Well, let him run, ultimately in that way he releases stress related with death. And when a child, calmly collects flowers, sticks or rocks then also allow him to do that. That is natural behavior. Later, he would carefully hide these rocks and they would be an heirloom from the deceased person.

I would like to mention one more thing. After the funeral, adults want to immediately (depends on the situation) change the child's room, apartment, town, his school, preschool, or at least decorations in the apartment for him to quickly forget about the loss. That is a grave mistake. Every child needs stability most of all. The loss that he experienced is enough and it would be for a long time. He already has a disturbed sense of security and you shouldn't change anything in his life. Only when he gets used to the loss should further changes be considered. Ensure a sense of security for the child. This could be achieved by keeping the same, old, daily habits when there was appropriate time for food, doing homework, play and sleep.

Sometimes adults experience their own despair and don't have the strength or time to take care of a child's emotions. This could cause the child to feel abandoned after a funeral and afraid of the silence because he doesn't understand the sadness which prevails around him. In this situation a third person is very helpful who could take care of the child and explain the situation at home to him, hear him out and answer any questions haunting him while comforting him. A lack of emotional support and the absences of any display of understanding for his pain, in other words, a lack of adequate care over the child's own pain could make him perceive the world around him as uncaring, unpleasant and incomprehensible.

CHARACTER

Dear reader, it's essential you deeply understand that your loved one, after the death of his physical body remains the same person as he was until his death. He still has the same mind, the same character with its positive and negative qualities, and if he had addictions then those remain with him. What we call "death" is only a separation of the person with the lowest, physical plane of existence. In contrast a soul unlike a real human is not a subject to change on higher planes, the same as a person doesn't change when he takes off his clothes at night. There is quite a large group of people who think the opposite. They believe that since a deceased person transitioned to the next world then he is automatically dealing with someone almost a saint who is capable of anything. They pray not only for his intervention, but most of all to him. They ask him for help and support in various things; they ask for advice even in matters that significantly go beyond his capabilities. A wise person could ask: "How could such a person answer specific questions on topics which he didn't have any knowledge about during physical life?" However, many people demand that from a dead person. Then instead of receiving help they become possessed, if not by the ghost which they pray to then by other one which is nearby and which could easily personate their loved one. Most of my clients were possessed exactly this way.

When it comes to the conditions that a dead person experiences after his death, it should be noted that he doesn't enter a new life, but continues the same life he had up to that point, the one which he led in the physical world, although based on a bit different rules. These are the basic and most important facts, which each person absolutely must have a deep understanding of them. Otherwise you risk missing you own death someday, as a great number of souls leaving for another world do.

When it comes to the deceased person's character then he has the same thoughts, feelings and desires as before. This explains the variety of intelligence levels among diverse souls in the astral world.

Quite often after death, a person doesn't recognize that he is free from the necessity to care about survival: free from the need to make money, eat or sleep. This is a very important fact. Unfortunately, souls are very rarely able to notice this. Usually, a lot of time needs to pass before a person would gradually and slowly start to notice the conditions of his new life. Then he stops feeling tired, feeling pain, he starts feeling younger, feeling fit, and in general freer. He starts gradually noticing a difference between his present reality and the physical world, which belongs to his past.

Only then he starts to understand that in reality he

doesn't see the physical bodies of his loves ones and friends, but their astral equivalent. He won't be able to follow, in detail events in the physical world like he did in his physical life, but immediately he gains the consciousness of feelings nurtured by others – love, hatred, jealousy and anger – because they display these in their astral bodies. These are for him the most important and are the basis for his existence, because he lives in the astral world, in other words the emotional.

The living people are convinced about the loss of their loved one forever, but a dead person is never, even for a second, under the impression that he lost those who remained in their physical bodies. Here I would like to express a few warning words. A dead person in his astral body feels emotions easier and deeper, and all the more if they come from his loved ones. He doesn't have a physical body anymore which until now suppressed his sensitivity to given feelings. That is why we should constantly remember and take into consideration the fact that living person's feelings have a very strong effect on dead people, especially when there is a connection between them. One cannot suddenly stop loving someone. When someone truly loves then he loves forever, because love is eternal on this and on the other world.

Continuing this thought – if the living persons despair and long for the dead person, the dead person that had already departed suffers greatly because of that, much more than the living people. I hope that after reading this book, dear reader, you would be more aware of the essence of death and in the future you won't put your deceased person at risk of extra, unnecessary agony.

PARTING

I believe that you already understand why once and for all you should stop fearing death and be in such great despair after losing a loved one. You never lose them, because our souls are eternal. You always meet them again on the other side, after death of your physical body, and if your shared work is not finished, you return with them, in other words reincarnate in human form. Sometimes your roles change, for example, one time you are a mother and in next incarnation you are a child – however as souls you remain the same and equally close to each other. Therefore, you have already met with your loved ones many times in physicality. Furthermore, all of us create spiritual families and on the level of the heart we are always together.

Sometimes by carefully inspecting our body we could recognize our identity from a previous life, for example, find characteristics in places where scars once were located. If you could take a look into your past lives, you would see that, for example, your beloved mother (son, daughter, husband etc.) was in a different time and place your beloved daughter (wife, parent, dear friend) and had already accompanied you for hundreds of years. When you are gaining deeper consciousness of yourself, you would feel with your entire self, that you have met again with someone very familiar on the physical plane (even though you would see a completely "foreign" person in front of you), only that it was at a different time and place. Hence, you never lose your beloved people. We return to physicality together and the energy for reconnection is love. When in our mutual relationships loves run out then our paths go separate ways. We could still meet if we desire to, but on different plane. Sometimes we very clearly sense in ourselves prior feelings even though we are conversing with someone who seems to be a complete stranger.

If you suffer due to a loss, I understand you perfectly. I went through it myself. However, this lasts only to a moment when understanding comes. Then suffering leaves us completely. Perhaps, you currently suffer so much, because your pain is strengthened by your earlier losses (experienced in your prior incarnations) which didn't lead you to understanding. Perhaps, many times you were separated from your beloved ones and now you are more sensitive to the loss of loved ones and you experience it more intensely. Each new loss awakens prior suppressed or forgotten feelings, which escalates sadness. This would last until the moment your full understanding comes, until the moment at which you grasp that your entire suffering comes from mistaken perceptions that you lost your loved ones forever. Death is only a transition through a door leading to another room, to another classroom. We certainly leave, but we also return to learn more lessons and qualities, such as love, compassion, forgiveness, understanding, patience, mellowness etc. Simultaneously we need to unlearn negative qualities such as fear, anger, greed, hatred, pride etc. which ensues from our old conditioning. When we get control over this, we can pass the exam and leave school, if we desire to do so. We are immortal and infinite, because we have been given God's nature. You suffer, because you forgot *Who You Are in Essence*.

I hope that with this knowledge you take a look at the losses you have experienced from a different perspective and allow your beloved soul its further journey. You could always make contact with him in the spiritual body and on the heart's level, when you think of the soul with love. Maybe you are not always aware of it, but your soul knows.

DEATH OF A BELOVED PERSON

When there is a lack of understating of death's nature, you always feel great pain and sadness when a loved one leaves. This is a quite natural reaction. If however you contemplated deeper over this sorrow, you would quickly notice (and with great surprise) that you don't despair over the person who left, but over your own fate. This sadness is in regards to that beloved person having left you alone. You wonder how you would manage without the beloved person. What bothers you most of all is the inevitability of death and consciousness that this would also happen to you in an unpredictable future. You fear this deeply. I hope that after reading this book you change your mind and come to understand that your life could undergo radical change. And if not, then I advise you to start to read it anew and contemplate and meditate over its content. Do this until you become a different, stronger person and around you changes for the better would begin.

It's different when we don't know the truth about death's nature. When a loved one dies with whom you were strongly, emotionally connected, with whom were bonded all your life, you feel as though you lack air to breathe, and your entire life is collapsing. Our connection with that person could have been so strong that we can't imagine how to live without him. His departure takes away our desire to live and act. It doesn't matter here whether his death was sudden or was preceded by a long illness. You may think that in latter case there is more time in order to, at least in a minimal way, prepare for it. Looking at it from the outside it could seem this way, however this is not true. When death comes, it strikes like lightning. I experienced this myself and know how it is. When someone is sick for a long time and suffers, at best we feel relief when his suffering comes to end.

Death comes suddenly, without announcement. We are very bewildered then, as if we were thrown into a different, paralyzing reality. Some despair so much that everyone around them experiences their suffering, while others remain immovable as if they don't care and they don't show any emotions on the outside. Yet others blame or curse at the world and God. Even though there are many ways to experience mourning, there is a common characteristic – great pain, which people who remain alive usually experience. Each death is a great shock, but the death of young mutually loving people is an even greater shock. Often the entire family suffers with them. Everyone sympathizes due to the misfortune experienced, and seeks to comfort and cheer them up. It's good to have support during tough moments. You should support as often and as best as possible as every person should experience mourning as strongly and for as long as he wants and needs. This is the best way to regain mental health and part with a beloved person. You should remember that one must part with his beloved person as quickly as possible in order for the beloved soul to transition to the other side of death's curtain.

I would like everyone who was left alone to realize that despite their suffering they are great, incredibly lucky people. I would like in a moment of mourning to appreciate what a great fortune you had that you loved and were loved, that you experienced something really wonderful which thousands and even millions of people never experienced. Take a look at yourself not from the perspective of your present loss, but from the perspective of what you gained thanks to love. Contrary to appearances true love is very rare. What we usually call love is only a fascination or attachment which sooner or later passes, leaving afterwards grey reality. True love never ends, but rather develops even more as time passes. No situation could separate love, not space, not even death. Know that your beloved soul after transitioning to the other side of death's curtain would always love you and remember you, and that when you die, would await you to welcome you upon your arrival.

However, often in the moment of death we don't want to remember all of this. Your thoughts would be absorbed with feeling of loss and nothing else. We won't take into consideration how greatly you harm yourselves and your beloved, departing soul as a result. At all costs we want to keep the departing soul next to us. This is a very egoistical approach which sooner or later would turn against us. This applies to all people who love each other but are forced to separate by death. It doesn't matter whether this is a loving couple, whether it is a parent and a child, or two friends. All partings hurt the same, however only when we don't know anything about death. Then we approach this seeming parting in an egotistical way (seeming, because in reality we never part). We behave like this because most often we don't realize the consequences. We don't know that by our great sorrow and despair we are binding our beloved's soul as though with great chains, by which we harm our beloved's soul very much, not to mention the harm we are doing to ourselves. Sorrow and despair doesn't allow for a soul to leave when it has the right and energy for it, and when there is adequate time for it.

Our attachment to beautiful, memorable moments becomes the reason for the soul's misfortune as well as ours. We don't take into account that the departing soul already has a hard time besides that, to leave everything that it loved, those for whom it lived and with whom it was greatly bonded. A soul is torn and doesn't know what to do. It wants to leave, and it feels that it should, but it would also want to stay, because it misses its life. This is why it's so important to not to add to the soul's indecisions your own sorrow and despair. An adequate time is given for each soul to leave. If we don't let it go, the time passes and it doesn't have the opportunity to leave on its own anymore. When after some time we get used to our loss, we become more willing to say goodbye to the soul, however it cannot leave at that point in time because the appointed time for its departure would already have passed.

Sometimes it's not you who stops a soul, but it's the soul who decides to remain. You don't have any influence when the soul makes this decision but you do in the previous situation. Unfortunately sometimes both cases cause tragic consequences which appear to us in the future as a possession. I wrote about this in a book *Possessed by Ghosts*.

When a mutually loving couple gets separated by a sudden, unexpected death, then it's hard for them to accept it. That is why it seems normal to you that after the funeral you recall your beloved one with tenderness, often thinking about moments you spent together. You think about each kiss, tender touch, the elation of your love. Your imagination would start to create more and more new images and your dreamy memories would have no end. Such fantasizing gives you comfort and thanks to it your heart would feel lighter. However this is a very critical period of time during which you have to be very alert. At the very beginning you were so very happy that you so intensively felt the presence of your beloved person that you were under impression that your beloved person still lived. You begin more often and more and more tangibly to feel the beloved person's touch and caress. You don't realize that you are moving further and further in that direction. You reach the point where you feel as if you were touching each other or physically making love. Soon this becomes normal to you and you finally start to have sex with the ghost. Such a state could last even to the end of life, but the moment you want to stop it, you encounter problems. You could ask what kind of problems? Weeks, months and maybe even years pass and what gave you so much happiness and comfort at the beginning, now isn't enough. You don't want to and you can't live any longer in loneliness, among ghosts. You want to be with people, with the living. You would like to meet someone, with whom you could feel happy, talk, go for a walk, see a movie, and go to a party. You would like to forget about the past, at least enough to be able to be among the living. Usually, however this doesn't work out at all, because the relationship with the ghost still exists. Very often ghost won't allow you to have contact with other people. The ghost gets rid of everyone who crosses your path or is around you. He got used to your dedication and doesn't want to share you with anyone. The ghost leads you into situations – these are very common – where everyone avoids you: family, coworkers, even people on the streets. Everyone in a weird way turns away from us. You begin to wonder what is wrong with you. You don't even come to the realization that each person who gets close to you is simply being pushed away by the ghost. You remain completely alone. In sporadic cases, you manage to have a relationship with someone, who is strong enough to withstand a ghost for a bit longer. You are happy then, finally you are not alone, and finally you have someone. You start new relationship full of trust that you have a bright future ahead of you. You still remember what love is, how to love and how to be loved. You have a wonderful partner. Unfortunately, in your relationship, from the very beginning something is not working out. You wonder what the cause is.

Maybe a period of time since the death of your previous partner is too short? Maybe everything in our apartment reminds you of the deceased person? Your new partner could put up with that due to love for you and respect for the deceased person, hoping that with time the situation would improve and you would be able to live happily. You don't realize however that there are three of you in the relationship, and not two as it seems to you. Neither you nor your partner notice problems which arise one after another because of the ghost's presence. Your partner may sense someone's presence. He would feel as if someone observes him nonstop, day and night. In so far as you consider that as normal, because you got used to it long time ago, for your partner that may seem extremely suspicious. You wait and delude yourself that everything would be alright, that things would fall into place. However every day it gets worse and worse. You constantly have a headache, at night you almost don't sleep and you are awakened multiple times. At work you are barely alive, constantly making mistakes and your coworkers start to move away from us. You think to yourself: "If this continues, I would lose my job".

While writing this I was thinking about a young couple, but the same situation could take place in relationships at any age, even in relationship between a parent and a child. Because you stopped the departing soul, now it demands from you exclusiveness. Your entire being is attracted to living people, but the beloved person's ghost doesn't want to allow you this.

In what way should two mutually loving people separate? Should they experience mourning at all? As I have already written, they should mourn in the way most suitable to them. But at the same time, they should not disturb the peace of a departing soul. Let that soul know, how much you love it and that at that moment you already miss them, but because of that love, you give it freedom and allow it to leave. That is a very tough period of time for dying person as well as for you. When this happens to you, it's already too late to think about it. That is why it's so important to contemplate over death before you experience it. In these tough moments you should realize that we all belong to God and at the moment of death we return to Him. When you come to understand that or at least start to think that way it would be already a lot easier for you. Death is nothing else than returning from school which is life on Earth, to Home, into the arms of our loving God, our Father-Mother. You came to Earth to learn something, most of all to learn love, and when you pass your lessons you return Home. When you attempt to retain a departing soul next to you, then that is as if you stopped a school friend in the classroom, not considering that you would soon see each other at Home.

People who are in different relationships should in their lifetime talk to each other about the fact that each of them would die one day. In many families this is a taboo topic. Nobody has the courage to mention the death of one family member until it actually happens. Unfortunately after death is too late for such conversations. If a person gets used to death during his lifetime he becomes stronger and know what to do with himself when the time arrives. This applies to the person who is departing as well as to the person who is staying. Then death doesn't surprise us that much and doesn't transfix us as much. I saw a loving couple that was saying goodbye to each other as if they were literally only separating for a second. Both of them knew that soon they would meet again. The person who was leaving had already worked through all of his own lessons, and the one that was staying still had to learn something. Most likely, the person wouldn't learn that at all if he stayed with his partner. There was no sorrow or despair during this separation, only great love and little bit of sadness.

Death on Earth is a birth on the other side of death's curtain. Even though for many people it seems to be painful, when we prepare for it, it turns out to be a blessing and stops causing pain.

Sometimes my clients during hypnosis went through their previous incarnations and times in between them. Often they said: "I never expected that death would be so simple, and life from a broader perspective made such great sense". Death is only terrifying when you are afraid of it. Your fear most often comes from a lack of knowledge about it. Just the thought of death transfixes us. We can't imagine that we could talk about death as though it were something completely obvious. This is why it's so important before death to learn to comfortably express own views about it, finish up all matters on Earth and reassure your partner that you would wait for him on the other side. The dying person should care about their partner's future and dismiss him from the promise. Many people need permission for a new relationship in order to not live in loneliness for many years or with the feeling of having betrayed a beloved soul. The fact that the person still alive falls in love with someone else doesn't mean that he would have forgotten about his previous spouse or loves her less. A person, who loves with true love, loves with his entire heart and there is a place in his heart for more than one person. Such a person is also loved, because love always returns to the sender like a boomerang. It's unknown from what side, but it's certain that it would return multiplied. A loving mother loves all her children equally, it doesn't matter how many she has. A loving person is never alone: he has friends and the entire universe supports him.

The person that allows for his heart to be clenched with despair, sorrow and loneliness is bitter. He is not capable of loving anyone and he is a burden for his surroundings. He never gives, but only takes and demands. The person who is jealous and greedy is most often alone and fears everything – old age and sickness. It's worth it to think about it when there is still two of you.

MOURNING

Mourning has various symptoms and phases. One shouldn't be surprised by anything, because everyone reacts in their own way. Some people cry, others don't find relief in crying. Many people start to feel physical pain or even get sick. They would work overtime to get tired and not have to think. This obviously applies to only those people who don't understand death's nature, who don't understand loss on a deeper level. In their case, it's necessary to experience mourning to be able to return to life. If you are currently in that situation, don't allow yourself to get convinced that you shouldn't despair. Allow yourself to cry and feel despair anger and sorrow as great as you could possibly express. Allow yourself from some time to ignore life happening around you. When the time of mourning passes, you would lift your head and return to the world of the living people. The deeper you experience mourning, the quicker you would return to equilibrium. You would never be the same again if you suppress the despair, anger and sadness inside of you. Inside you would remain an open wound which would be hard to heal.

It's hard for you to imagine this, but at some point everyone has to go through this. The loss of a beloved person is part of life. Mourning doesn't only apply to death, but any other loss, such as betrayal, abandonment, or even theft, fire or flood. The more you are attached to someone or something, the more you would suffer.

Earlier, I also went through such painful moments. Currently, it's completely differently due to understanding the Truth. If you are experiencing a tragedy and you lack an understanding of Life as a whole, then for a long time you won't understand how life could keep going forward and why it surrounds you with happy, pleasant people. Someone else's happiness irritates you and even a beautiful day seems to be a punishment. You find that colors, sun, greenery instead of lifting your spirits, overwhelm you. It's hard for you to stand other people's laughter, good luck, and even their simple babble or music. Why do they exist since you are so unhappy? Why don't they die, why didn't I die with my loved one? In such a situation, reality stops having meaning. All that exists is pain, negation, anger at fate, God, yourself and people close to you. Later s despair with no limits, crying for days, weeks or even months comes. Finally, that which seemed impossible becomes your reality – a return to life.

One more time I repeat: mourning applies to each loss, not only death, but also to each parting. Going through it is not easy, because in our culture deeply rooted tendencies exist which pretend that you must be "tough". Instead of understanding the suffering a person feels and support him, we repeat: "Get yourself together. You have to be tough. Don't show any weakness". As an alternative we offer pills to calm you down or even worse substances that strongly deepen our subconscious, like alcohol or drugs. People who close themselves in like shells have the hardest time when they go through a loss. They are afraid that at any moment their heart would be broken, but they have to get through it somehow. In your thoughts you should send to such people understanding and love, and that would lift their spirit and would help them endure this tough period.

In the past it was easier for people, because in old families everyone was close to the dying person and each other – family, friends, and neighbors. They burnt candles, prayed a lot, and covered windows and mirrors with heavy curtains. There was plenty of sympathy and understanding there. Today this has changed for the worse. Hundreds of times people told me how they were left alone with their pain and there was nobody next to them. People who are getting closer to death complain as well. They remain with their pain by themselves. Meanwhile even one person would have been enough. He doesn't have to say anything, it's enough that he just sits and listens, or only sits, because the most important thing is presence. People can take turns while doing such a favor, ensuring care and support for the suffering person. Perhaps, the person who is caring for such a fellow human has to witness unending monologs and laments. This shouldn't bother him. If it is needed, one should hug and allow the suffering person to cry loudly. The worst alternative is to suppress his suffering. The consequences of this could show itself throughout his entire life.

Mourning is necessary. There is no other way and the ideas of modern psychologists don't help. They benefit only the psychologists. These ideas only ensure that suffering person sees a psychologist for many years and sometimes to the end of his life. I often get phone calls from people who despite the fact that their loves ones passed ten, or even twenty years ago, they still feel deeply affected by it, because in the past they weren't allowed to cry out.

I think for religious people it's a bit easier in such tough moments. They believe in God and no matter what is happening, after some time they experience some sort of spiritual alleviation. It is hardest for people who are convinced that after death we simply disappear and remains only emptiness, void and nothingness. Often such fear affects them for the rest of their lives, and as a result they don't manage with their own existence on Earth.

Most of us avoid people who are mourning. We do this most often because of the fear of suffering. Also, we don't quite know how to behave in those situations. We convince ourselves that it's best not to get involved. Meanwhile, it's exactly the opposite. Every person's responsibility is to care for others and not leave them alone in great despair. Often during mourning we forget about children. Children are in the same, or even a worse situation, because they still don't understand many things.

A GRIEVING CHILD

There is not a way to prepare a child, as well as adult for death. In each situation, death is a surprise, causes great pain and sadness. In regards to children these feelings are even more intense. It doesn't matter here whether a child knew that his beloved one would die and whether this is the loss of an adult or sibling. In each case this is a great despair, even though sometimes the child doesn't show that on the outside, because it goes to play. When a child is in despair, don't calm him down, just allow him to cry and feel despair, anger and sorrow. Allow him to negate life, be naughty and misbehave. Inside him everything is rebelling, the same as in you. Don't push or criticize him when he can't manage something, don't get mad at him when he gets worse grades. When the mourning passes, he would come to desire living again, everything would fall into place and he would make up for lost time. I am talking here about softening requirements, not about completely abolishing them. Despite the tough situation a child still needs to eat, sleep, keep good hygiene, do homework, and help with daily responsibilities.

Each child reacts to loss in a different way. One child would be apathetic, he would not want to play, and another child would be rebellious and would react aggressively to everything. That is why we should inform teachers about the loss of loved ones as well as other children at the school or preschool. That would allow a child to be treated warmer and when he demonstrates bad behavior it would allow others to react with encouragement rather than criticism. A child sometimes talks nonstop about a deceased person and because of that is sometimes ridiculed or pushed around by other children who don't understand that. Child should be protected from such actions so that it doesn't add additional stress on him.

I know this topic perfectly from the point of view of grown up children, meaning adults. They often tell me what was happening with them then and how some intrusive feelings bother them to this day, even though they have their own children or grandchildren already. It turns out that in the case of a loved one's death, it doesn't matter whether death is sudden or due to a long sickness, children almost always feel guilty about the death. A child notices misfortune around him and is sad, anxious and blames himself thinking: "Probably I was naughty, and that is why daddy died", "I took away a toy for my sister and that is why she is not with us anymore", "I was hitting my brother and he left me", "I didn't want to have a sister and that is why she had to die". It is very important for parents not miss that and constantly repeat to a child that he is not at fault for death. The situation is even harder when the loved one dies suddenly, in an accident or a catastrophe. Then basically each child bothers himself with questions: "Why did I live and he didn't?", "Do I have the right to live since he died?", "Did I steal life away from him? That is a very hard to handle, crippling feeling. That psychological state is called "survivor syndrome". Things that earlier belonged to the deceased person could bother a child. For one child these things would give comfort while another child would feel uncomfortable with them. Parents very rarely notice these very important concerns of their children. That is not surprising, because parents feel hurt themselves by the loss of the loved one and it's hard for them to notice what is happening in the child's psyche, especially when the children don't express that on the outside. Someone's help from the outside of the family is very important here because that person would not have been affected by the death as much. A helping hand can be extend by a neighbor, a teacher at school or kindergarten. It could also be helpful to see a psychologist, but only when y you explain to the psychologist that the child is suffering because of a loss. Otherwise, it won't bring benefits as explained in the case described earlier. It's enough to talk to a child about a tragedy that touched him. It's better to take preventative actions than allow things to fester leading to disturbances which could affect him for the rest of his life. Children whose siblings (or mother, father, grandmother, grandfather) are sick for a long time, already suffer during the illness, because their parents are absorbed with helping the sick child. After death children suffer twice as much, because they lost a loved one and additionally see what their parents go through. Some children in this situation try to cheer up their parents, be unusually polite and helpful. Adults could take this as something good. However such behavior would only be positive if it doesn't result from great feelings of guilt. In the meantime, other children would feel aggression towards their parents, because they didn't defend, for example, their brother and didn't prevent his death.

A child, by experiencing mourning suddenly realizes that he could die as well. He could experience fear in at the moment he reaches the age of his deceased sibling or parent. This emotion could be suppressed or forgotten, but it would resurface on its own when that age is approaching. It was like that with many of my clients, but I would use my dad as an example. When he was eight years old both of his parents died in the same month due to the flu. One parent was thirty five years old and the other thirty seven. He was left alone with eight of his siblings and nobody was there to explain this painful loss to him. As time was passed he forgot about it. He grew up normally, even enjoyed life. When he reached adulthood, he met a wonderful girl – my mom – started a family, had children and good job. Everything was alright until he started to approach the age at which his parents died. The fear started to escalate rapidly, but he wasn't able to determine the cause of it. With each day he was more and more terrified until his fear completely paralyzed him. He started to greatly fear death, and with that also life as well. So as not to die young like his parents, he started to take care of his health, however he did so excessively, almost in a pathological way. He was afraid of anything that could in the smallest way threaten him. Nobody could sneeze next to him, open a window due to a draft, because he would immediately panic and think that he could get flu. Day by day he became a hypochondriac. This lasted many years until I grew up. I started to inquire what was the cause of such odd behavior and why only my dad behaved like this, but not the rest of his siblings. I asked all the living relatives for details. When I understood what the cause was I started talking to my dad about it. I told him what he didn't realize and

was denying. That lasted quite a long time, but he slowly overcame that problem. At the moment my dad understood what
bothered his it seemed as though a miracle happened. He gained
enough control over his fear to once again live normally. And so
in complete health and happiness he reached the age of ninety
five years old. When he was asked about his wellbeing and
health one could always hear his enthusiastic assurance: "You
know, out of all the stages of my life, old age is my favorite",
which abolishes the banal stereotype. Many people repeat endlessly: "God definitely didn't do a good job with old age", instead of "I didn't do a good job with my old age". Not everyone
is able to manage or completely eliminate their fear of death.
Everything depends on the age at which the child experienced
the trauma. The younger a child was, the harder it is to overcome this fear. How many people don't even realize they are
dealing with this fear?

A child's life during mourning could be very tough if
you give him excessive care because you fear he might die as
well. It is even worse when a child is being compared to a deceased child and when the deceased child is idolized. Many of
my clients told me in anger or despair they screamed to their
children: "Why didn't you die instead of her" or "Why do you
still live if she is not around". Nobody is able to erase such
words from their memory. They continuously return to these
children, even though they themselves now have children or
grandchildren themselves.

PROPHECIES

Dear reader, we live in times in which fear about the future intensifies in us more and more.. Most people feel this fear. They are terrified by what the prophecies say, because they don't realize that each prophecy, no matter how negative, indicates only that prophet's ability to see into the future. It's based on recognition of what is currently happening in the world in terms of energy.

Indeed, a prophet creates sort of a map, because he references about course of our destiny, however this is never the final matter. There is always room for changes. Therefore, the danger with prophecies is that they are approached too seriously. They are mistakenly treated as the foretelling of actual events, and not as a probability. That is why predictions and prophecies concerning catastrophes on Earth cause such great anxiety in people. Dear reader, treat prophecies as talking about things that could possibly happen, as talking about the probability of events. Prophecies present an understanding that something could happen in the future, but only if the course of your life doesn't change. In order for you to understand correctly, I would give you an example.

Let's just say if you are sitting on a branch and you are cutting it from the branch side, it could be said with confidence that you would fall when the branch is cut off. If you took that prophecy as a warning, and change your behavior you sit down on the trunk side) you would avoid an accident. If you took that prophecy as a fact, which cannot be avoided you would continue cutting the branch and sitting on the branch side. When you fall off the tree, it could be said that the prophecy came true and you were already destined to fall. You would recognize this as destiny, bad fate, and you would be convinced that you didn't have any influence over your life. Meanwhile the truth is that you didn't consider other options, in other words changing your behavior, because you blindly believed in the prophecy.

Dear reader, never be afraid of a prophecy. Even after hearing about a catastrophe, you shouldn't think about it at all, in order to not to attract to you what you wouldn't want to experience. If there was supposed to be a catastrophe of global reach, trust and know, that nothing bad would happen to you. Nothing would happen that isn't good for you, in other words the Higher Good. Trust and realize fully that God never sends down destruction on Earth. Humanity does this to itself. When you live in love, with God and in God, no catastrophe would reach you. Love would lift you so high; you won't experience any defeat or catastrophe. This doesn't mean at all, that you would have to go through the transformation known as death. If however your soul's choice would be death then you already know that after abandoning your physical body you would transfer from one classroom to the other. There is no point to assign blame because no matter what happens, this would be good for you as well as for your loved ones. Besides that, you don't have to live in constant fear, because nothing ever happens suddenly, instantaneously. You would be warned in time.

So, the real function of prophecy is to warn people what could await and happen to them in a future, if they don't change their behavior. A prophet who is foretelling a future only says in what directions we are heading. Certainly, he warns us, but simultaneously he proposes to us to think about whether we still want to follow that path. We could then think about what we do wrong and have the chance to change course. Therefore, a prophecy is not in any way a sentence, but a suggestion. It tells how to correct a course towards the direction of safer waters.

Remember! True prophecy (there are also many prophecies up there that are untrue, and they shouldn't be taken into consideration at all) is never based on presenting a vision of the future that doesn't leave people with the choice or possibility to change. There is always choice, however people don't always want to take advantage of an opportunity that presents itself. They do nothing with their life and postpone things for later.

Many people proclaim upcoming catastrophes on Earth. One of the prophecies talks about the end of the world. However the "world" doesn't mean here on Earth. Certainly, the idea of the "world" in prophecy relates to the human's world; however it is seen rather as a system, as government order, a way to organize society. Meanwhile, Earth, in other words our world is an alive, sensitive, loving being, and the "world" from prophecy relates to the order of human relations. Besides that this prophecy doesn't talk about the end of the world as a great, total, catastrophe, but about human's awakening. Thanks to an awakening, humans can renew this wonderful legacy. Their current "world"

will end, and in its stead would begin the "world" of the Kingdom of Heaven. For people interested in this knowledge I recommend the book *In the Wheel of Life,* Vol. III.

Many enlightened people also claim that we are approaching the end of the world, however in any case it's not
about Earth's doom, but about Earth's rising. They refer there to
the end of the "world" of humans for the Divine "world", about
the transition from the third dimension to the fourth dimension.
That process started at the beginning of past century. Dear reader, I think that you already noticed for yourself that long ago we
have entered into an accelerated state of affairs and this rate is
continuously increases. We are entering greater and greater into
the Light, and we have at our disposal more and more information. What humanity used to assimilate during hundred or
more years, currently only takes a few years. Many people can't
handle these growing intense vibrations of Light and die. They
declare in such their unwillingness to change. Many people are
also seriously sick. This is an opportunity, a great chance to, in
the shortest amount of time, transform your own body, mind and
soul and rise to the Light.

We should know that whenever there was a change in
Earth's history Earth itself evolved as a being. It does it in the
same way people do it. During the changes we are now going
through, there will be great opportunities, but also a great
amount of danger. You could evolve with Earth to the fourth
dimension, or you could also close yourself to changes, fall out
of the rising process and start everything from the beginning.
Such possibilities happen cyclically every 26,800 years. These
changes are tightly related to the precession of the Earth's axis
meaning with the change of the inclination angle of its axis.

In order to find ourselves in the fourth dimension, in other words in The Kingdom of Heaven, we don't have to go

through death like some religions teach. It's enough to raise our own consciousness, enough to start to touch "Heaven". In this way we come to next conclusion that Heaven is a state of consciousness, and not a place to which we go to after death.

One should know that in The Kingdom of Heaven there are in effect different rules to those in our world, to which one should adjust in advance. The key to higher worlds are our vibrations. When you vibrate on lower frequencies, you automatically don't have an entry to places that vibrate a lot faster. It's a must to have this knowledge intellectually, and also use it in practice. For you could be in The Kingdom of Heaven already at this moment and not after death like religion promises you. For this, you would have to love God from your own, unforced will, and not because as a follower you are forced to do it. Otherwise these words would remain and empty cliché. Only when with your own free will you love your Creator above all, with a clean heart would you be able to connect with the Spirit, and then would come peace in you and your world, you would find yourself in His Kingdom.

You paramount desire would then become achieving everlasting happiness. You would stop chasing after passing happiness which satisfies your external senses. In your heart you would start having faith, hope and love permanently, and not only from time to time. Showing compassion and leniency to your neighbors would become your second nature. You would also gain permanent harmony and balance. You would get a feeling like you were born again. This would mean that you have completely freed yourself from the past. You won't enter a new, unknown world; you would just call upon The Kingdom of Heaven where you lived once. If such a state of spirit was embraced on the entire Earth, the problems of hunger, poverty, illness and any other unfortunate circumstances would disappear for you and everyone around you once and for all.

Unfortunately, in today's world people have a complete-ly different state of spirit which is incompatible with Nature. Until humanity reaches a different state, we won't radiate with love, compassion and simplicity; it won't be enough to clean up and get rid of omnipresent fear and rise higher. However no matter what other people do, this is their problem, and not yours. You create your own life, and they create theirs.

For the same reason, don't accept any prophecies as facts, but only as possibilities. It is true that currently there are many great changes happening on Earth. They are the result of the Earth's evolution as well as yours. These changes don't have to be catastrophic on a global scale as many people proclaim, even though for some it could turn out to have catastrophic con-sequences (if they won't change).

CONCLUSION

Dear reader, I am full of hope that thanks to this book you stopped once and for all fearing the phenomenon commonly called "death". If at the deep levels of yourself you have reached the understanding that there is no death that after getting rid of your physical body you are the same then certainly the question of whether the life you lead right now fully satisfies you would arise. Your positive answer would mean that you are in a comfortable situation and a negative answer would mean that it's about time for changes. The best way to start is with forgiveness. Forgive everything and everyone, but most of all yourself. How long and how intensively this should be done? Until at some point you get a sense of relief and you feel that you are completely cleaned inside.

Perhaps it could seem to you that you have nothing to forgive yourself and others. That would mean that you are deceiving yourself. If you approached yourself and life honestly, you would start to recognize inside you various hurts from the past and present. If despite good intentions you don't know who and what to forgive, then at the beginning make a list of people, situations and things which you were mad at and the reasons for your anger. When the list is read you would know who and what to forgive.

On that list also include yourself. Don't you have any pretension towards yourself? Believe me that you have, and a lot, but you just don't realize it. Ultimately, many times you allowed yourself to t be hurt, cheated and used. Did you always stand up for yourself? Why didn't you do that? And how many times you didn't take care of yourself so you could have a better life? These are the things that you have to forgive yourself most of all. Approach this matter with honesty and you would begin to live better, not only on this world, but on the other world in the future.

This is not an easy path, especially at the beginning when there is still so much doubt inside you, and who knows, maybe you are overwhelmed by many things. When you find the courage and with determination you make even one step forward, with each next step it would be easier, until suddenly you discover that everything negative left you. It still remains somewhere far behind you, but it doesn't have any influence over you. I wish you this from the bottom of my heart.

If despite everything you don't want to forgive, know that everything that you experienced was pushed off to your subconscious. You may not realize that consciously. If something negative happened to you and you don't forgive it in time (it doesn't matter whether to yourself or to others) then this great burden would still rest in your innermost subconscious. Then the subconscious classifies the given act for you and considers it either good or bad. That would determine what consequences your subconscious mind creates for you. If it recognizes that you committed a violation, your subconscious would feel guilty and that would automatically attract to you some sort of punishment.

Your subconscious mind already punished you in that way many times by creating illness, or other unfortunate circumstances, the character and strength of which depended on how it classified the event. The greater the violation according to its subjective assessment then the greater was the punishment. If currently you were able to discover the true cause for such difficulties (your illnesses, problems, etc.) most likely they would seem to you trivial, nonessential, and possibly even funny. However at the moment of inception they were seen as serious violations against your value system by your subconscious. Therefore, you administer each punishment for yourself; in other words, create problems, and even tragedies which happen to you. I emphasize this again: the greater the violation according to your subconscious, the greater is the punishment. This mechanism works in this and the other world, because what we experience there depends on our experiences up to that point, it is based on how we look at certain things. This explains why some souls who have serious violations on their consciousness are able to forgive themselves and go to the Light, while others can't do that despite trivial ones (for which they are unable to forgive themselves). A lot depends on whether the soul loved itself, others and God during its lifetime. If there was in a person's heart only despair, sadness, and lack of hope then there was little room for the love and courage (meaning trustfulness) needed to transition to the Light. Therefore, what you desire, what you fear, what you care for in the physical world would dictate what your existence in the astral world would be like and whether it would be rewarding. A lot depends on how you currently imagine it, during your lifetime.

If you fully understood my message, you would know that you need to decide now what you would do after the death of your physical body. In what direction your soul would go? This would depend on how it lived and what you believed in, in the physical dimension. It is extremely important how you take the loss of your physical body. If you separate from it without sadness, then you would be happy. However, if you get a sense of lacking, then most likely you would experience suffering. I trust, that you don't read these words shallowly, so that this does not happen to you.

Dear reader, always remember that only you can discover your own reality. Nobody could do that for you, because it exists inside you, deep in your heart. Aim your life exactly in that direction and you would find the greatest treasure. That is why no matter what is happening around, always listen to you, on this as well as on the other world.

In any case, don't condemn anything. It doesn't matter whether is about matters that apply to this world or to the next one, whether they apply to your family or to yourself. Don't feel sorry or pity for others. If you condemn or feel sorry for them, you always strengthen with your energy what you condemn or feel sorry for. You should be fully aware that by condemning something you don't destroy that at all. It's quite the opposite – you help that to grow and become stronger. It's the same with feelings of sorrow and pity – instead of helping, they bring you down even more and deepen the person's misery to whom it is being sent. However, you can help when instead of condemning or pity, you sent true love. It lifts others and you as well, unto a higher vibrational level; as a result you are able to neutralize negative action force which were a cause of discomfort up to that point.

Dear reader, perhaps you are trying to help your love

ones and you strive for them to also understand the text of this book. Know that you are not allowed to force them into anything. You can only gently try, show, and encourage them, nothing more. Accept the fact that no matter how hard you try there are people (and there would be a lot of them) who don't want to join you, who don't want to awaken. This could make you sad, but you must respect their free will, even when their incorrect choice today could mean a spiritual loss in the future. You have to accept the fact that if your good example doesn't influence them, then certainly they have to learn from their own mistakes. Otherwise, you won't help them at all, but could harm yourself greatly. You are not able to transfer any matters from yourself to another person, even the most precious persons to you. By the way, there is no need for it, since they are as equipped in everything as you are. Perhaps, you don't recognize this clearly at this moment, but when you do develop more and raise the level of your consciousness, it would become completely clear and readable.

Dear reader, by reading this book for the first time you would understand it in a different way than after reading it once again. While reading it the first time you would only attain the amount of knowledge relative to the level of understanding you are at currently. When you accept and assimilate this knowledge, you would process it inside you, you would become more and more open to it and with willingness and easiness you would absorb the next level of knowledge. Therefore, each time you reach out for this book after the first reading (and it's written on many levels of understanding), you would notice more and more things, new aspects of things which you missed earlier. Return to this book from time to time until this knowledge solidifies in you and you get rid of the omnipresent fear in you. When once and for all you stop fearing death, you would become fearless. It's because in reality there is nothing scarier than this fear. Besides death, what else is there to fear? And then you would finally become free and really begin to live. I hope that this happens to you soon.

I am certain that with the knowledge you currently have, death won't surprise you in any case, because you would be ready for it at all the time. And after putting off your physical body without any burdens, fully aware and with trust, you would make your way towards the Light, into the arms of a loving God, Your Father-Mother. I wish this for you from the bottom of my heart.

Dear reader, if you are in a situation where you cannot cope you may turn to me and ask me to help at the following address:

IN POLAND:

Wanda Pratnicka
P.O. Box 257
81-963 Gdynia 1 / Poland

IN THE UNITED STATES:

Wanda Pratnicka
46-02 21st Street, PO BOX 1544
Long Island City, NY 11109 / USA

E-mail: info@WandaPratnicka.com
Web: www.WandaPratnicka.com

You may also phone my office at:

Phone in **Poland**: +48 58 555 9815
Fax in Poland: +48 58 550 6812

Phone in the **United States**: 631 402 1254
Phone in the **United Kingdom**: 02032 984727
Please take a look at our website ("Contact") for current phone numbers in the country of your residence.

I will need to have the following information:

    1) Forenames and surname
    2) Date of birth
    3) Place of permanent stay

For the help to be effective I will most often need to have the details of all the people residing in the house/apartment because in the majority of cases the whole family is in need of help.

If you are a public person or for any reason you are unwilling / unable to pass to me your personal data (which I fully understand and respect) you still can use my services (checking and cleansing of you and your near ones) without passing to me or to my associates any of your personal information.
That option is certainly making it more difficult for me and I am willing to grant that option only in rare, justified cases and for a higher fee. Please call to receive more information on that matter.

Please note that I am also giving private consultations for problems not connected to the presence of ghosts. Ask my staff to receive more information about that option.

If the subject of this book has aroused your interest then I will be happy to hear your opinion of it.

BOOK ORDERING

You can order this book at the following address:

IN POLAND:

Centrum Publishers
P.O. Box 257
81-963 Gdynia 1 / Poland

IN THE UNITED STATES:

Wanda Pratnicka
46-02 21st Street, PO BOX 1544
Long Island City, NY 11109 / USA

e-mail: info@WandaPratnicka.com
www.WandaPratnicka.com

You may also phone my office at:

Phone in **Poland**: +48 58 555 9815
Fax in Poland: +48 58 550 6812

Phone in the **United States**: 631 402 1254
Phone in the **United Kingdom**: 02032 984727

Please take a look at our website ("Contact") for current phone numbers in the country of your residence.

All books can be ordered from Amazon.com for the US and Amazon.co.uk for the United Kingdom. The books are also available for purchase from Ebay.

WANDA PRATNICKA
*Possessed by Ghosts –
Exorcisms in XXI
century*

This book is
aimed at all readers, not
just those who are
interested in the esoteric
arts. It presents in an
accessible and surpris-
ingly clear way the
causes of the toxic
associations that arise
between people and
ghosts. It contains a
large dose of the psy-

chology of soul. Ghosts are the souls of people who, for various reasons, overlooked their own death, did not have the courage to depart for the other world or were detained, or even dragged from the road, by their dear ones weeping for those souls. When they remain in the world of the living they possess people and this can be the cause of very unfortunate, and sometimes even tragic, experiences. The presence of ghosts within a person causes powerful mood swings from strong negative emotional outbursts to profound depression. They evoke powerful anxiety attacks, persuade those who are possessed to commit suicide, have strong influences on the psyche and are the cause of mental illnesses. Additionally, the physical illnesses of the person who died are very often transferred by the ghost to the person possessed.

The subject of this book could be a panacea for very many of our world's misfortunes. From various states of mental disturbance, deviations, dependencies, severe psychiatric illnesses including those requiring isolation, through to chronic diseases or those that are considered to be incurable.

The question of ghosts also applies to various everyday situations like the demanding behavior of a family member, difficulties with learning, with people close to one, work colleagues or business associates. They often lead to helplessness, loneliness, isolation, or to difficult financial, health and social situations.

What is a frequent cause of various diseases, misfortunes, lesser or greater failures? How can one deal with them, how can one guard against them in the future? That's what this book is about. It is also a reply to the endless questions asked by people turning to Wanda Pratnicka for help. They often believe that the things that have happened to them are unique, they happened only to them. They wonder why they are suffering so much. They think that maybe they did something bad and that now they're being punished. Or maybe it's the work of some curse or black magic.

Possessed by Ghosts is a very exceptional work. Nobody before has described the dependencies that exist between the world of ghosts and that of people in such an extensive, comprehensible and profound way. It allows you to understand the causes of these dependencies and shows how to free yourself from them. It is a guide that leads to a life of peace, satisfaction, enthusiasm and wealth.

It is a handbook for anyone who is pursuing personal and spiritual development. It shows the universal laws that govern our world and is a testament to the author's spiritual maturity.

WANDA PRATNICKA about *Possessed by Ghosts – Exorcisms in XXI century*:

"For many years I really wanted to read a good book about exorcisms, but I never found one. Unfortunately, till now nobody had written one. So I had to do it myself. In it there are answers to questions asked every day by my patients, but also answers to questions I asked myself.

In it, I address those who have tried everything, every method, every remedy to ease their problems or those of their near ones. Unfortunately, none of them worked or if they did work they did so for only a short time. I wrote it also for those who are only at the beginning, they sense that something bad is happening to them or their families, or that not everything is as it should be. I wrote it for those who are healthy and happy, too, those who have nothing wrong with them or their nearest. They are the very ones who could help in many tragedies which are taking place inside their neighbors' homes, or to an unhappy family nearby, or to some hooligan or drug addict in the street where they live. Sometimes one can help simply with a piece of advice about what can be done in a given situation or with the information that something can be done at all.

Usually, the fact is that the person who is possessed is unaware of his or her state. By helping such a person we are really helping ourselves since we no longer hear the fights the other side of the wall, or our neighborhood becomes quieter. In extreme cases we may even prevent a suicide, a rape or even worse. It affects, therefore, not just the individual but most often all of us."

WANDA PRATNICKA
In the Wheel of Life
Volumes I-IV

Wanda Pratnicka presents the Universal Laws ruling our Universe over the span of approximately **two thousand pages** in her new book **consisting of four volumes.** These laws have the same impact on our daily lives as they do on our overarching concepts of spiritual development. The author often raises extremely complicated and deep questions, presenting them in an exceptionally simple way. Her work is easily comprehended by experts in the esoteric field and novices alike. An expert will find the correct way to interpret the studies of the greatest Teachers of humanity, and the beginner will find explanations full of truth, peace, and light concerning all areas of daily life. The book discusses the entire range of what human experiences consist of. It raises questions corresponding to physical space, as well as higher worlds including the etheric, astral, mental, causal, and higher. This work is intended for people interested in spiritual development, as well as people who constantly work on improving their situation, whether it be emotional, material, interpersonal, etc.

Volume I and II contain further explanation of all phenomena mentioned in the author's previous book, ***Possessed by Ghosts: Exorcisms in the 21st Century.***

A note from the author regarding **Volumes I-IV** of *In the Wheel of Life*:

"This knowledge will help you discover meaning in your experiences and what the purpose of your life and the lives of those close to you is. You will find out how the distant past influences your present life and what will happen with you when you are separated from your physical body. These are very essential matters because this knowledge has an influence not only on your journey here on Earth, but on the entire range of experiences each human shares while going through the transition commonly known as death of the physical body.

Information contained in this book will allow you to look at life from a completely different perspective, free of fear and the illusions you have accepted as the truth until this point."

Wanda Pratnicka
about **Volume I:**
In this Volume I
would like to present to
you, dear reader, Life
from a broader perspec-
tive and guide you step
by step through all its
stages. I discuss your
soul, illuminate *Who
You Are in Essence*, and
explain what caused you to come to Earth. Consequently,
you will come to understand the goal of your own and
other people's lives.

By learning about your energetic bodies, you will
come to understand how significant they are not only in
this life, but also after the death of the physical body.
Then you will come to understand your role here on
Earth and you will find it easier to take responsibility for
your life.

I explain specific chakras in detail and outline
their functions in our daily lives. By learning about each
individual chakra, you will realize that each one presents
a given situation from a completely different angle.

Furthermore, you will find out how the distant past
influences your current life, which will help you look at
your life from a new, fearless perspective and free your-

self from the illusions that you have accepted as the truth until now. You will also stop postponing your growth for later because you will understand that avoiding taking responsibility for your life will disturb your energy. Consequently, this will manifest in your life as troubles, difficulties, and even tragedies with serious illnesses included. Thanks to the knowledge contained in here, you will recognize what functions in your life incorrectly and why you have certain experiences. As a result you will be able to exchange them for more satisfying ones.

You already know everything I present here in the deepest levels of Your Being. Hence, my role is to only remind you of what you already know.

WANDA PRATNICKA
In the Wheel
of Life
Volume II

Wanda Pratnicka about **Volume II**:

"In Volume II, I present Life from an even broader perspective. I wrote Volume I assuming that you lived on Earth only once. In this book, I describe your Life from the perspective of many incarnations and gently

lead you step-by-step from life here on Earth, through so-called death and all levels of existence that follow, and into the next life in physicality.

Essentially, it will help you realize what we commonly call death is not the end of life, but a transition from one state to another. This will lead you to the conclusion that you never die, you only exchange bodies like clothes, and as a soul you exist eternally.

This knowledge will spontaneously and completely change your view on Life and free you from both fear of death and life. It will also free you from the fear of a dangerous, vengeful, unjust God.

Taking a look at one's own life from the perspective of many lives answers a very essential question about ostensible injustice.

Who knows? Perhaps you will stop blaming God for injustice when you will realize why He, who ultimately is only Love, put people on earth in such extreme diverse conditions.

By accepting this broadened perspective you will come to understand why some people are happy, healthy, beautiful, and wealthy, while others lack everything. People in the latter group struggle greatly every day and deceive themselves into believing that there is no chance for a better future.

You will become convinced that you are not a victim of your life, but your life's creator. This will allow you to take responsibility for your life. The knowledge contained in my book gives you this responsibility, but also the tools to introduce your psyche to changes that will lead to a better, happier, more secure and wealthy life on all fronts. I wish you this from the bottom of my heart."

WANDA PRATNICKA
In the Wheel
of Life
Volume III

Wanda Pratnicka about
Volume III:
In Volume III I de-
scribe the existence of the
human soul from the
perspective of all of Earth's
prior civilizations. The
book begins with my
description of the time that
humans came to Earth due
to their own free will to

join with other souls and create a wonderful, Light civilization.

The main building material of this civilization was
True Love and Faith in God. Because of true Love and
deep Faith, this civilization worked out the Eternal Higher
Laws of Life, which remain in each human being today.
This civilization created a great power which became the
impetus behind all mental activity. This inborn Divinity
was passed over without a slightest change from generation
to generation. Peace and complete satisfaction emerged
from this great activity of the Higher Mind for millions of
years.

Dear reader, looking at Life from this perspective
will help you understand what life is truly about, which will
allow you to correct your own life. I will narrate each stage
of the downfall of this great civilization, which will give
you the opportunity to not only recognize own mistakes,

but also avoid them in the future.

The Laws of Life that were worked out in the First Civilization are still present in each human being but are almost completely forgotten by most people. The Laws of Life will enable you to free yourself once and for all from compulsive thinking about the lack of Good in which you live in on a daily basis and locate your true being.

You will become convinced that the control that your compulsive, mistaken pretensions have over you is only an illusion. In reality, you have power over them but you don't use it because you don't realize you have it. The knowledge contained in this book will lead you to Power and Wisdom. You cannot be serene, strong, persistent, and secure without them.

WANDA PRATNICKA
*Know the Truth
And Be Free*

A note from the author:

I am addressing this book to everyone irrespective of race or religion because one day we will all deal with our own or someone else's death. We should adequately prepare for this event, especially when we are sick, elderly or

have someone in our family who is rapidly approaching the transition we call "death". If you have lost a loved one and have been grieving then this book is perfect for you. The wisdom contained here will also help you to heal from past traumatic experiences that followed the passing of loved ones.

Most people fear death. Do you realize that the fear of death is the cause for most, if not all, misfortunes in this world? It is not caused by death itself, but rather from a lack of information on this subject. Therefore, knowledge about death while you are alive is as important as the air that you breathe.

By familiarizing yourself with this text you will stop living your life with constant frustration. If on a deep level of your being you adapt to guidance from this book, you will get rid of your fear of death once and for all. And having rid yourself of this fear you will begin to make different, more conscious choices. Then it's not out of the question that you will become amazingly wise and happy.

From the chapter "Preface":
"Do you realize that the fear of death is the primary cause of most, if not all of our internal adversities? The fear of death is like the interior of a simmering volcano. It is that hidden, constant fear that no amount of money or superficial effort can neutralize. This fear is the essence of all things. It is a fear that emanates not only from death itself, but also from a lack of understanding of this very emotional subject. Traditional media is not making it any easier to understand death. Death is either not shown or, for example in movies and video games it is presented in a banal or unrealistic way.

Therefore most people leave things up to chance, not

knowing how to control their life on Earth as well as after death. When you familiarize yourself with the information introduced in this book you will no longer waste your life. You will begin to make different, more conscious choices. Who knows, maybe you will become amazingly wise and happy. Once and for all you will get rid of your fears and stop living in constant frustration. You will understand that what you fear the most (most often unconsciously) doesn't even exist, because what you call death is just taking off your body in the same way that you take off and throw away the old clothes that you don't need anymore. Meanwhile you, the essence of you, moves forward. Where? Well, to understand this is extraordinarily important because what you know about death, what you think about it during your life and what you expect from it, will determine what you will experience in the future. Therefore, the knowledge you acquire about death in your lifetime is as important as the air that you breathe because your future depends on it. I hope that you will come to understand that everything that happens to you depends only and solely of you. You must take your life into your own hands because nobody else will help you with it.

Nobody can get by in life without the knowledge provided in this book. It is especially important when you are sick, aged or you have someone in your family who is quickly approaching the transition commonly known as "death". If you have lost someone close to you and you are mourning then this book is appropriate for you. This book will explain every tragedy and it will help you heal any wounds in your heart caused by the loss of someone dear to you."

From the chapter "Introduction":

"Dear reader, we are living in times of great change. We should be very happy about this, but many people are constantly worrying about impending doom. It is causing people great, unconscious fear. I took on this task to not only mitigate this fear, but to permanently remove it. It is not possible for us to live with such a burden and function normally. It will negatively affect not only your life, but life in general.

No matter what you are afraid of right now, with this fear there is a fundamental, overarching fear associated with your death and non-existence. You are not even conscious of this fact. This is the reason why many people object to closely looking at this subject. These people are thinking naively deluding themselves into thinking that if they don't touch this subject, death will pass them by. In reality, it is the other way around. Only when you get to know the phenomenon commonly known as "death", when you understand and accept it then you will have a chance that this so-called "death" won't return to haunt you."

Perhaps, like many other people you are afraid to think about death. This is because you know nothing or very little about it. Therefore, you don't understand what happens in the moment of "death" and as a result a great fear paralyses you about this occurrence.

The word "death" should be written in quotes because in reality there is no death. You never die. Only your physical body dies. During so-called "death" you take off your body in the same way you take off old, used, unneeded clothing and you - as the essence of you - still exists, and this is the eternal life. The transformation called death is in reality a movement from one state of consciousness into another one. It is as if you were moving from one classroom to another.

WANDA PRATNICKA obtained Ph.D in Philosophy; M.A in Psychology; and B.A in Parapsychology. She is an international lecturer, spiritual teacher, psychic and clearings professional. During her 45 years of practice she has helped tens of thousands of people around the world. Her first book *Possessed by Ghosts – Exorcisms in XXI century* became a bestseller in Poland shortly after publication of its first edition. The book was translated to English, German, Spanish, Russian, Japanese, Chinese and currently other translations are being prepared.

Dr. Wanda Pratnicka's next literary work *In the Wheel of Life* consists of four volumes and around 2,000 pages. Her books are aimed to all readers, not just those who are interested in the esoteric arts.

These books present, in an accessible and surprisingly clear way, the universal laws of the Universe, a soul's psychology, deep matters in regards to true human origin and the causes of toxic associations that arise between people and ghosts. Ghosts are the souls of people who, for various reasons, overlooked their own death, did not have the courage to depart for the other world or were detained by their dear ones weeping for those souls. When they remain in the world of the living, they possess people and this can be the cause of very unfortunate and sometimes even tragic experiences. Starting from the mildest symptoms, the presence of ghosts within a person causes powerful mood swings from strong negative emotional outbursts to profound depression. They evoke powerful anxiety attacks, persuade those who are possessed to commit suicide, have strong influence on psyche and are the cause of mental illnesses. Additionally, the physical illnesses of the person who died are often transferred by the ghost to the person possessed.

Dr. Wanda Pratnicka's newest book is *Know the Truth and Be Free* which cures such problems as fear of death/life or traumatic experiences that result from loved ones' loss/death.